India's National Security: Military Challenges and Responses

India's National Security
Military Challenges and Responses

Capt. (Retd.) Prem Singh

PRASHANT PUBLISHING HOUSE
DELHI-110094

Published by :
Prashant Publishing House
C-34, 28 Foota Road, Gali-3,
West Karwal Nagar, Delhi-110094
Phone : 011-22963970, Mob. : 9810396373
e-mail.: prashantpublishinghouse@gmail.com

India's National Security: Military Challenges and Responses

First Published 2017

ISBN 978-93-80565-8-59

PRINTED IN INDIA

Published by Mr. R.K. Jha M/s Prashant Publishing House and Published at H.S. Offset House Press, Delhi.

Contents

Preface

India's national security and defence is equally the responsibility of all its citizens. They must not only study matters military, but also be alive to dangers to India's security, both from external and internal threats. As regards India's parliamentarians and politicians are concerned, their responsibility in this respect is far more.

India presents a regrettable phenomenon where political opposition parties, in the absence of any other political issue, tend to politicise national security issues. In this process and in their zeal to discomfit the ruling party at any cost, they fail to realise the impact it has on the Armed Forces of India – their morale, their will to fight and their entire confidence in the political structure of the Indian nation state is seriously jeopardised.

National security issues have hardly been discussed by political parties during Defence budget debates in Parliament. The parliamentary attendance then presents a sorry spectacle. Yet when grave national crises occur every second politician becomes a master strategist or tactician minus the grasp of the essentials of strategy and the intricacies of military operations and oblivious to the fact that the parliamentarians own strategic incompetence brought about the military aggression in the first place.

The Indian security establishment also needs to carefully monitor the growing military collusion of the Pakistan- China strategic axis. Most analysts conclude that it would not be possible for Islamabad to wage its proxy war against India without Beijing's military backing and financial support. China has 'guaranteed Pakistan's territorial integrity' but it is not clear against whom. Beijing has also furnis hed much military hardware to Islamabad.

The Modi government, as it works to establish good neighbourly relations, has to make it clear to Pakistan that the sooner the Pakistanis rid themselves of their Kashmir fixation and India centricity in all their formulations, India-Pakistan relations may move beyond a zero-sum game. Pakistan has to rid itself of its propensity of planning terror inside India and rein in its infamous ISI from its anti-India machinations. Pakistan needs to be strongly told that India has not exploited Pakistan's many fault lines, but India's patience should not be taken for granted. Relations cannot improve in a one way alley.

slamic terrorism spanning increasingly wide swathes of the globe has emerged as one of the harsh realities of our age. The concept of the "global jihad" –whatever one thinks about the perverse interpretation of such a movement –is related to the Caliphate or "khilafat", meaning an "Islamic world empire". The Islamic State (IS), the brutally cruel terror organization earlier called the Islamic State of Iraq and the Al Shams (ISIS), presently straddles parts of Syria and Iraq, though the envisioned Caliphate of Salafist orientation includes areas of the Middle East, Central Asia and South Asia, including India. All the matter that has been given in public domain and we have just compiled it.

This book makes an interesting reading for historians, defence and policy analysts, researchers and general readers alike.

—*Editor*

1

Introduction

INDIA'S NATIONAL INTERESTS AND OBJECTIVES

National interests and objectives establish a nation's strategic requirements. Policies provide the guiding rules for satisfying them. National strategy integrates all elements of national power to achieve national interests and objectives, both during peace and war.

National strategy includes a political strategy, that addresses internal as well as international issues, an economic strategy, a national security strategy and so on. National security strategies together constitute "grand strategy" that is "the art and science of employing national power under all circumstances to exert desired degrees and types of control over the opposition through threats, force, indirect pressures, diplomacy, subterfuge and other imaginative means, thereby satisfying national security interests and objectives."

However, unlike solitaire, grand strategy is not a game that a nation can play all by itself. Actions and reactions of adversaries who will invariably seek to promote their own national interests and further their own objectives must always be vectored in, in as much as this grand strategy must be flexible and adaptable to emerging situations.

The four basic national interests of nation states are the defence of the homeland, economic well being, the creation of a favourable world order or external environment and the promotion of values. These national interests are generally graded on a four-tiered scale of priorities or intensities. The foremost among these are survival interests which deal with the very existence of a nation and are of broad, overriding importance to the survival, safety and vitality of a nation. There can be no compromises with survival interests, no matter what the diplomatic, political or financial cost because the survival of the nation cannot be imperilled under any circumstances. Vital interests are those which if not duly safeguarded, have the potential to result in serious harm to the security and well being of the nation. The next in the order of priority are major interests with a much reduced potential for serious harm than vital interests and at the lower end of the scale are peripheral or minor interests that are unlikely to require precipitate action. The time dimension provides another yardstick for measuring the intensity of an interest. Survival interests invariably require immediate attention. For example, the Japanese bombing of Pearl Harbour in 1941 had directly threatened the survival of the US and an immediate US reaction was necessary to ward off the threat. Vital interests require urgent planning and preparation to meet threats to national security, particularly if they have the potential to approach the survival level. Major interests require a serious approach but are generally those that can be handled through negotiations and an accommodative attitude based on give and take. In the case of peripheral interests, a wait and watch policy normally suffices.

The most basic national interest is the survival of the state. A state must ensure its survival "with an 'acceptable' degree of independence, territorial integrity, traditional life styles, fundamental institutions, values and honour intact. Nothing else matters if the country is exterminated as a sovereign entity. No other end is worth risking national extinction to attain." Post-World War II, the Cuban missile crisis was the most challenging example of the survival of the US being at stake. It is the survival instinct that will keep the Pakistan leadership, military or civilian, from launching a nuclear first strike on India knowing full well that Pakistan will cease to exist as a viable nation state after massive punitive Indian nuclear strikes in retaliation. No matter how irrational the Pakistani leaders make themselves out to be, India knows that they cannot afford to act irrationally as far as the very survival of their country is concerned.

It has been said that nations have no permanent friends or permanent enemies - they have only permanent interests. This is not really true. National survival is the only abiding national interest. All other interests can and do change from time to time. Vital interests include the physical security of territory, the safety of citizens, the economic well-being of society and the protection of critical national infrastructures from paralysing attack, both physical and cyber attack. These include banking, finance and stock markets, energy, telecommunications, transportation systems (roads and railways, airports and air traffic controls and shipping and inland waterways), water supply systems and emergency services. Threats to vital interests pose potential rather than imminent dangers and hence allow policymakers time to resolve those threats through diplomatic means and to convince an adversary that confrontation would prove extremely costly. A recent example of military action to safeguard a vital interest is that of the Coalition Forces campaign to evict Iraqi troops from Kuwait during the 1990-91 Gulf War.

India's foremost national interest is India's survival as a nation state. Despite several wars and low intensity conflicts having been thrust on it by inimical external powers, India has successfully survived the first half-century after independence. It is well known that India has no claims or territorial ambitions beyond its borders. Ample proof of this was provided after the 1971 war with Pakistan when India declared a unilateral cease-fire on the western border despite being in a position of immense military superiority after the Pakistani forces in East Pakistan (now Bangladesh) surrendered at Dacca. The Indian armed forces also vacated all Bangladesh territories by March 1972. However, Indian territory remains under the occupation of its adversaries. Pakistan is in occupation of approximately 80,000 square km of the state of J&K since 1947-48 despite a United Nations resolution calling upon it to vacate. China is in occupation of about 38,000 square km of India's Aksai Chin since November 1962. Also, Pakistan has illegally ceded 5,800 square km of Indian territory in J&K to China through which the Karakoram Highway has ben constructed.

India's first vital national interest is independence and autonomy in decision-making. There can be no compromises with national level decision-making in important matters, particularly those relating to national security. Whether it is the decision to sign the CTBT or to join the FMCT negotiations, Indian decision-makers must be guided purely by the national interest and not by any extraneous considerations. The next vital interest in order of importance would be to create a secure environment conducive to India's unhindered economic development. India should aim to achieve the status of a fully developed country by 2020-25 and the Indian Government must not tolerate any external interference in this national effort. The early resolution of the territorial and boundary dispute with China is a vital interest for India's security and so is the resolution of the ongoing low intensity limited conflict along the Line of Control (LoC) in J&K and the Actual Ground Position Line (AGPL) at Siachen Glacier. Ensuring that Pakistan's sponsorship of trans-border and trans-LoC terrorism and insurgency in J&K and other parts of India is brought to an early end would also qualify as a vital interest. In fact, finding a long-term solution to the internal and external dimensions of the Kashmir problem is India's foremost vital interest at present.

Another vital interest would be to ensure that a credible nuclear deterrence is firmly in place with China and Pakistan. If nuclear deterrence were to ever fail, this interest would be instantaneously upgraded to the level of a vital or even survival interest and immediate retaliatory action would be warranted. Parallel to this would be work towards total, universal nuclear disarmament and disarmament of other weapons of mass destruction. The protection of Indian citizens against threats to their lives and to care for their well-being at all places and at all times would be vital interests. Other vital interests would include a conflict and tension free internal security environment and the protection of key national infrastructure from physical and cyber attack. Effective control over and the protection of India's airspace is a vital interest that cannot be compromised. As 97 percent of India's trade (by volume) is ship-borne, the guaranteed, unhindered passage of Indian ships and foreign-owned ships carrying goods to and from India through India's sea lanes of communications (SLOCs) would also be a vital interest and the Indian Navy would need to be structured to ensure the protection of these SLOCs both during war and peace. India must spare no effort to defend its vital interests, including the decisive use of military force when necessary and appropriate.

Major interests are important but not crucial to the well-being of a country. Major economic, political and ideological issues that cause serious concern can be negotiated with adversaries even if the negotiations are protracted. Confrontation is rarely desirable to protect major interests. A confrontation free regional security environment is a major national security interest. An early end to the Afghan conflict and the resolution of the ethnic conflict in Sri Lanka would be major interests with diplomatic and military overtones. To enable India to exercise a degree of influence over the nations in India's regional neighbourhood to promote harmonious relationship in tune with India's national interests would be a major national interest. Safeguarding India's interests in its two million square kilometre Exclusive Economic Zone (EEZ) is an important major interest. The maintenance of the Indian Ocean as a zone of peace is a major interest that also has a bearing on the prevention of armed intervention and the establishment of military bases by inimical external forces in India's regional neighbourhood. India would like to promote the United Nations (UN) as the world's premier peacekeeping, peace enforcement and peace support organisation and continue its support to such operations worldwide. As a corollary, it is in India's interest to oppose the growing tendencies to marginalise the UN since the end of the Cold War.

Another major interest is the resolution of internal ethnic conflicts with fissiparous tendencies and the prevention of terrorism. Linked with this are the proliferation of small arms and narcotics trafficking and organised crime, including the circulation of fake Indian currency to undermine the Indian economy. Since these internal problems have a major external dimension, they need to be approached in a comprehensive inter-ministerial and inter-departmental manner at the national level in conjunction with the concerned state governments. Energy, food, water and environmental security are major interests that require synergised civil and military action plans at the national level. India must at all times maintain access to sources of energy supplies, natural resources and world markets for Indian goods. The prevention of demographic invasions from India's neighbours would also qualify as a major interest. Promoting democracy abroad, particularly in the Southern Asian region, is as important for India as it is for the US. India would need to find ways and means to promote democracy in Afghanistan, Pakistan, Myanmar and even Tibet without direct interference in the internal affairs of these countries.

A peripheral interest is one that does not seriously affect the entire nation's well being even though it may be detrimental to the private interests of Indian citizens and businessmen. Peripheral interests are lower order political, economic and ideological interests.

Concern for the well being of the Indian Diaspora could be called a peripheral interest. However, such interests may at times have to be upgraded to major interests due to the impact of the prevailing situation. The events in Fiji during the summer of months of 2000 when the democratically elected government was overthrown and the Indian minority was subjected to undue harassment provide an example.

While the promotion of democracy abroad is a major interest, the promotion of secular values could be termed as a peripheral interest. Humanitarian interests would also qualify as peripheral interests.

China's human rights violations in Tibet are of immense concern to India because of India's long-standing affinity with the Tibetan people. Pakistan's suppression of the human rights of the people of Pakistan Occupied Kashmir (POK) and the Northern Areas of Gilgit and Baltistan are also a cause for concern. The people in these areas do not enjoy any fundamental rights and those in the Northern Areas have no representation or say in their governance. India needs to bring international pressures to bear on these countries to stop these wanton and unchecked human rights violations.

The two national interests that are most likely to determine whether a country would engage in war are serious military threats to its homeland and major potential dangers to its external environment. The real test of the worth of a nation's political leadership is to correctly assess vital national interests and the likely costs involved in upholding them. Failure to appreciate the intensity of an antagonist's interest, or for that matter an ally's stake, can lead to blunders in foreign policy and disasters in war. The United Kingdom's invasion of Egypt in 1956, the US intervention in Vietnam in the mid-1960s, Argentina's seizure of the Falklands Islands in 1982 and Saddam Hussein's capture of Kuwait in 1990 are examples of such blunders. The US intervention in Vietnam is a classic example of the political leaders deciding that the issue was a vital interest and merited armed intervention and the US Congress and public thinking otherwise. No issue that is not supported wholeheartedly by the public can be graded as a vital interest without the risk of ultimate failure if the use of force is resorted to. This is, of course, more true of open societies and modern democracies than of totalitarian regimes. India's intervention in Sri Lanka in 1987 was not supported by the public and had finally led to an ignominious abandonment without having achieved any strategic goals.

National interests cannot be easily sub-divided into vital, major and peripheral ones, as they tend to change with changes in the international environment and the prevailing situation at any point in time. The sub-divisions tend to be judgmental and even experienced analysts can and often do wrong. It must be recognised that various political leaders, government functionaries, scholars and academics would have their own concept of what qualifies as a vital, major or peripheral interest. It is necessary to have a parliamentary and wider public debate on these issues to assess whether there is a national consensus. After that it should be left to the National Security Council and its various groups to evaluate India's interests holistically and draw up a list that is both meaningful and achievable.

EMERGING SECURITY CHALLENGES

Even as India grapples with diverse external and internal threats to its security, many new challenges are emerging on the security horizon. Before the dangers evident in them can be addressed, the emerging threats need to be identified and understood. The major emerging threats are outlined below:

- Increasing demands for electric power to meet the requirements of industry and the growing population will make energy security a primary concern. Energy security will be particularly important in future, as fossil fuels will become more and more inadequate for the nation's increasing energy needs. Domestic oil production has been declining while the demand has been rising steadily. Hence, oil will continue to be a strategic resource and the security of India's oil supplies from abroad as well as that of all oil reserves and installations will need to be ensured.
- India's growing population and the likelihood of mass migrations into India, for example from Bangladesh, will threaten the existing food reserves and endanger food security. The nation will find it extremely difficult to cope with successive failures of the monsoon, if they occur, and the consequent famine-like conditions that are likely to prevail. For almost a decade now, the monsoon has been bountiful in most parts of India.

Quite obviously, this cannot continue for long and the law of averages will catch up sooner rather than later.

- The ravages of global warming and changing monsoon patterns are likely to deplete India's water sources and threaten water security even as the increasing population, rapid industrialisation and the enhanced requirements of irrigation raise the demand for water. The Tata Energy Research Institute has estimated that the demand for water will almost double from 564 billion cubic metres (bcum) in 1997 to 1,048 bcum in 2047.14 The situation will be further exacerbated when the Himalayan nation-states begin drawing more water for their own consumption. The amicable sharing of the Ganga River waters between India, Bangladesh and Nepal has already been posing problems. Successive droughts have ravaged some of India's western states during 1999 and 2000 mainly due to groundwater levels having fallen to extremely low levels.
- Information warfare is another emerging threat through which, besides nation-states, non-state actors, individual terrorists and even disgruntled elements within a state can play havoc with a nation's telecom, banking, stock exchanges, power grids, railways and air traffic control infrastructure, besides military communications and networks. The prevention of large-scale damage through a complex cyber-security system requires an inter-departmental approach in concert with industry and private entrepreneurs and can only be undertaken by a duly empowered apex organisation.
- The threats to India's maritime security are increasing exponentially as the world turns more and more towards the exploitation of ocean resources for food, energy and raw materials. This long- neglected aspect needs to be incorporated in the management of national security so that India's ocean resources in its exclusive economic zone (EEZ) are not poached at will by state and non-state actors. Increasing piracy at sea and the possible

use of India's island territories by terrorist organisations and for trade in contraband goods are other serious maritime threats.

- Security of the environment is another emerging challenge. The continuing increase in the population will threaten the already depleted forest resources as the area of cultivable land comes under pressure. Also, over exploitation of the oceans may upset the delicate marine balance. Increasing urbanisation is causing its own environmental problems. Soil erosion in some areas, specially in hill states due to the impact of deforestation, and the irreplaceable loss of vital nutrients due to the tendency to harvest three to four crops a year in some other states, will eventually lay waste vast areas of cultivable lands and severely curtail agricultural production.
- In future, the Indian government will have to increasingly plan for the security concerns of the vast Indian Diaspora, particularly the migrant Indian population employed on temporary work permits in the Gulf countries. The Gulf War in 1990-91 had resulted in the most massive airlift since the Berlin airlift as over 100,000 Indian workforce personnel had to be evacuated from Iraq. The increasing persecution of ethnic minorities of Indian origin in countries like Pakistan will create its own tensions and may force India to intervene in future. The May 2000 coup in Fiji, where the Indian minority was specifically targeted, may be a pointer of the shape of things to come.

Still newer challenges that are emerging include those from organised crime and narco-terrorism. India is flanked by two of the most notorious narcotics producing regions in the world - the Golden Crescent (Afghanistan, Iran and Pakistan; annual production approximately 2,500 tonnes) on the west and the Golden Triangle (Laos, Myanmar and Thailand; 1,500 tonnes) on the east. Money laundering and the issue of fake currency by inimical neighbours are new problems to be contended with. The Asian financial crisis demonstrated that a nation's currency can be undermined through external intervention and its economy can be de-stabilised. The Ministry of Defence (MoD) Annual Report 1995-96 listed several other non-military 'pressures' on the national security environment which could not be ignored. These included "...those relating to trade, intellectual property rights, environment, human rights..." The existing and emerging threats to national security are becoming more and more complex to evaluate and manage in the prevailing era of strategic uncertainty.

Need for a Formal Defence Policy

These threats and challenges to national security require systematic evaluation by an apex body and the formulation of a comprehensive national security strategy to ensure that they are managed well and not allowed to spin out of control. Indian defence analysts have for long lamented the lack of a national security vision and strategy. With his characteristic frankness, K. Subrahmanyam minces no words in bluntly stating that, "It is now well recognised all over the world that India does not have a tradition of strategic thinking... mainly due to the incapacity of our political leaders and top civil servants to take a long-term view of national security. This is compounded by their consequent failure in giving a lead to the armed forces in preparing the country to face its long-term need for defence preparedness." In Brahma Chellaney's view, "The lack of an integrated, long-term national security approach stands out as the biggest failure of nation-building in the half-century that India has been independent. In the absence of such an approach, national security policy-making has been characterised largely by ad hoc decisions to meet new threats and realities." M. D. Nalapat says that national security policy has generally been one of reacting to threats and events and, "A holistic view was avoided as this would have reduced the powers of the separate bureaucracies (in the home and defence ministries especially) dealing with the problem... this uncoordinated response to security threats is a major failing in the system." And, K. N. Daruwalla asks, "Can a country have a military doctrine if it does not posses a strategic one? If your overall objectives and goals are ambiguous and undefined, how can you lay down objectives for your armed forces? How can a military doctrine be embedded in such amorphousness?.... Since the armed forces are required to safeguard national interests, foreign policy objectives should go hand in hand with the development of the military machine." However, Jasjit Singh has expressed the view that, "... the reality also must be recognised that (despite the absence of a formally articulated defence doctrine) the country has managed its defence and military affairs well during the past half century."

Indian policy planners have traditionally fought shy of formally articulating the country's defence and national security policies. Perhaps this reticence owes its origins to an innate sense of refraining from hurting the sensibilities of India's adversaries and neighbours. In its Nineteenth Report, the Estimates Committee had recommended that the country should have a formal National Security Doctrine. When the Standing Committee on Defence (1995-96) in the Tenth Lok Sabha enquired about the action taken on this recommendation, the Defence Secretary replied: "... there is a policy; the only thing is that it is not written down as a separate document and published as such... As a matter of policy we have not published such a document and the Government has not been in favour of publishing a separate document. It is only the United States in my knowledge which annually publishes a document called National Security Doctrine. Non-publication of the document does not mean in any way non-existence of policy." Replying to the debate in the Lok Sabha on the Demands for grants of the MoD, on May 10, 1995, Prime Minister P. V. Narsimha Rao, who was also the Defence Minister, stated: "We do not have a document called India's National Defence Policy. But we have got several guidelines which are followed, strictly followed and observed... This policy is not merely rigid in the sense that it has been written down, but these are the guidelines, these are the objectives, these are the matters which are always kept in view while conducting our defence policy..."

Similarly, the Ministry of External Affairs (MEA) avers in its Annual Report 1998-99 that, "We view foreign policy as an integral part of the larger effort of building the nation's capabilities: through economic development, strengthening social well-being and the quality of life and of protecting India's sovereignty, territorial integrity and security, not only in its defence and economic aspects, but in the widest strategic sense of the term." It says that India's external relations are guided by "well-established principles" which have formed the "basis of our foreign policy for decades" and "enjoy a broad national consensus, thus providing a strong foundation of stability and continuity." However, the report does not spell out what those principles are in specific terms and how they translate into practical execution in furthering national interests and objectives.

It is due to this lack of a long-term national security perspective and the failure to initiate a public debate for the formulation of a national consensus on the vital interests, national security objectives and a synergised national security strategy, that the security pendulum has swung between the interventionist "Indira Doctrine" of the 1970s and 1980s on one end and the conciliatory "Gujral Doctrine" of the mid-1990s on the other. The Indira Doctrine stated that, "India will neither intervene in the domestic affairs of any state in the region, unless requested to do so, nor tolerate such intervention by an external power. If external assistance is needed to meet an external crisis, states should first look within the region (that is, to India) for help." The ill-conceived IPKF intervention in Sri Lanka, as also the stand-off with Nepal on the trade treaty and the successful crushing of the coup in the Maldives could be attributed to the practical application of the Indira Doctrine (dubbed as a "muscular" foreign policy by some non-Indian South Asian commentators). The Gujral Doctrine reflected the recognition that India's policies towards its smaller neighbours within Southern Asia should show greater concern for their security perceptions, instead of sticking to hard-line attitudes that have created tensions in the past. The essence of the doctrine was that India would not insist on reciprocity and would be prepared to go more than half way to improve its relations with its smaller neighbours. Inder Gujral, India's Minister for External Affairs, expected the implementation of his ideas to result in a "fundamental recasting of South Asia's regional relationships... to create a climate of greater confidence and close and mutually beneficial co-operation." The two doctrines would require fundamentally different national security strategies to implement though these would not be mutually exclusive and would even overlap in certain areas. Radically different approaches to national security from decade to decade can only lead to a mismatch between capabilities and intentions and must be resolved through wider national debate.

The closest that government documents in India come to articulating national security and foreign policy objectives are the annual reports of the MoD and the Ministry of External Affairs (MEA). In fact, it was only with the 1997-98 annual report that the MoD for the first time spelt out India's national security objectives. Commenting on this interesting development, Raja Menon wrote recently: "The Annual Defence Report of 1997-98 has many welcome changes and for the first time, the notion of 'sacred territory' has been watered down. In all the previous years the role of the armed forces was depicted purely and solely as the 'defence of our territorial integrity', exhibiting a mindset that was not conducive to understanding coercive diplomacy, the manipulation of risk and the threat of military action."

In its opening chapter entitled "National Security Environment", the Annual Report of 1997-98 stated that India's national security objectives are served by:

- Defending the country's borders as defined by law and enshrined in the Constitution and protecting the lives and property of its citizens against terrorism and insurgencies.
- Promoting further co-operation and understanding with neighbouring countries and implementing mutually agreed confidence-building measures.

- Working with countries of the Non-Aligned Movement to address key challenges before the international community and engaging in co-operative security initiatives such as the ASEAN Regional Forum (ARF).
- Pursuing security and strategic dialogues with major powers and key partners.
- Following a consistent and principled policy on disarmament and international security issues based on universality, non-discrimination and equal security for all.
- Having a secure and effective deterrent against the use or the threat of use of weapons of mass destruction against India.

Post-Pokhran II in May 1998, in the 1998-99 Annual Report, the issue of deterrence against weapons of mass destruction was moved up from the last place to the second place in the national security objectives and was re-worded as follows: "Having a secure, effective and credible minimum deterrent against the use or threat of use of weapons of mass destruction against India. The profile of this deterrent, including accurate and refined delivery systems, will not be circumscribed in range and payload by any outside pressure or influence but will be determined by the country's threat perception at any point of time." Also, a new sub-para on technology control regimes was added: "Insulating the country from the effect of individual or group restrictions on the transfer of material, equipment and technologies that have a bearing on India's security, particularly its defence preparedness. This involves a greater emphasis on in-house research, development and production of the nation's requirements and recourse to feasible alternative sources." In the 1998-99 Annual Report, in the objective on the country's disarmament policy, the phrase "based on the principles of supreme national interest" has been added after the words "and international security issues". Curiously, the report refers to the territorial dispute with China as a "boundary" dispute. A careful reading of the national security objectives enunciated in the annual reports of the MoD reveals a tendency to mix objectives with policy in some cases and shows that the objectives are mere statements of intent in others.

According to the MoD, "... although there has been no specifically written document called India's National Defence Policy, yet it has been articulated clearly and unambiguously through various policy statements over the years. The policy articulated since independence is as follows:

"That our military capability is to be so directed to ensuring the defence of national territory over land, sea and air encompassing among others the inviolability of our land borders, island territories, offshore assets and our maritime trade routes. Government have repeatedly made it clear that it is not our objective to influence/interfere/dominate (the) region on the basis of military strength."

In a submission made by the MoD to the Standing Committee on Defence, it was stated that the following aspects "fully depict the national security interests":

- Defence of national territory over land, sea and air, encompassing among others the inviolability of our land borders, island territories, offshore assets and our maritime trade routes.
- To secure an internal environment whereby our Nation State is insured against any threat to its unity or progress on the basis of religion, language, ethnicity or socio-economic dissonance.
- To enable our country to exercise a degree of influence over the nations in our immediate neighbourhood to promote harmonious relationship in tune with our national interests.
- To be able to effectively contribute towards regional and international stability.
- To possess an effective out-of-the-country contingency capability to prevent destabilisation of the small nations in our immediate neighbourhood that could have adverse security implications for us.

Though national security interests and objectives have been

spelt out in bits and pieces by the Government, in annual reports and while answering the queries of the Standing Committee on Defence, as brought out above, these have tended to change from time to time and have not been subject to direct parliamentary oversight. These policy statements are of a transitory nature and could sometimes even be based on the personal predilections of policy makers who may be in power at a given point in time. A case in point is the question of whether or not China poses a threat to India. It is well known that while the Defence Minister was reported to have named China as India's number one threat, the Minister for External Affairs subsequently ruled out such an assessment. Hence, these transitory policy statements do not amount to a comprehensive, nationally debated approach that is sanctified by parliamentary consensus transcending the political divide.

Brahma Chellaney has written: "... it needs to be recognised that national security is much more than defence policy. The defence of India means the defence of its national interests. National security demands integrated planning and co-ordinated use of India's political, military, diplomatic and scientific resources to advance its core interests... Unfortunately, India lacks a long-term national security strategy despite the pressing problems it confronts. There is no integrated policy-making process that seeks to make specific policies compatible with each other... serious efforts have (not been) made to establish institutionalised methods so that policy-making is driven less by personalities and more by long-term integrated planning. A host of functional inefficiencies continue to burden Indian policy-making constricting any government's ability to manage national security in a prudent, cost-effective and result-oriented manner..."

Even the Kargil Review Committee Report has recommended an overhaul of the present system: "The Committee strongly feels that the Kargil experience, the continuing proxy war and the prevailing nuclearised security environment justify a thorough review of the national security system in its entirety."

It clearly emerges that the manifold existing and emerging external and internal threats to national security demand a comprehensive and mature system for their handling and management.

Present Government policies appear to reflect individual ministerial approaches rather than a holistic integrated approach. Coherence in application can only flow from a synergised national security strategy. Only an all-encompassing national security management system can take into account all the prevalent inter-ministerial, inter-departmental and civil-military diversities. The emerging asymmetric threats require systematic evaluation and meticulous planning, so that long-term projections can be made in respect of military force structures and the development of the necessary capabilities.

Only when a comprehensive national security strategy is formulated to deal with the existing and emerging threats on a long- and mid-term basis, can the responsibilities of the armed forces and concerned government departments be clearly visualised. Based on the security objectives and the responsibilities assigned, the Services can review their organisational and force structures and make recommendations to the government to institute the changes necessary to translate policy into action. The virtues of long-term defence planning cannot be over-emphasised. Ad hoc functioning on a year-to-year basis leads to imperfection in decision-making and tends to result in avoidable waste.

INDIA'S NATIONAL SECURITY STRATEGY

National interests lead to the drawing up of national security objectives and the formulation of national security policies. India's national security objectives have been adequately stated in the MEA Annual Report of 1998-99, reproduced above. The only aspect that really needs to be added is to strive to weaken the China-Pakistan collusive nexus in nuclear and missile technology and military hardware. It should be India's objective to marginalise Pakistan's military power by 2010-15 and eliminate its interference in India's internal affairs. India's national security policies must be so formulated that India is in a position to provide leadership to other countries in the Southern Asian region so as to be able to exercise a reasonable degree of influence over their policies and actions to further its own security interests. India's security lies in establishing a confrontation free external environment. For this, India must be prepared to use all elements and instruments of national power to influence the actions of countries that follow policies and initiate measures inimical to India's national interests. Such policies would require matching strategies backed by necessary resources being devoted to diplomatic, military, intelligence and other efforts to achieve the desired objectives.

India's strategic frontiers extend to Tibet in the north, the Central Asian region, including Afghanistan, in the northwest, include the Saudi Peninsula in the west, extend to Mauritius and Diego Garcia in the Indian Ocean and the ASEAN countries in the east, including the Malacca Straits. India's national security strategy must reflect India's strategic interests in these regions. In the prevailing uncertain geo-strategic environment and unstable world order, with the primacy of the nation-state being gradually eroded, no country can afford to "go it alone" in organising its national security. Even the US, the world's only remaining superpower, has formulated a well-crafted strategy of alliances to further its wide-ranging security interests. In this age of globalisation and trade blocks, the trend is inexorably towards collective security. India too needs to form strategic partnerships with countries sharing a mutuality of interests to countervail its adversaries. India's abhorrence for military alliances and its efforts towards pursuing a fiercely independent foreign policy have been well founded. However, India has found it difficult to single-handedly eliminate or even reduce the external threats and foreign-sponsored internal security challenges. India needs to establish strategic linkages with the US, Russia (as it will once again rise from the quagmire it is in at present to become a major power), Israel, Iran, Myanmar, Vietnam, Taiwan, Japan and South Korea to counter-balance China's growing power and influence.

One of the major reasons for the continuing violation of India's borders and the destabilisation of India through proxy wars is the prevalent perception of India as a soft state that is if not unmindful at least not adequately concerned about its external and internal security. This perception is founded on India's failure to exploit the advantages gained during the 1947-48, 1965 and 1971 conflicts with Pakistan and on its purely reactive handling of Pakistan's proxy war over the decade of the 1990s. India's continuously reducing defence expenditure throughout the period 1985-1999, even as the threats to its security increased manifold due to Pakistan's nuclearisation in 1987 and its proxy war against India from 1989-90 onwards, also sent a message of being relatively unconcerned. Inimical neighbours have always exploited such weaknesses to their advantage and so has been the case with India. Quite clearly, India now has no option but to adopt pro-active strategies to deal firmly with the threats confronting its security.

While India's nuclear doctrine of no first use and a credible minimum deterrent has been clearly stated, the strategies to be followed to give effect to this doctrine have not been spelt out except in passing in the recommendations of the National Security Advisory Board (NSAB) while formulating a draft Nuclear Doctrine. In fact, till the time of writing, the issue is yet to be debated in Parliament. The first inescapable ingredient of India's nuclear strategy would be overt signs of weaponisation - mere declaratory statements are not enough. If India's "nuclear capability is to become a source of power and influence during crises rather than only a strategic deterrent to total war... (a) public stance on the actual nuclear capability, the range and accuracy of delivery systems, the kilotonnage of warheads... the authorisation (procedures) for launch, and the custody of codes and interlocks for authorising a launch..." will be necessary. Having consciously abjured a first use doctrine, India's retaliatory strike strategy has to be based on destroying the adversary's large industrial and population centres if deterrence is to be successfully maintained. Only if the adversary's political and military leadership is convinced that the cost of a first strike would prove to be unbearably high, will it be deterred from doing the unthinkable. If India's retaliatory response strategy lacks credibility and the adversary is convinced that he can bank on an ambivalent Indian response, he may be tempted to risk a first strike. Deterrence is ultimately a mind game and turns on credibility.

Some other aspects that would enhance the credibility of India's nuclear deterrence include the establishment of a viable command and control system with well publicised procedures for nuclear decision-making, a clearly enunciated chain of succession, at least the partial transfer of the custody of nuclear warheads to the armed forces units designated to launch them and a well-conceived targeting philosophy. However, real credibility will stem from a demonstrated delivery system capability and an established programme for building the required number of missiles. While India's delivery systems are adequate to retaliate against nuclear threats from Pakistan, India is yet to develop a 5,000 km class missile to retaliate against a Chinese threat and other threats that may manifest themselves in future. In fact, unless the N-5 agree quickly to adopt a time bound nuclear disarmament programme, only a remote possibility at present, India has no option but to develop an inter-continental ballistic missile (ICBM). Some commentators have written about such a programme named Surya but there has been no official confirmation. The status of the advanced technology vehicle (ATV) project for a nuclear powered submarine is also not clear. Unless India demonstrates the will to develop the required delivery systems and commits sufficient funds and efforts to their development, India's nuclear deterrence will continue to lack credibility.

In view of the doubts expressed by leading Indian nuclear scientists like Dr. P. K. Iyengar regarding the viability of the thermonuclear test carried out in May 1998[42] and the need for more tests if weapons in the megaton class or even 200 kiloton (kt) fusion warheads are to be developed, India will have to develop a suitable strategy to find a way around the CTBT to enable further testing without inviting a fresh round of sanctions and international opprobrium. In case India's nuclear warhead capability remains confined to 15 to 30 kt fission warheads, it will lead to the sub-optimal utilisation of India's meagre fissile material stockpile. With negotiations for the FMCT staring it in the face and the likelihood of an early agreement being reached, India would be hard put to stockpile adequate fissile stockpile for the total number of warheads that its retaliatory strategy and targeting philosophy may require. These are the tough issues confronting the development of a potent nuclear strategy. While there are no easy answers, a determined diplomatic stance and a tough negotiating position with some hard bargaining can achieve the desired results. The world is gradually getting used to the idea that a "cap, reduce, eliminate" policy is no longer feasible and that India's nuclear weapons, born primarily out of the need to safeguard national security, cannot now be rolled back.

Simultaneously with developing a credible nuclear deterrent, India must continue to pursue its nuclear disarmament efforts. The best nuclear strategy would undoubtedly be the total elimination of nuclear weapons from the face of the earth. However, this is one aspect in the affairs of mankind where progress will continue to be excruciatingly slow. This will have to be vectored into India's nuclear calculations. India must also seek to discuss and agree upon mutual nuclear risk reduction measures (NRRMs), particularly with China and Pakistan. Since neither China nor Pakistan is willing to negotiate a mutual no-first-use treaty with India, it would be in the interest of all the protagonists to ensure that sufficient safety checks are mutually in place to reduce the risk of knee-jerk responses in situations of panic and accidental nuclear war. The holding of discussions for NRRMs need not be linked to the lack of progress on other issues of concern such as a halt to Pakistan's sponsorship of terrorism in India. The possibility of the unleashing of nuclear weapons, even if unintended, is too horrific to make its reduction contingent upon other political and diplomatic considerations, no matter how deeply vexatious the issues concerned might be. The first aim of a well-rounded nuclear strategy should be to ensure that deterrence does not fail, whether by design or by default, and that the nuclear genie remains tightly bottled up - as it has been since August 1945.

It is apparent that India's world view has changed since Pokhran-II to one that is more assertive and more willing to reach out to safeguard national security, even if the new thinking is not very clearly and lucidly articulated officially. Indian defence analysts are becoming increasingly more forthright in spelling out specific policies and actions to reduce and gradually eliminate the manifold threats and challenges to national security. Bharat Karnad strongly advocates that Vietnam should be propped up as a nuclear counter to China to ensure the same level of discomfiture to China as China's collusion with Pakistan is causing to India. He rationalises that India would not be violating any international treaties in offering nuclear know-how to Vietnam and the international opprobrium that is bound to result would be justified in terms of India's larger security interests. He recommends that India must exploit the growing anti-Pakistan sentiments in Pakistan Occupied Kashmir (POK) and the Northern Areas of Gilgit and Baltistan and that India should sponsor and support an Azad Kashmir Liberation Front and provide its members "diplomatic, political and moral support" exactly like Pakistan claims to do to Kashmiri militants.

Bharat Karnad is also of the view that India's special operations capability needs to be increased to about a division worth of Special Forces troops to sustain covert special operations inside POK on a long-term basis to counter Pakistan's proxy war through pro-active trans-LoC operations. Appearing as a defence analyst on a TV programme, Lieutenant General Satish Nambiar (Retd.), Director, United Service Institution of India, New Delhi, recommended that trans-LoC operations be launched by the Indian army to raise the cost for Pakistan to sponsor foreign mercenary terrorists for operations in J&K. Mulayam Singh Yadav, a former Defence Minister and a member of Parliament, has publicly demanded "hot pursuit" operations across the LoC to stop Pakistan's trans-LoC terrorism. Ever since Lashkar-e-Toiba's brutal massacres in J&K on the night of August 1, 2000, in which 100 innocent people were killed, there has been a spate of editorials and opinion pieces in leading Indian dailies demanding hot pursuit and other trans-LoC operations. Leading Indian analysts like Brahma Chellaney have questioned whether a strong, stable and prosperous Pakistan is in India's interest.

It is emerging quite clearly that the limit of tolerance of the Indian people has been crossed and there will be greater demands on the government in future to adopt pro-active trans-LoC measures to put an end to Pakistan's proxy war against India. "... India will have to exploit Pakistan's weaknesses with a strategic blueprint that incorporates military, political and unorthodox elements. The main aim should be to start hitting Pakistan wherever it will hurt and whenever it least expects such counteraction." Since it is necessary to raise the ante on the LoC, India will have to be prepared for a larger conventional conflict with Pakistan that may not remain confined to the LoC and may spill over to the international border. Hence, India's strategy must be to further develop its conventional superiority to fight and win a limited war with Pakistan in a nuclear environment. Victory in such a limited war should be measured not through inflicting a comprehensive military defeat on Pakistan, as that in any case is not possible below the nuclear threshold, but by destroying a substantial portion of Pakistan's war waging potential so as to marginalise the Pakistan army as the force majeure in Pakistan's polity. It should be clear to all perceptive observers that the real problem between India and Pakistan is not the Kashmir issue or any other issue but the Pakistan army that drives Pakistan's foreign policy and is the progenitor of Pakistan's proxy war strategy to "bleed India through a thousand cuts". The early marginalisation of the Pakistan army should be a major national priority.

With China India faces a "capabilities-intentions" dilemma. While China has systematically resolved its long-standing, complex and seemingly intractable territorial and boundary disputes with Russia, Vietnam and the Central Asian Republics through protracted negotiations in a spirit of mutual accommodation and there is peace on these borders, it has shown remarkable intransigence in following the same approach with India.

China continues to profess its willingness to resolve its territorial and boundary dispute with India through peaceful negotiations. Despite the Border Peace and Tranquillity Agreement signed in 1993 and the Confidence Building Measures in the military field mutually negotiated in 1996, there has been little change in the ground situation. China either fails to or does not deliberately wish to accept that the best confidence building measure would be to first delineate on the map and ground the Line of Actual Control (LAC).

As long as the LAC is not clearly demarcated, border clashes can occur between the two opposing armies at any time in the disputed areas and these can lead to another border conflict. Though there is a fair possibility of such a conflict between the two nuclear-armed adversaries being fought below the nuclear threshold, it could rapidly escalate to nuclear exchanges that may not remain limited to battlefield targets. China is known to be engaged in modernising its armed forces and acquiring offensive conventional capabilities, including the creation of rapid reaction forces based on strategic airlift. It is also engaged in developing information warfare capabilities. Since China has successfully resolved its territorial disputes and boundary problems with most other neighbours, the new capabilities would be available to be used against India.

The only deduction that can reasonably be drawn is that China wishes to put its territorial dispute with India on the back burner for the time being, while it consolidates its economic and military power and is engaged in resolving the Taiwan dispute and in settling its claims to various islands in the South China Sea. Michael D. Swaine and Ashley J. Tellis have written that the basic logic underlying China's "indefinite postponement" approach has been to "steadfastly avoid conceding any Chinese claims with respect to the dispute, while simultaneously seeking to prevent the dispute from vitiating the pacific environment that China needs to complete its internal transformation successfully." Swaine and Tellis list several advantages of this approach:

- It positions China as a conciliatory state seeking to resolve all outstanding disputes peacefully.
- It does not increase the demands on China's military's forces at a time when the PLA is relatively weak and when the Chinese economy needs all the breathing room it can get.
- It prevents balancing coalitions from arising against China in the event Beijing pursued more coercive strategies.
- And, it delays the resolution of these disputes at least until the balance of power changes substantially in favour of China. At that time, both simple usurpation and coercive bargaining might become more attractive, although it is unclear today whether the Chinese leadership would conclude that the benefits of such actions easily exceed the costs.

China may choose to settle the territorial dispute with India at a time of its own choosing when it is militarily far more powerful. It may opt to do this either through coercive diplomacy or even by seeking a military solution. It is in India's interest to strive towards an early resolution of the territorial dispute with China so that India has only one major military adversary to worry about.

India would also be able to re-deploy at least some of the 10 to 12 mountain divisions and perhaps four to six squadrons of the Indian Air Force from the Tibetan border in the east and the northeast to the western border to gain a decisive military edge against Pakistan. India may even be able to "downsize" a few army divisions and utilise the savings that will accrue for the long-overdue qualitative upgradation of the army. Perhaps these are the real reasons that compel China to drag its feet in resolving its territorial and boundary dispute with India so that it can support Pakistan, its friend and ally, to continue to destabilise India through its proxy war without fear of major military retaliation.

India's strategy should be to develop adequately powerful leverages to make it incumbent on China to act quickly to resolve the territorial dispute between the two countries. Developing the strategic linkages mentioned above could do this. There would be immense advantages in commencing the sale of modern military hardware to Vietnam, including some quantities of Prithvi missiles with launchers under government-to-government soft loans.

The Defence Research and Development Organisation (DRDO) could provide technical know-how to Vietnam's nascent armament industry. If it becomes necessary, India should also be ready to play the Tibet card, something it has consciously avoided doing for almost half a century since China launched its brutal suppression of the human rights of the Tibetan people. The Chinese people's latent yearning for democracy could also be discreetly encouraged. The large number of multinational companies (MNCs) that are unhappy with their business ventures in China could be persuaded to invest in India instead through attractive offers. This would make both business as well as strategic sense.

Attempts to ensure a stable and peaceful external security environment would be meaningful only if internal security was first ensured. Throughout the last two decades of the 20th century, India's handling of militancy has lacked a firm and well-coordinated approach. India's reactive strategy of fighting Pakistan's proxy war through security forces' operations limited within its own territory has not produced the desired results. In addition to the trans-LoC pro-active measures mentioned above, India's internal security strategy needs to follow a three-pronged approach. Firstly, all security forces' operations in the states affected by armed militancy should be conducted in a comprehensively coordinated manner with well-streamlined procedures for the acquisition and sharing of intelligence. Secondly, there is an inescapable need to organise a national level para-military counter-insurgency force with the army's ethos and standards of training and, at least initially, army leadership. Such a force could be based on an existing police force like the CRPF that could be designated as the Central Government's primary counter-insurgency strike force. Its charter will have to be modified accordingly to relieve it of other law and order duties. Or, a new elite force could be raised from scratch for the purpose. The haphazard raising of additional police force battalions, guided more by turf battles rather than hard-nosed national security considerations, must stop.

It is also imperative that the army's involvement in counter-insurgency operations must be reduced gradually from the peak level of approximately 120,000 (six divisions equivalent) in 1998[49] as it is by now well recognised that the prolonged employment of the army for such tasks hampers its training and operational preparedness for conventional military operations. Ideally, internal security problems should be handled by the Ministry of Home Affairs without seeking the army's help.

However, in proxy war situations involving well-trained foreign mercenary terrorists equipped with sophisticated weapons, it may become necessary to deploy the army. Such deployment should be for short-duration surgical operations only and even then, the army's specialised counter-insurgency strike forces like the Rashtriya Rifles (RR) should be employed and not regular infantry battalions. If the present level of Pakistan-sponsored militancy is not rapidly reduced to more manageable levels by trans-LoC pro-active operations, it will be necessary to increase the number of RR battalions to between 75 to 80 to reduce the involvement of regular infantry battalions. Finally, armed militancy can never be eliminated only through security forces' operations. Ultimately it is a battle of hearts and minds and only a political solution can eliminate the root causes of militancy and assuage the feelings of hurt of the alienated people. The government must initiate a political dialogue with all parties concerned to find a lasting solution to the complex problems confronting the nation in J&K and the northeastern states while simultaneously expediting developmental activities. Good governance is also an important ingredient of a successful internal security strategy.

Effective border management strategies go hand in hand with well-conceived internal security strategies. The infiltration of well-armed mercenary terrorists from Pakistan, mass migrations from Bangladesh into lower Assam, narcotics and small arms trafficking across India's vast land borders and long coastline, the smuggling of consumer goods and fake Indian currency from Nepal, the operations of ULFA militants from safe hideouts in Bhutan and the sanctuaries available to the insurgent groups of the northeastern states in Myanmar and Bangladesh, have all added to India's border security challenges. While the BSF should be responsible for manning all settled borders, the responsibility for unsettled and disputed borders, such as the LoC in J&K and the LAC on the Indo-Tibetan border, should be that of the army. The principle of 'single point control' must be followed if the borders are to be effectively managed. Divided responsibilities never result in effective control. While full operational control on the LoC is already with the army, it is not the case on the LAC with China. On the LAC, the ITBP, which is under the Ministry of Home Affairs (MHA), is responsible for the Ladakh, Himachal Pradesh and the Uttar Pradesh segments while the army is deployed in Sikkim. The Assam Rifles, another MHA force but under the army's operational control, manages the LAC in Arunachal Pradesh. On the other hand, on the Tibetan side, Border Guards divisions of the Chinese army under a single commander manage the entire LAC. The BSF must be withdrawn from its internal security commitments and reverted to border management that is its primary role. Ad hoc measures in utilising police forces for operational tasks for which they are not trained, invariably leads to the lack of a cohesive response to critical situations affecting national security and further complicates the resolution of existing problems.

Achieving self-reliance in critical weapons technologies is another important ingredient of India's national security strategy. Stringent technology control regimes have been applied by the western powers as a consequence to India's independent line on nuclear weapons even though India has behaved extremely responsibly as a nuclear power and has refrained from proliferating nuclear weapons and ballistic missile technologies, unlike China that is a signatory to the NPT and the MTCR. Though such technology denial regimes have only slowed down India's quest for self-reliance and not stopped it altogether, the present dependence on imports for major defence equipment needs to be reduced quickly and eliminated by 2020-25. The efforts already underway in indigenous weapons research and development need to be further stepped up. At the same time, India should establish closer strategic ties with countries like France and Israel that may be willing to enter into joint weapons development agreements with India. The leverages provided by India's weapons procurement programmes should be exploited to gain access to cutting edge defence technologies. Defence cooperation programmes need to be made more meaningful to establish strategic linkages with countries of consequence. The full importance of military diplomacy and its vast potential in furthering national security is yet to be realised in India. Other important national security strategies that need to be instituted include those for maritime and energy security, food, water and environmental security and for security against organised crime and cyber terrorism.

INDIAN COUNTERMEASURES POST MUMBAI ATTACKS

Immediately after the Mumbai attacks several measures were taken by the Indian administration amidst much public debate- mostly criticism as to how vulnerable Indian cities are to terrorist attacks. These measures were:

- Creation of NSG hubs in the major metropolitan cities
- Diplomatic pressure on Pakistan for the arrest and trial of Lashkar-e-Taiba's top leadership
- Creation of a new National Investigation Agency (NIA)
- Amendment of Unlawful Activities (Prevention) Act
- Increased budget allocation for Homeland Security Agencies

- Coastal Security Scheme
- Creation of a Police Commando Force in Mumbai
- Arrest of key Lashkar-e-Taiba operatives

Within a week of the attacks Indian Prime Minister Manmohan Singh announced the setting up of NSG hubs in different parts of the country. The first phase included setting up of hubs in Mumbai, Kolkata, Chennai and Hyderabad. All four of the hubs have been established and the last one was inaugurated in the winter of 2011. The regional NSG hubs were set up with the intent of reducing response time in case of a terrorist attack. In a country like India, which faces terrorist threat not just from external terrorist groups like Lashkar-e-Taiba but from homegrown terrorist and insurgent groups, even though it is necessary to have these regional hubs for quick deployment and response, security experts also feel that increase in the number of personnel or hubs is not going to solve the problem. Former National Security Advisor M.K. Narayanan said at a conference that the idea of setting up of NSG hubs was 'archaic' and a 'major mistake'. "I am concerned about the current emphasis on increasing the size and numbers of the NSG. I also have reservations about the establishment of four regional hubs. The NSG is an elite special force intended to meet a specific situation and not intended to confront the normal law and order situation... Its strength does not lie in its numbers, its uniqueness lies in the fact that it consists of the bravest of brave personnel, of great virtue and ability, specially trained for undertaking the most difficult tasks... increasing numbers, to my mind, is bound to dilute both quality and capability of the force"

The National Security Guard which was established in 1986 was modelled after the German GSG-9 and raised as an elite anti-hijacking, anti-terror and bomb disposal force. In the years before as well as after the attacks in Mumbai, they have mostly been used for VIP security. In 2012 the NSG for the first time in many years pulled out its 900 commandos from VIP security details and put them to train for and perform counter-terrorism and anti-hijacking operations. The boost that the

NSG got after the Mumbai attacks was a step in the right direction but no Mumbai like attack after 2008, the force seems to now be caught up in a fight for budget allocations, equipment acquisition and improving their capability in terms of personnel and training.

As the interrogations of the lone surviving terrorist, Ajmal Amir Kasab, proceeded and reports of Pakistani state support as well as Lashkar-e-Taiba's involvement surfaced, Indian officials blamed Pakistan for providing sanctuary and letting terrorist activities emanate from their soil. Indian administration since then has been trying to pressure Pakistan through diplomatic channels as well as through the international community to crack down on Lashkar- e-Taiba and bring the masterminds of the Mumbai attacks to book. In early January 2009, India sent evidence to Pakistan which linked the Mumbai attacks to Pakistani terrorists including data from the satellite phones which were used by the 10 gunmen to keep in touch with their handlers as well as what was described as 'Kasab's confession.' The evidence dossier was also sent to countries whose citizens were the victims of the attack such as the United States, as India tried to corner Pakistan diplomatically into bringing the perpetrators to justice.

In a time frame of three years since, 15 such dossiers have been provided to the Pakistani administration by the Indian government and officials of both countries have met on 13 different occasions. And even though Pakistan has acknowledged that the plan to attack Mumbai was hatched on Pakistani soil, India feels Pakistan has done little to cooperate and hasn't taken any real hard steps to crack down on terrorist activity. It has been almost 5 years since the first dossier was provided and on the 5th anniversary of the attacks, Indian officials still press for a speedy and just trial of the masterminds.

Another major initiative taken by the government was the setting up of a federal National Investigative Agency by passing the National Investigative Agency Act and making relevant amendments to the already existing Unlawful Activities (Prevention) Act. Both these measures were taken within a month of the Mumbai attacks and were passed by both Houses of the Parliament almost at the same time.

At present the NIA is functioning as the Central Counter Terrorism Law Enforcement Agency in India and has dealt with 72 cases till date. Even though there was a dire need for a Federal Investigative Agency, the haste in which this Act has been conceived has left unresolved many issues about the NIA's constitutional validity, functioning, and scope.

The constitutional basis for the creation of the NIA remains a matter of debate. The areas of policing and public order lie within the exclusive legislative competence of the States and not with the Centre (Central government). States would be extremely chary of accepting or cooperating with any agency that encroached on that power. Furthermore, the NIA Act has been drafted in a way that it focuses only on investigation but not on prevention. In order for the NIA to be effective in preventing federal crime, it needs to be able to warehouse, process and coordinate the flow of critical information.

The Amendments to the Unlawful Activities (Prevention) Act which were brought about almost parallel to the NIA Act also felt significant but were vague in character and meaning. The amendments define 'an act of terrorism' but for the Act to have any real prevention or enforcement powers the definition needs to be more specific in sketching out the difference between civilians and combatants as well as between political and personal motives.

Further the Act lacks any kind of provision for a review mechanism. It grants immunity from prosecution or other legal proceedings to the central and state governments, and their employees.

One of the more progressive steps which seems promising and likely to have a real effect on India's counter-terrorism policies is higher budget allocation for the Ministry of Home Affairs which is responsible for internal security, border management, para military forces etc. The allocation for India's homeland security agencies was increased by 25 percent in the budget 2009-2010. The allocation of budget for the Ministry has since increased yearly. The budget in recent years also included the Coastal Security Schemes which were initiated in 2005, well before the Mumbai attacks in 2008, and completed its first phase in 2011.

The Coastal Security Schemes were initiated with the aim of improving surveillance and patrolling along the Indian coast with the strengthening of the Marine Police Force. Under Phase-1 of the scheme 73 Coastal Police Stations, 58 Out Posts and 30 Barracks were approved with 204 boats and vehicles. Phase-2 was approved in 2010 and is set to be completed by 2015. 131 Coastal Police Stations, 180 boats/vessels, 60 jetties and 373 vehicles have been approved under Phase-2.

The issue of maritime security and the lack of it surfaced and gained much attention after the Mumbai attacks. The fact that 10 men could easily enter Indian waters and gain entry into India's financial capital armed with explosives, made the Indian government a target of the civil society's outrage and frustration.

Candle light vigils and heated public debates forced the administration to review the matter of coastal security and accelerate the implementation of the Coastal Security Scheme. But even though the Home Department and police are regularly claiming to have enhanced the coastal security system, the projects launched for this still remain on paper. Many coastal states failed to reach the target number of coastal police stations under Phase-1 and yet more have been sanctioned under Phase-2. States are also struggling with the maintenance and repair of equipment and vehicles. The intelligence community in Mumbai has got around 250 intelligence inputs this year with some referring to the possibility of terrorists using the sea to carry out attacks. Despite this, coastal police stations have not been built and the boats have been under repair for nearly two years. Yet another example of an ineffective counter-measure is the creation of an elite commando force under the Mumbai Police Department. The commando force called Force One was created for swift action in an event of Mumbai style attack and again it failed to even stand up on its feet. Till 2012, three years after its formation, the force was struggling to get the funds allocated to it by the State government and was struggling to cope with shortage of equipment such as special rifles, bulletproof vests, pistols and even ammunition for training and practice.

The most successful of all countermeasures though has been the arrest of key Lashkar-e-Taiba operatives. In 2013, Indian security officials arrested Abdul Karim Tunda- an expert bomb maker for the terrorist outfit. In 2012 approximately 61 operatives were killed in encounters with Indian security forces including Lashkar Division and District Commanders. Around 48 were arrested and 8 sleeper cells were neutralized. The arrests included key recruiter for Lashkar from India and Nepal Mohammad Omar Madni and Chief Coordinator for Jammu and Kashmir Manzoor.

Looking at the numbers, it certainly seems like the intelligence community is successful in gathering critical information as well as preventing further attacks but in my opinion they still have a long way to go. In 2013 itself, there has been a record of 254 infiltration bids made by terrorists along the India-Pakistan border. In 133 cases, the terrorists were made to 'return' to Pakistan territory, while they successfully crossed over in 84 cases. The operatives that crossed over in these 84 cases could well be planning another Mumbai. As seen in most of the counter measures analyzed above, they were carried out in haste without much deliberation or debate after the attacks in Mumbai. The poorly formed and impulsive decisions were then tangled in bureaucratic processes, slow paper work and murky politics. A senior journalist, Praveen Swami, commenting on the police reforms after the Mumbai attacks wrote in an article, 'The Indian Fine Art of Faking Security'- "India's post-26/11 police reforms painted stripes on a donkey — and passed it off as a tiger." But the alarming as well as disconcerting fact is that it is not just the police reforms which are being passed off as a tiger but India's counter-terrorism policies as a whole seems to be a striped donkey which when under attack will shed its stripes and show its true colors. Indian authorities continue to boast and reiterate the fact that they have launched many counter measures post Mumbai and they have been successful because there has not been another Mumbai like attack after 2008. Although that it is true, it is hardly a metric that can be used to measure success for counterterrorism policies. Most of these measures were taken to show to the world as well as to pacify the public sentiment that 'we are doing something.' Instead, for a review of the success or failure of these measures some basic questions should be addressed: Is the dependence on certain factors that terrorists or anti-terrorists can exploit as vulnerabilities increasing or decreasing? How seamlessly do terrorist organizations and networks interact? How seamlessly do new government anti-terrorist organizational structures and networks interact? Is the international operating environment becoming more or less inviting or restrictive for terrorists or for those combating them? Is it easier or harder today for terrorists to inflict the damage they seek to do?

ENTER SECURITY ISSUES FROM A GROWTH PERSPECTIVE

Security is widely considered the Number One issue for Afghanistan's reconstruction and development agenda. Dealing with the legacy of nearly a quarter-century of protracted conflict, and with the difficult security issues currently facing the country, has been and will continue to be a major challenge. The main security issues in Afghanistan from a development perspective (not necessarily in order of importance) are outlined briefly below. Needless to say, many of them are closely interrelated with each other.

Continuing conflict/insurgency/terrorism and associated insecurity. Although outright insurgency and significant military conflict are concentrated in areas in the south and east of the country (where much terrorist activity is occurs as well), this conflict has been continuing on a significant scale albeit with seasonal and other fluctuations, and is adversely affecting security in these areas with important development implications.

Elsewhere, sporadic acts of terrorism have occurred from time to time, but not on a widespread scale or in a sustained manner. These have a disproportionate impact on perceptions of the security situation particularly from outside the country, and hence deter foreign investment. Another adverse implication is movement restrictions on aid agencies and higher security costs for development activities, as well as for private business. For example, highway reconstruction projects reported that their direct spending on security added 3-15% to project costs, and a recent survey of private business firms found that their reported spending on security infrastructure accounted for close to 15% of sales revenue, and that an additional 3% of sales was reportedly spent on protection payments to commanders, government officials, or organized criminals (World Bank, 2006).

Lack of rule of law and poorly functioning judicial system. This is a fundamental problem, seriously affecting Afghans in their daily lives, which is both a manifestation of underlying insecurity and itself contributes to continuing insecurity. Rule of law and the judiciary were weak during most of the past quarter-century, and restoring let alone enhancing these critical components of the security system will be a major challenge. More specifically the police, weakened and largely captured by factional forces during the conflict, has often been more a source of insecurity than of security for most Afghans. Anecdotal evidence indicates that District officials are unable to reliably resolve local disputes in their official capacity, unless they have personal prestige through their traditional connections to do so. Few police officers in rural areas have professional training, and many are former mujahedin or militia members who became police officers when their commanders joined the Government after 2001. Police forces continue to operate largely independently from a centralized command structure under the Ministry of Interior, and many remain loyal to their former commanders. The police force is overwhelmingly male, and many districts lack detention facilities for women. The lack of women police officers to handle the arrest, detention, or transport of female detainees places any woman arrested at heightened risk of abuse.

The formal judicial system was devastated during the conflict, and its rebuilding since 2001 has been slow. In addition to the lack of recourse for Afghans and inability to effectively punish serious crimes (including those committed during the conflict), the weakness of the formal judicial system is a deterrent to business activity in the formal sector and to foreign investment. Although historically Afghanistan has relied much more on customary and traditional practices and adjudication mechanisms, these also were significantly eroded in many respects during the conflict, and/or "captured" by warlords and commanders, with adverse effects on local security as well as on business activities and livelihoods.

An important manifestation of these problems is the widespread uncertainties and disputes over land, leading to ambiguities and insecurity related to land tenure as well as theft and illegal appropriation of land. Confirming other information, recent fieldwork in Nangarhar and Laghman provinces found that conflict over agricultural land (and related water supplies) was the most common source of violence (Koehler and Zurcher, 2005). Access to land is the second most widely cited constraint on business activity in a recent survey of firms (World Bank, 2006).

Finally, there is a long tradition of the Judiciary being an exclusively male domain, and only around 3% of judges currently are women. With the exception of the heads of the juvenile and family courts in Kabul, women are not found in key positions within the judiciary. Where women do serve as judges, reports indicate that they do not perform the same functions as their male counterparts. Female judges tend to act in the capacity of judicial clerks and are rarely involved in the adjudication of cases, which severely limits the ability of Afghan women to approach the courts.

Dominant drug industry. The opium economy, which is estimated to comprise more than a third of total economic activity in Afghanistan, is a direct source of insecurity (drug-related conflict and violence, financing of armed groups and warlords and commanders who provide protection). But even more important, the drug industry is a major force working against state-building and good governance, and thereby has a major adverse effect on security indirectly as well. The drug industry can thrive in a situation where there is a weak, corruptible state and security forces, no or ineffective rule of law, and inadequate sanctions or negative incentives to discourage the whole range of actors - from farmers to drug traders to their sponsors inside and outside of government as well as regional drug industry actors. Therefore the drug industry comprises a powerful interest group diametrically opposed to the heart of Afghanistan's reconstruction agenda and thereby promoting insecurity.

Remaining factional forces. Although as noted earlier the DDR process has been completed, there are numerous "illegal armed combatants" not included in DDR. The new program for Disbandment of Illegal Armed Groups (DIAG) is intended to address this problem; however, this is expected to take several years. Moreover, Afghanistan by tradition and even more during the conflict has had an armed population, and this is not expected to change very quickly. Widespread ownership of small arms can be a source of insecurity as long as there is not basic rule of law and a minimum adequate level of government functionality in the security sector. Popular revulsion against warlords and commanders and their armed groups potentially can be a very powerful force, but it has not yet been harnessed. The Government's MDG report makes strong reference to the urgent need for licensing of arms.

Violent and other crime, including corruption. Although it is difficult with available data to ascertain whether violent crime and other forms of ordinary crime are more pervasive than in other low-income countries, anecdotal evidence and surveys suggest that crime is an important issue for Afghans. Criminality can thrive in a conflict or post-conflict situation where legal, law enforcement, and social checks are weakened. The same is true of corruption; rough indicators compiled by the World Bank, which have substantial margins of error, suggest that Afghanistan is perceived to be among the countries most severely affected by corruption. The recent Transparency International index of perceptions of corruption similarly indicates that Afghanistan has a serious corruption problem.

It should be noted that while corruption in government contracting, the tax regime, licenses and permits, etc. may be significant problems in Afghanistan, the enormous role of the drug industry in promoting corruption, as well as to a lesser extent the role of other parts of the informal/illicit economy, must be emphasized.

The huge sums of money involved - in 2004 gross value of opiate production in Afghanistan was roughly estimated at $2.8 billion, of which $2.2 billion went to traders and processors and only $600 million to farmers - virtually guarantee massive levels of corruption. Moreover, narcotics-related corruption most likely to a considerable extent takes the form of "grand corruption" and capture of parts of the state apparatus, which is profoundly damaging to the state-building agenda as compared with smaller "petty corruption". Corruption contributes to personal and business insecurity, as the "rules of the game" are not clear and can change depending on who is in particular government positions, and also can take coercive forms like extortion of payments.

Landmines. Afghanistan inherited from its long period of conflict one of the worst landmine problems in the world, as well as enormous amounts of unexploded ordnance. While progress has been made in clearing mines in urban areas and some other parts of the country, enormous numbers remain and continue to kill and maim people, harm livestock, and render many areas unusable.

Finally, from a developmental perspective the impact of insecurity on vulnerable groups like women continues to be very serious. In the absence of effective mechanisms to investigate gender related violence, the vast majority of such violations are not reported to the criminal justice system and almost none are subject to investigation or prosecution. The practice of detention and prosecution of women for *zina* crimes (adultery and consensual sex outside marriage) is common in major cities, while in more conservative rural areas the family might deal with such a case by killing the girl or woman involved. The predominance of customary law in traditional jirga/shura decisions by and large works to the disadvantage of women, as customary law tends to grant fewer rights to them than Islamic law or civil law in matters relating to inheritance, property, and marriage, as well as in relation to crimes like so-called "honor killings" for which the perpetrators are generally not punished.

Customary law's bias against women is also illustrated when for example murder cases are resolved by the jirga ordering that the alleged perpetrator provide the family of the alleged victim with a young girl or girls, usually below the legal marriage age, to compensate for the alleged crime. The girl is then forcibly married to a male member of the victim's family. Such arrangements are also sometimes used to settle large opium-related debts. A sign of the impact of conflict, violence, and lack of access to justice on women is the reported dramatic upsurge of female suicides, often to escape unwanted arranged or forced marriages.

EXTERNAL SECURITY THREATS TO INDIA

India has the disadvantage of being situated in close proximity to what is being described as "the epicenter of global terrorism". Tribal region near the Afghanistan-Pakistan border is constantly drawing attention of America's Global War on Terror (GWOT) since 2001. India's increasing relevance to the US strategic canvas, troubled relationship with Pakistan since the independence of the country, deteriorating and unpredictable relationship with China, unstable political climate in Nepal along with Maoist insurgency, mistrustful relationship with Bangladesh, civil-war ravaged and still-healing Sri Lanka, authoritarian Myanmar have rendered any fair estimation of Indian preparedness to deal with these security challenges an onerous task. We will now analyse capabilities and interests of each of these players and then asses their influence on India's strategic calculations.

The United States of America

India's relationship with the sole military and economic superpower of the world has been on the rise during the previous decade. A new shift in Indo-US relations was witnessed during President Clinton's visit in 2000, fortified by Presidents Bush and Obama's visit to the country. That said, although India remains ideologically non-committal to signing the CTBT and NPT regime; there has been tremendous improvement in the nuclear energy field through singing the Indo-US Nuclear Treaty in 2006.

The US has always been a practitioner of hard real-politick, its policies have always been defined by its own interests in the region. The US support to Pakistan's military through CEATO arrangements in 1960s, later President Nixon's visit to China in Feb 1972 which was secretly facilitated by Pakistan and resulted in melting the ice between the two nations, support to Pakistan‘s defense apparatus and Taliban through 1980s and now military offensive in the Af-Pak tribal region have all been calibrated on the US self-interests.

All these steps have had a profound impact on India's external security environment. The continued US presence in our North-West border is cited to be one of the main reasons behind Pakistan's belligerent attitude in the aftermath of the Parliament attack in 2001 and 26/11mayhem in 2008. The Pakistani Army knows Indian options are severely limited to strike across Pakistani territory owing to military assistance she is providing to GWOT.

Apart from limiting India's punitive capability against Pakistan for its sponsoring terrorist attacks and their infrastructure in India, the US has also provided substantial financial and military to Pakistan which have adverse consequences to our strategic calculations.

Nonetheless the US is likely to dominate world affairs for at least another two decades. India has to work towards minimizing adverse impact of the US-Pak assistance on our external security. On a lighter note, India should emphasize to the US that for fighting tribal insurgents in its North-Western region; Pakistan does not need F-16s and nuclear submarines!

People's Republic of China

Indo-China relations have been marked with distrust and fear on both sides after 1962 border clash which resulted in China usurping Aksai Chin area in J&K giving it easy road access from the Tibetan plateau to remote Xinxiang region in the West. Additionally China's rise in the past three decades has given it tremendous weight in international political and security circles. China has patiently been working towards building military-economic and political alliances around India's periphery – termed as "strings of pearl strategy". China remains India's number one security threat. It has provided consistent military assistance to Pakistan for use against India, funded armed rebels in the North-East and has continued to up the ante in diplomatic circles through stapled visas, visa denials and spying on Tibetan Diaspora in India. Although India needs to be sensitive towards Chinese sensitivities towards Tibet, India has failed to play an assertive role in communicating its interests to the Chinese side. On the other hand, China has built up superior civilian and military infrastructure along Indo-Tibet border. Our defense preparedness vis-à-vis China leaves much to be desired. As has rightly been enunciated by one of our Army Chiefs, the possibility of Two-Front War scenario with both Pakistan and China should be factored in while preparing our doctrine of war and operational readiness.

To match China's might and thwart any misadventure from our Northern neighbour, we should invest heavily in our infrastructure in border areas, phase out obsolete military hardware, raise at least 3 mountain divisions for the Eastern sector and shore up anti-ballistic missile capability through expedited Agni programs. Fortunately Indian economy's healthy growth in the past decade has ensured greater defense outlay but even now our defense budget at 2.1% is way below 4.5% and 4.7% of Pakistani and Chinese budgets as % of their respective GDP and even the allocated funds do not get fully utilized for modernizing the forces but for the lack of speedy and transparent procurement procedures.

A look at the following chart shows the yawning gap between the defense expenditures of China and India. China is widely known to have unders tated its publicly announced defense budgets. The defense expenditure for Pakistan does not include capital outlay hence actual spending should be higher than shown here. Hence the need to selectively utilize our limited defense outlay for maximizing lethality of our forces.

To that end recent successful trial of indigenously designed and developed Light Combat Aircraft (LCA) Tejas is a welcome development. Similarly other big-ticket purchases for example C130s and Medium Multi-Role Combat Aircraft (MMRCAs) should also be expedited for induction into the Indian Air Force. Indian Navy's recent announcement of forming an Andaman specific command is a right step towards influencing Malacca strait area which can be one of the pressure points on the Chinese Navy in the event of a prolonged conflict. But our Navy needs much awaited aircraft career to project military power away from the shores. Unfortunately Russian aircraft carrier Gorshkov is waiting for about a decade for acquisition. Other steps should be towards economically integrating countries in our immediate neighbourhood to balance strategic Chinese investment in these countries. A strong political will is required to transform the forces and provide them necessary resources to successfully face the challenges on the external front.

Pakistan

The perennial challenge before Indian defense apparatus to manage external covert and overt threat from Pakistan does not need any emphasis. Since the birth of that country, we have fought them four times in war - 1948, 1965, 1971 and 1998. Besides the country is facing low intensity conflict in J&K abetted and sponsored by Pakistani military, in the North-East and through support to various fringe extremist group within the country. The country also faces huge challenge before its economy in the form of fake rackets being operated from Karachi and Dubai and widely believed to have blessings of Pakistan's infamous Inter-Services Intelligence – its external spy agency.

Thus Pakistan remains one of our principle worries at both external and internal security fronts. Besides on the basis of its long-standing strategic partnership with China, it can stretch our armed forces capabilities in the Eastern sector.

The modernization plans of Karakoram highway, the development of Gwadar as an aval port by the Chinese Navy and covert assistance to Pakistan's nuclear and missile program are on the anvil; these two countries should be watched very carefully in our defense planning. Rapid implementation of the mooted Cold-Start Strategy should be pursued by the forces to neutralize Pakistani threat quickly in a two-front war scenario and deny the bigger neighbour to our North an advantage from the Western sector.

Immediate Neighbourhood

Unfortunately our other neighbours with the exception of Bhutan also don't provide any succour to military planners and political leaders and are equally as challenging as China and Pakistan. While Nepal is in the grip of political turmoil since the ouster of unpopular King Gyanendra, India has to play its cards carefully lest it be seen with a big brother agenda. India and Nepal share an open boundary with free exchange of people and currency across the borders. Although few contentious points remain in the Indo-Nepalese relations; they should not be allowed to obstruct our efforts in ensuring political stability in this strategically important neighbour of hours. Perhaps Indian leftist parties can be utilized by the Central government to persuade Maoist leadership in Nepal to desist from mollycoddling too much with the Chinese to our and Nepal's detriment.

Bangladesh on the other hand is showing signs of delivering on the stated policy of the Government of Prime Minister Sheikh Hasina of not letting her country's soil for anti-India activities. Bangladesh has recently handed over many high profile terrorist leaders hiding in their country. India has also reciprocated with huge USD 1 billion economic assistance in the form of line of credit to Bangladesh. But India should actively continue to manage her somewhat uneasy relationship with the Opposition leader in Bangladesh former PM Mrs. Begum Khalida Zia. Seeking active Bangladeshi cooperation in destroying the terrorist infrastructure of Harkat-ul-Jihad-al Islami (HuJI) remains a challenge for Indian security agencies.

Although India at first neglected their relationship with Burmese military rulers, there have been improvements in the past few years in our bilateral relations. China has been investing in Kyaukryu and Sittwe as commercial ports on the west coast close to our NE states. Both of these ports can be used as a naval base and should be a cause of concern. India also needs to co-opt Myanmar for curbing the North Eastern rebel groups e.g. NSCN, ULFA and Manipur rebels which find shelter in dense forests along the international border. For that increased economic and military cooperation without inviting international limelight is a challenge as recently the US has started objecting to our strengthening relationship with the junta.

India also faces competition from China in keeping Sri Lanka attuned to our interests. The recently finished Civil War in the North-East Sri Lanka has incurred huge emotional and economic costs for the Indian Tamils. Thus encouraging cordial linguistic relations in Sri Lanka through persuading Lankan government towards equitable distribution of resources and fair treatment of ethnic minorities is a priority for Indian foreign policy mandarins. Bhutan has demonstrated sensibilities to our concerns by wiping off ULFA rebels in their territory in 2003 and India rightly assists in their economic, social and defense developments. Similarly India should also manage our closest ally during the Cold War era – Russia – to counterbalance China and procuring critical defense supplies.

2

India's National Security, Defence Policy and Planning

It is generally acknowledged that the approach to national security requires a comprehensive view of various political, social, economic, technological and strategic aspects. National security implies not only safeguarding territorial boundaries but also that the nation is able to build a cohesive, egalitarian, technologically efficient and progressive society with a good quality of life. Compared with national security, defence policy is more focused, concerned with the protection of the state and its citizens from direct and indirect (proxy) military threats and actions of other states. In defence planning, the emphasis shifts to national security concerns that are mainly military in nature. There are two concepts at this level: deterrence (including coercive diplomacy) and defence (dissuasion).

Deterrence refers to policies designed to discourage the adversary from taking direct or proxy military action, by raising the cost so that it outweighs the gains that he may wish to attain. Defence (dissuasion) policies are designed to reduce the capability of the adversary to cause damage—and own costs and risks—in the event deterrence fails. Deterrence and defence are two interwoven strands of defence policy. Defence planning involves the conceptualisation of plans and decisions for the execution of defence policy. Long-term planning for defence is essential for the following reasons:

(a) The existence of a highly fluid strategic environment, which results in continuous shifts and changing profiles of threat and power equations.
(b) To ensure judicious allocation of resources and cost effective utilisation.
(c) Revolution in Military Affairs (RMA), i.e. advances in technology, which result in weapons and equipment systems becoming obsolete at a fast rate.
(d) Lead time required to raise and prepare defence units; to produce or acquire and introduce new weapons and equipment systems.
(e) The changing nature of conflict and reduced reaction time.
(f) Coordination problems between defence, economic, science and technology, infrastructure and industrial activities, as well as among the Defence Forces.

The defence planning process attempts to match the budgetary resources likely to be made available for the requirement to establish the defence capability necessary to face the threats and challenges. This exercise is undertaken in two phases: (a) What should be the proportion allocated to the defence effort as against other areas of national security concerns and economic growth? This exercise involves a 'visionary' analysis of external and internal security threats (often linked) and challenges. In order to minimise adverse affects of high military expenditure on socioeconomic development, it is necessary to harmonise national development planning with defence planning. (b) Optimisation of allocated resources, i.e. distribution of resources within the Ministry of Defence (MoD) based on Force planning (Force and weapons mix, command and control, logistics and human resources management) by the Defence Services to combat current and future threats, and development of required capabilities by the Defence Research and Development Organisation (DRDO), defence production and other agencies concerned.

The quantum of indigenous production and the requirements to be procured from outside are decided in this phase. The objective is to achieve maximum defence capability from the given resources. Both allocation and distribution are closely linked. They need to be reviewed periodically but not so frequently that the planning process becomes ad hoc. In India's case, this is done at five-year intervals.

INDIA'S STRATEGIC CULTURE: THE NEED FOR RE- INVENTION

India's geographical boundaries stood changed after 1947 and so also the nature and relief of terrain configurations on which present boundaries rest.

Historically and culturally, India went through three widely separated stages–Hindu, Muslim and British, Each of these periods had a religious and cultural disconnect and therefore do not provide the consistency of the evolution of a strategic culture, like China for example.

India today stands faced with the daunting task of re–inventing its strategic culture for two good reasons :

- India today faces strategic threats to its national security both external and internal, which are in marked variance to its earlier geographical, historical or cultural configurations.
- Secularism does not define or arise from any strategic culture. India's strategic culture needs to be reinvented by drawing on its most ancient and indigenous roots and blending it with India's contemporary strategic ambitions and the global strategic environment. It is India's political leadership and its elites who have failed to grasp this critical strategic requirement.

India's history of the last fifty years indicates that India was unable to re-invent a strategic culture, appropriate and commensurate enough to meet the threats to its security. India was passive, defensive, reactive and soft in her strategic cultures. India needs to re-invent its strategic culture in a more resurgent mode of proactive, directed and aggressive responses to threats to her national security.

NATIONAL SECURITY ISSUES SHOULD NOT BE POLITICISED

India presents a regrettable phenomenon where political opposition parties, in the absence of any other political issue, tend to politicise national security issues.

In this process and in their zeal to discomfit the ruling party at any cost, they fail to realise the impact it has on the Armed Forces of India – their morale, their will to fight and their entire confidence in the political structure of the Indian nation state is seriously jeopardised. The most recent examples of this politicisation of India's national security issues pertain to the then opposition parties reaction to India's nuclear weaponisation in 1998, their ill- informed criticisms during the Pakistan aggression in Kargil in 1999 and thereafter and their attitudinal problems to the Indian Army operations against the Pakistan sponsored proxy war in Jammu and Kashmir State. National security issues have hardly been discussed by political parties during Defence budget debates in Parliament.

The parliamentary attendance then presents a sorry spectacle. Yet when grave national crises occur every second politician becomes a master strategist or tactician minus the grasp of the essentials of strategy and the intricacies of military operations and oblivious to the fact that the parliamentarians own strategic incompetence brought about the military aggression in the first place.

India's political leaders need to get together and work out conventions where during a crisis they can discuss the issues away from the glare of publicity and arrive at a consensus on how the Indian nation state has to meet the security challenges that arise.

NATIONAL SECURITY AND INDIAN MEDIA

The Indian media both print and electronic has developed imperialistic attitudes towards the coverage, analysis and projection of national security issues.

Nothing exemplifies this more than the 'Tehelka Tapes' episode. In a bid to make money, national security interests were given a go by this portal. A noble mantle was sought to be worn by depicting it as a crusade against corruption. The media elite including notable editors-in-chief ganged up to support Tehelka not on the grounds of objectivity but for sheer defence of one of their flock.

Some Indian journals, indulged in politicising the issues of military commanders performances on the basis of leaked classified documents.

They did not even bother to think that such irresponsible journalism not only affects the national security of the country but also the morale of the Indian Armed Forces.

It also affects the confidence of the uniformed personnel in the Indian media, who should really strive to be a pillar of the state rather than a money-spinning enterprise of some industrial house, depending on sensationalism for its wider circulation. India as a nation state is still in the formative stages and many challenges both external and internal threaten its existence and integrity. The Indian media should refrain from applying western templates of journalism as neither the political & strategic context nor the national cohesion as existent in the West is presently obtainable in India.

DEFENCE PRODUCTION AND SUPPLY

The Defence Production Department created in 1962 and the Department of Defence Supply set up in 1965 were merged in 1984 to constitute the Department of Defence Production and Supplies. Presently, 39 Ordnance factories and eight Defence Public Sector Undertakings (DPSUs) come under this department. The Directorate of Quality Assurance, Air Technical Development and Production (Air), Standardisation, and Exhibition Organisation also form part of this Department.

The Ordnance Factories produce more than 1,500 items of arms, ammunition, equipment and components. Most of these products constitute relatively low to medium technology items.

Twenty per cent of the output goes to non-defence customers. Due to the very high cost of production, delivery delays and suspect quality, it has not been possible to meet export targets and, sometimes, even orders given by the Services. Ordnance factories as well as DPSUs need to shed the manufacture of low technology items to the private sector and focus on hi-tech products. They should also be in a position to take up substantial product improvement themselves and not be dependent on DRDO.

Defence Planning Tools

In recent years, defence economics and management techniques have made an important contribution to defence planning. A number of techniques such as Operational Research and Systems Analysis (ORSA), Planning Programming and Budgeting System have been developed to make the planning process more systematic and to maximise the benefits obtained from the given amount of resources. Systems Analysis can assist in developing rational procedures for procurement of new weapons systems. Systems performance at design stage can be evaluated through computer simulation. Planners all over the world are using computerised war-gaming techniques and structure analysis. Prospects exist for a more enlightened approach that can bring together military officers, historians, technologists and quantitative analysts.

In many countries, there is a growing interest in analytical realism, operational relevance and integrated defence planning. In India the Services are far behind in introducing these aids in our defence planning system. The planning directorates in Service Headquarters do not even have data banks which can provide relevant information on a specified subject. Most of the planners have high combat and command qualifications but little clue of the modern techniques. There is an urgent need to introduce modern planning aids into our planning system. Defence planners should also learn the basic principles and techniques of economic analysis and not leave it to their 'Finance' colleagues.

Management of Defence Budget

A major lacuna in defence planning and implementation has been lack of financial commitment for the Plan period. Financially, the defence plans are treated more as annual plans rather than composite five years plan. There is a rush to spend the annual capital budget by the end of the financial year since the amount not spent has to be surrendered. In FY 2004-05, the previous government had proposed to institute a non-lapsable Defence Modernisation Fund of Rs 25,000 crore. This was a long awaited reform in the defence-finance mechanism as budgeted capital expenditure worth thousands of crores was surrendered year after year. However, the new government, being of the view that there are no provisions in the budgetary rules and regulations to carry forward unspent funds for three years, has done away with this reform.

It needs to be pointed out that a similar procedure was being followed in the 1930s and 1940s. The provisions invoked at that time need to be studied carefully and could be used as a precedent. Action should be taken expeditiously to revive the Defence Modernization Fund. Otherwise, funds earmarked for capital expenditure on an annual basis will continue to lapse, leading to lack of systematic defence preparedness.

In the Revenue Budget, there is a need to include incentives to save and reduce annual maintenance expenditure without adversely affecting operational efficiency. It is also necessary to exploit the increasing domestic industrial capability to support the existing infrastructure and thus reduce maintenance costs and enhance the quality of maintenance.

Human Resources Management

The development of human resources must keep pace with the modernisation of the armed forces so that new, state-of-the-art equipment can be optimally exploited by well trained and motivated soldiers, sailors and airmen. The age profile of military personnel, particularly in the Army, and the age of commanders at battalion and brigade levels needs to be looked into. Currently, a soldier has to serve for 15 to 17 years to earn his pension.

When he retires, besides the lifelong pension that has to be paid, a trained individual is lost to the nation. Similarly, while there is a shortage of approximately 14,000 officers, most officers retire in rank of Lieutenant Colonel or Colonel at the age of 52-54 years when they still have years of productive life ahead though they are no longer fit for active combat. Innovative measures need to be adopted to reduce the effects of the current national loss on this account. The best method would be to institute a procedure of 'lateral induction" under which both officers and personnel below officer rank can be transferred to central police and paramilitary forces(CPMFs). The colour (active) service of jawans should be reduced to 7-10 years with no pension liability after which the volunteers are transferred to the BSF, CRPF, ITBP, CISF and other such forces. Similarly, the Shipping Corporation of India, National Port Trust and other such maritime organisations can fruitfully employ Naval personnel. Ex-servicemen will be expected to serve in these organisations till superannuation, after which they would be entitled to pension. This will improve the age profile of the Services, provide trained manpower to the CPMFs, ensure productive long-term employment for a large number of trained men till superannuation, and also reduce the pension bill of the Central Government.

The Army should increase the recruitment of Short Service Officers to make up its shortfall. Induction of these officers to the CPMFs after five years of service will improve junior leadership and effectiveness of these forces in internal security and counter insurgency operations.

Recommendations

- Given the fluid strategic environment and the rapid advances in defence technology, there is a need for judicious allocation of the limited budgetary resources. Long lead times are required for creating futuristic Forces, hence the need to make long-term defence planning mandatory. Greater synergy between defence and development plans is required.

- The lack of a cohesive national security strategy and defence policy has resulted in inadequate political direction regarding politico-military objectives. The Government should prepare a clear national security strategy, defence policy, and review it every 4-5 years.
- In view of the time taken to create the capabilities necessary for facing future threats and challenges, it is essential for the Defence Services to evolve 10 to 15-year perspective plans with the required budgetary support.
- The Chiefs of Staff Committee has not been successful in preparing comprehensive 'integrated defence plans' due to emphasis on single Service planning and constant competition among the Services for a bigger share of resources. The civilian bureaucrats in the MoD do not have the professional expertise to decide on inter-Service priorities. Hence, the early appointment of Chief of Defence Staff (CDS) is essential as he will be the cornerstone for integrated defence and operational planning.
- A non-lapsable Defence Modernisation Fund must be expeditiously created to ensure that allocations are optimally utilised and funds earmarked for capital acquisitions are not allowed to lapse.
- The Revenue Budget of thc Services needs to be better managed. Annual maintenance expenditure can be curtailed by greater exploitation of the available public and private sector industrial infrastructure capability and offering incentives to the Services to save.
- To ensure smooth progress towards self-reliance in defence technology, the Government must undertake a periodic performance audit of the DRDO plans and projects. The review should reinforce efforts in areas of success and weed out unproductive projects.
- Ordnance Factories should produce only hi-tech products and shed the production of low-tech items to the private sector.

- Integrated Defence Staff and the Services' perspective planners should acquire expertise in operational research and systems analysis, as also financial planning, for evolving complex integrated defence plans.
- In order to improve the age profile of the Services and simultaneously reduce the pension bill of the Central Government, personnel below officer rank should be transferred to central police and paramilitary forces (CPMFs) after active service of 7-10 years.
- The Army should increase recruitment of Short Service Officers to make up its shortfall. Induction of these officers to the CPMFs after five years of service will improve junior leadership and effectiveness of these forces in internal security and counter insurgency operations.

Defence planning has been neglected for long in India. This has led to ad-hocism in decision-making and adversely affected the modernisation plans of the Services. The key issues needing immediate attention include the need for formal prior approval for five-year defence Plans, better management of the defence revenue and capital acquisition budgets, streamlining of the defence procurement process and better human resources management.

The Government of India should appoint a group of eminent experts to study the present defence planning process, identify the lacunae and grey areas in the process and recommend structural and procedural changes. The aim should be to streamline defence planning, harmonize it with national development plans, and make the process more responsive in order to deal effectively with the rapidly changing geo-strategic and regional security environment.

PUBLIC-PRIVATE SECTOR PARTNERSHIP

The public sector possesses excellent infrastructure, manufacturing facilities and a highly experienced task force. It will be a waste of national resources if these assets are duplicated by the private sector. The private sector, on the other hand, can bring in latest technology, managerial practices, marketing skills and financial management. Therefore, a well-blended fusion of both will result in synergising of their strengths through economies of scale and prove mutually beneficial. A strong and fruitful relationship can be built with mutual accommodation. The public sector should not regard private players as a persistent irritant and adopt a confrontationist attitude towards them. Similarly, the private sector must not seek to replace the public sector. Such an approach may be perceived by the public sector as a threat to their primacy and existence. It may make them close their ranks and resist all interaction with the private sector. That shall be counter-productive.

The Government has to realise that both public and private sectors are national assets and harnessing of their potential is essential if India wants to achieve self reliance in defence production. It should not play favourites and treat both as equal partners in progress.

The then Defence Minister of India, Mr Pranab Mukherjee, in his address at New Delhi in June 2005 had stated: "The Government is committed to the development of a vibrant and proactive defence industry in India. It should be ensured that the available capability, infrastructure and resources including intellectual capital are harnessed to the fullest extent as our national assets and optimally utilised in achieving this objective." He further advocated a strong and healthy partnership between the public and private sector for enhancing the defence capability and in sustaining a powerful domestic industrial base for the future.

During the last three years, a serious and concerted effort has been made by the Government to reform and streamline the entire acquisition process. The Government has come to appreciate the potential of the private sector and wants it to complement the efforts of the public sector. A number of praiseworthy initiatives have been taken and policies reviewed. Yet, the results on ground have very little to show. There has been no appreciable inflow of anticipated foreign funds. Even today all major defence deals are signed with foreign producers. The public sector continues to get bulk orders under transfer of imported technology. The private sector continues to be a peripheral participant with the production of some low-tech items and indigenisation of some components.

The present process of interaction and integration should be continued, albeit with renewed vigour and purpose. All joint committees should be represented at the level of decision makers so that the follow up action can be implemented in a time bound manner. There is no point in having committees and joint task forces if their reports are going to gather dust with no follow up action. Technological prowess of the private sector should be given due recognition and considered a national asset. The objective of achieving self-reliance will remain elusive unless the private sector is duly integrated and its potential fully harnessed to build a viable indigenous defence industrial base. The Government has to create an environment wherein the private sector feels assured of just business opportunities, level playing ground and fair play.

And finally, India plans to spend USD 100 billion on capital expenditure during the 7th Plan Period (2007-12). Imports account for close to 70 percent of capital expenditure and offsets are required equal to 30 percent of import contracts. Thus, India expects offset trade worth USD 21 billion during the next five years. Currently, Indian defence exports amount to paltry USD 50 million annually, i.e. USD 250 million in five years. From USD 250 million to USD 21 billion, it will be a quantum jump of enormous proportions. The public sector cannot handle it by itself. The private sector has to be closely integrated and its potential fully harnessed for beneficial absorption of the projected offset business.

SECRET SECTOR IN DEFENCE PRODUCTION

The Government of India has been reiterating its commitment to achieve the much-publicised target of procuring 70 per cent of its defence requirements from indigenous sources by 2010. Despite its best efforts over the last two decades, India is nowhere near that figure as yet. The Government is well aware of the emergence of private sector as a vibrant and dynamic force, especially in information technology, service sector and manufacturing fields. It has come to realise that self reliance would remain a pipe dream if it continued to bank on public sector alone. One of the objectives mentioned in the new defence procurement procedure is to achieve self-reliance in defence equipment. But the whole procedure is silent about the role of the private sector and no worthwhile initiatives have been proposed to integrate its potential in India's quest for self reliance.

In addition to economic factors, defence industry is generally considered to be an instrument of national sovereignty and pride. Defence industry comprises of all industrial undertakings engaged in the production of hardware and services for use by the defence forces. The origin of the Indian defence industry can be traced to the establishment of Gun and Shell Factory at Cossipore in 1801. At the time of the Independence, India had 16 Ordnance Factories, established by the British to produce low tech items. Bharat Electronics Ltd was the first Defence Public Sector Undertaking (DPSU) established in 1954 to manufacture electronic equipment for the forces. Today, India has 39 Ordnance Factories and eight DPSU.

The Industrial Policy Resolution of 1956 divided industry into three parts:-

- Schedule A: Basic industries which are the preserve of the state, including defence and heavy engineering.
- Schedule B: Industries in which private industry was allowed to operate.
- Schedule C: All other industries.

Manufacture of components, assemblies and sub-assemblies was thrown open to the private sector in 1991. With a view to promote defence-industry partnership, the Ministry of Defence (MoD) constituted six Joint Task Forces in collaboration with Confederation of Indian Industry in 1998. Consequent to their recommendations, the Government opened defence production to the private sector in January 2002. It allowed 100 percent private equity with 26 percent Foreign Direct Investment (FDI). It was a major policy change. Subsequently, the Department of Industrial Policy and Promotion issued detailed guidelines for the issuance of licence for the production of arms and ammunition.

The Kelkar Committee, constituted in 2004, made many radical recommendations. The Government has accepted a majority of them but their implementation has lacked earnestness and focus. The Department of Industrial Policy & Promotion (DIPP), in consultation with Ministry of Defence, has so far issued 37 letters of intent for the manufacture of various types of defence hardware which include armoured and combat vehicles, radars, electronic warfare equipment, warships, submarines, avionics, military aircraft, safety and ballistic products, armaments and ammunition.

Despite the above measures, there has been no discernible change in the ground situation. Only a handful of India's top companies are involved in small value defence contracts. The private sector has to remain content with the supply of some low-tech items to the public sector. Its supplies to DPSU and Ordnance Factories grossed over Rs. 1200 crores and Rs. 1900 crores respectively last year. Whereas these figures signify the contribution made by the private sector, they also highlight the fact that the private sector continues to be merely an outsourcing base for the public sector.

CONTINUED NON-PARTICIPATION OF THE PRIVATE SECTOR

A number of defence-industry seminars, conferences and exhibitions have been held in the recent years. Given decades of insulation and prejudices, this was no small achievement. But old mindsets, complexity of procurement procedures and clout wielded by the public sector have been acting as major deterrents to any meaningful participation of the private sector. New aspirants, in particular, find the whole regime to be highly forbidding.

Policy and Procedural Issues

Decisions are taken by the Defence Acquisition Council to categorise a proposal as 'Buy' or 'Buy and Make' or 'Make' based on the advice given by Defence Research and Development Organisation and the public sector. No inputs are sought from the private sector. Its competence and potential are given no consideration. In all deals where transfer of technology is negotiated, the nominated recipient is always a DPSU, even if a private sector company is better placed in terms of infrastructure and know-how to absorb the technology. A DPSU may have to establish complete facilities ab initio, whereas a private sector company may need only incremental technology.

Requirements of the armed forces are not made known to the private sector sufficiently in advance, with the result that it does not get adequate time, either to scout for foreign tie-ups or to establish the necessary facilities. The time given for the submission of technical and commercial proposals is grossly inadequate for a new entrant in the field. Parameters for the equipment to be procured are formulated with foreign equipment in mind, after reading manufacturers' brochures. Private sector is not consulted in this process, whereas minor acceptable changes in parameters may make the Indian equipment eligible for consideration. As Requests for Proposals (RFP) are issued to foreign original equipment manufacturers as well, they prefer direct bidding. They decline joint ventures with Indian companies as it helps them to guard their technology and perpetuate their monopoly with consequent financial gains. All trials are carried out on 'No Cost No Commitment' basis. Whereas foreign vendors can incur the expenditure involved, many upcoming indigenous companies do not possess the necessary financial strength. This acts as a major disincentive.

Functional Issues

Due to the very nature of its usage, defence equipment has to meet highly exacting standards. There can be no failure in the face of the enemy. Regrettably, many Indian vendors have not fully grasped the import of this requirement and find the quality control regime to be extremely irksome. Every producer seeks economies of scale and assured continuous orders. Unfortunately, Indian procurement regime precludes both. RFPs are issued for one-time piecemeal quantities without indicating the envisaged total requirement over a period of time. Additionally, no long term commitment is made regarding regular flow of orders. This deters Indian companies from committing resources for establishing production facilities as the venture can prove both expensive and risky.

Lack of Mutual Confidence

The Indian public sector has got used to a position of pre-eminence. Its hold over defence orders is total. It thrives because of its monopolistic clout and not because of any displayed excellence. It is fully aware of its weaknesses and knows that it cannot survive an open competition with the private sector. This sense of insecurity makes it wary of any move to facilitate the entry of the private sector and it tries all stratagems to block it. On the other hand, many functionaries feel that the private sector is out to make a quick buck and lacks required perseverance. They tend to view the private sector as traders rather than committed manufacturers who can endure the travails of long drawn procurement procedure. According to them, anyone desirous of entering defence industry has to be fully aware of the fact that defence orders take inordinately long to materialise and vacillation invariably proves unproductive.

The Communication Gap

There is a total absence of an effective institutionalised interface between the MoD, the services and the private sector for regular interaction at the policy making level. There are a number of 'groups' or 'partnership forums' in place, but their utility is limited to exchange of views only.

Procurement Agencies are Unaware of Industry's Potential : The procurement agencies are extremely keen to encourage indigenous production and limit imports to the minimum inescapable requirements. They, however, are unaware of the capabilities and potential of different private sector companies, as the competence of Indian companies has not been authentically catalogued as yet. They do not know whom to invite for submission of proposals. It is much easier to acquire details of numerous foreign producers.

There is no data bank of Indian industries available with the MoD. Requests for Proposals (RFPs) are issued only to a few highly visible companies, while many others lose by default. Although, the Acquisition Wing has been tasked to create the necessary data bank, the process has hardly taken off as yet.

Industry Lacks Knowledge of Defence Requirements and Procedures : On the other hand, many private sector companies have the capability to manufacture the whole range of defence requirements but do not know whom to approach to ascertain details. They are ignorant of the procurement agencies, their policies and procedures. This ignorance makes them wary of dealing with the defence. To compound the problem, there are over 150 different defence procurement agencies with different procedures. There is no system of centralised notification of requirements and vendor registration. Due to this lacuna, a new entrant finds the whole environment highly dissuasive.

The Way Forward

The present process of interaction between the Government, public sector and private enterprises should be continued, albeit with renewed vigour and purpose. All joint committees should be represented at the level of decision makers, so that follow up action can be taken in a time bound manner.

Structural Reforms

A representative of the designated industry association should be a permanent invitee to the Defence Acquisition Council, depending on the security sensitivity of agenda points. His inputs as regards the technical prowess of the private sector will prove invaluable while deciding whether to import technology or not. Similarly, selected agenda points of Defence Procurement Board, Defence Production Board and Defence

Development Board should be circulated to the industry association for advice. These steps will go a long way in integrating the private sector.

DEFENCE PLANNING SYSTEM

Before independence, the defence services worked on a system of contract budget. Defence expenditure was pegged at Rs 55 crore per year, which was more than half of the Central Government's revenue. There was no serious threat from outside (except during World War II, when a fresh agreement was signed) and this amount was more than adequate to maintain the establishment.

The savings were not allowed to lapse but put away in the Defence Reserve Fund that was utilised to finance measures for re-equipment of the Defence Services, thus freeing the Government from having to provide fund money greater than the contract amount. Expenditure on defence rose steeply soon after independence. However, there was no planned effort and defence programmes consisted mainly of outright purchases from abroad, drawing heavily on available Sterling reserves. In the late 1950s, some efforts were made to initiate domestic weapons production by the Ministry of Defence when Mr. Krishna Menon was the Defence Minister. The Sino-Indian conflict in 1962 aroused a new defence consciousness in the country. After taking care of immediate postwar requirements, systematic defence planning started in 1964. Defence requirements were assessed on a five-year basis and the First Five Year Defence Plan (1964-69) was drawn up. This plan took into account the resources available and assistance which could be expected from friendly foreign countries. The plan was primarily based on an expansion and modernisation programme considered necessary by each Service in the light of the respective threat perception assessed. It also proposed a defence production base that would gradually reduce the country's external dependence, provide for improvements in border roads and communications, and a modest expansion of DRDO. The Government recognised the imperative need to synergise 'defence' and 'development' instead of planning each on a separate and unrelated level. The MoD emphasised the "inevitable need to harness all resources of the country for the country's defence and for the defence effort to derive full sustenance from the country's economic development plans".

Thereafter, the National Development Council authorised the Chairman of the Planning Commission to review the needs of both development and defence. A Planning Cell was established in 1965 in the Ministry of Defence 'to deal with the wider aspects of defence planning'. The new system was intended to facilitate medium and long-term defence planning and to maintain constant liaison with the Planning Commission and other ministries. It was expected that the MoD would derive maximum advantage from the development effort by being able to place its priorities for consideration along with the overall economic and industrial plans drawn up by the Planning Commission. The experience of the First Five Year Defence Plan showed that the development of weapons and equipment was a long drawn out process. The Government realised that there could be no forward movement in attaining self-sufficiency in weapons and equipment unless these requirements were planned over a reasonably long period, long enough to cover the span of development and production of new weapons systems and other fighting tools.

The inadequacy of foreign exchange reserves was another hindrance in planning and implementation. In order to mitigate some of these drawbacks, the Second Five Year Defence Plan (1969-74) was instituted on a "roll-on" basis. After a year, an additional year was added so that the Defence Services would have before them a revised and updated five-year plan. In this context, the MoD commented: "Opportunity is taken by this annual exercise to take note of and reflect the change in priorities, the shifts in emphasis and the latest concepts and programmes to reorient the plan within the scheme of resources so that the aims and means are most effectively balanced." This system was expected to facilitate the planning of projects that took five years or more and to revise or eliminate projects, depending on the prevailing foreign exchange situation and availability of domestic resources.

For a period of five years, firm assurances were to be given on the availability of resources. This, unfortunately, never happened. In 1971, it was impossible to adhere to the discipline and the pattern of the roll-on plan. Instead of roll-on annual revisions, immediate requirements dominated the Government's attention that pre-empted plan efforts. In its 1971-72 Annual Report, the MoD acknowledged that having a Planning Cell in the ministry was an insufficient and unsatisfactory method of meeting a crisis.

The Planning Cell was not taken seriously in the crucial stages of economic planning and the argument that defence needs would be adjusted in the over-all allocation of resources was proved wrong. In 1974, an Apex Group headed by the Union Minister for Planning again suggested that steady long-term defence programmes would be more cost effective and economical rather than fluctuating allocations due to periodic economic and security crises. In order to integrate defence planning with the overall economic planning effort, defence and economic development plans were made co-terminus.

Planning Machinery

Most of the defence planning machinery and planning methodology was developed in the decade 1964-74. The Joint Intelligence Committee (JIC) was established in the Cabinet Secretariat to provide external and internal threat assessments. Inputs for this purpose were to be provided by all Intelligence agencies of the Government. The Service Chiefs were to assess the broad military aims and a strategy, coordinated in the Chiefs of Staff Committee, was to be approved by the Defence Minister. However, this was seldom done. Each Service ended up planning its own force level, choice of weapons and equipment, and build-up of infrastructure. In 1977, the Government formed a Committee for Defence Planning (CDP) to "undertake regular assessments relevant to defence planning in the light of all factors having a bearing on national security and defence". However, this committee could not function smoothly nor meet the desired goals.

Planning units were also established in the Department of Defence Production and DRDO. A Planning and Coordination Cell was created in the MoD to coordinate and compile various plans into a 'Defence Plan' for Cabinet approval. As the bureaucrats in the ministry had no professional knowledge or background, this cell could only compile different requirements without any analysis. In Army Headquarters, the Deputy Chief of Army Staff was made responsible for preparing the Army plan. A Perspective Planning Directorate was established in the late 1970s. Naval and Air plans were prepared in the respective Planning Directorates. Financial considerations, nonexistent at this level earlier, were introduced through Finance Planning Sections attached to these Directorates. In 1986, the Directorate General of Defence Planning Staff (DGDPS), comprising officers from the three Services, DRDO, and Ministries of Defence and External Affairs, was established under the Chiefs of Staff Committee (COSC) to coordinate and harmonise defence planning. Civilian officers from the Ministries probably did not find the job professionally satisfying and were gradually withdrawn, thus leaving the DGDPS a tri-Service set up.

All these measures enabled each Service headquarters to prepare defence plans in a more rational manner. But due to lack of clear political direction and each Service primarily planning for itself, joint planning, coordination between Services and other departmental plans of the MoD, were largely ignored. After the Kargil conflict in 1999, the Group of Ministers (GoM) and later the Cabinet Committee on Security (CCS) approved several reforms. An Integrated Defence Headquarters (IDH) was established and the DGDPS was merged with it. The creation of the post of Chief of Defence Staff (CDS), whose tasks would include ensuring intra and inter-Services prioritisation of defence plans and improvement in joint functioning of the Defence Services, was recommended. The reforms also included establishment of a Defence Intelligence Agency and creation of

Defence Equipment Production, Research and Planning councils in the IDH and MoD, respectively. Unfortunately, the CDS, who would be the cornerstone of integrated operational planning for defence, has not been appointed.

Analysis of the System

Despite several years of planning efforts, defence planning in India is characterised by seesaw bouts of frenzied activity followed by long periods of relative inaction. Five-year defence plans have rarely been formally approved before commencement. The Tenth Defence Plan, now in its third year, is yet to be accorded formal government approval. Adhocism is the order of the day, leading to knee-jerk responses and haphazard planning, making India a reactive rather than proactive nation in matters pertaining to national security. Whenever India's major adversaries plan a big defence purchase, there is an outcry for similar acquisitions, resulting in piecemeal decisions regardless of long-term impact and overall requirements. The Defence Forces are forced to follow "a case-by-case" approach to modernisation and procurement of arms, ammunition and equipment to replace obsolescent items, in many cases long after their life cycle is over and they cannot be maintained in a cost effective manner. The Army's Vijayanta tanks, MiG-21s of the IAF, and IL-38 maritime reconnaissance aircraft of the Navy are some examples. Weapons development, procurement and absorption are complex processes. A lead-time of 15-20 years is required to plan and execute major projects. Despite this, for several years, a large amount of the capital acquisition budget has been surrendered. In the prevailing era of strategic uncertainty, the changing nature of warfare demands a judicious mix of threat and capabilities-based forces that can operate efficiently as combined arms, joint Services teams and components of multinational coalition forces.

DEFENCE PLANNING AND POLICY

As regards the planning process, the Government has taken a number of measures to improve the structure, process and procedure relating to defence planning based on the recommendations of Group of Ministers on 'Reforming the National Security System'. The preparation of Long Term Plans, Five Year Defence Plans and Annual Budgetary proposals have been brought under the newly established Integrated Defence Staff (IDS) to bring about greater inter-service coordination in planning. The IDS also interacts closely with Defence (Finance) in the formulation of Plans and Budgets.

The Government has set up a Defence Acquisition Council headed by the Raksha Mantri and consisting of Raksha Rajya Mantri (s), the three Service Chiefs and Defence Secretary, Secretary (Defence Finance), and Secretary (Defence Production) to assist the Raksha Mantri in taking decisions in the totality of the new planning process, including capital acquisitions and major modernisation projects. The Government has also set up a dedicated institutional structure for defence procurement, the Defence procurement Board, headed by the Defence Secretary for acquisitions on the capital account. Planning processes have been further tightened under budgetary pressures and the need to establish greater synergy and jointness amongst the Armed Forces. This has also necessitated greater coordination in planning and procurement among the three services.

The Ministry in its written note submitted on the current status of the implementation of the 10th Plan has inter alia stated that: "The projections of the Ministry of Defence for the Tenth Defence Plan were reviewed thrice between March 2003 and July 2004 bearing in mind the needs of defence modernization and the likely constraints to the availability of funds for defence in the Tenth Plan. The Ministry of Finance have now agreed in principle to the latest projection made by the Ministry of Defence of Rs. 4,18,101 crore. However, a firm indication of annual outlays for the remaining year of the 10th Plan has not yet been given by the Ministry of Finance.

Meanwhile, in the absence of a formal approval of the allocation for defence in the Tenth Plan, defence planning has been harmonised with the allotments for defence in the annual budgets of the Government. Actual expenditures in 2002-2003 and 2003-2004 were Rs. 55,620 crores and Rs. 60,300 crores respectively. An allocation of Rs. 77,200 crores has been made in the Budget Estimate for 2004-2005 against a projection of Rs. 90,928 crores. About, Rs. 11,000 crores additional funds have been allocated beyond the Budget Estimate for the capital head.

The projected expenditure in 2005-2006 and 2006-2007 are Rs. 1,00,960 crores and Rs. 1,10,251 crores respectively. However, an amount of Rs. 83,000 crores only has been allocated in the Budget Estimate (B.E.) for the current financial year 2005-2006.

While some compromises are inevitable in the absence of a formally approved Plan, every effort has been made to ensure that the annual budgets have been utilized in accordance with the Plan projections of the Ministry of Defence and that any negative impact on ongoing modernization, infrastructure development and procurements of equipment is minimized. Ongoing projects and commitments have been reviewed and prioritized so that the main objective of the Tenth Defence Plan to carry forward the process of modernization of the Armed Forces is not adversely affected. A modest outlay of over Rs. 950 crores has been made for new schemes for the Army. (No increase is being sought)".

In response to a query regarding the existence of a core plan the Ministry though a written reply has inter alia stated that : "There is no formal draft core plan to make up for the delay in the finalization of the Tenth Defence Plan. Meanwhile, in the absence of a formal approval of the allocation for defence in the Tenth Plan, defence planning has been harmonised with the allotments for defence in the annual budgets of the Government. While, indigenous production/Research and Development is being made in accordance with the decisions flowing from the Defence Acquisition Council, defence procurement is being made in accordance with annual acquisition plans for the three services as approved by the Defence Procurement Board. Adequate measures have been taken to minimise any adverse effect on ongoing modernisation schemes. On-going projects and contractual commitments have been reviewed and prioritised to minimise the effect of any shortfall in actual allocation vis-à-vis projections, both in respect of modernisation plans and in essential procurement. Keeping in view, the rising competing demands on limited resources, the budgetary framework has been fine-turned in such a manner to ensure most effective utilisation of Government resources".

While presenting a detailed picture on the entire planning exercise that has been undertaken in the recent past, the representative of Ministry has stated as under:

"In the year 2001-02, projections for the 10th Plan were examined in the Ministry of Defence. These projections were made by the different Services and the Departments. They added up to Rs. 4.97 lakh crore. In January, 2002 the Ministry of Finance indicated the likely availability of Rs. 4.21 lakh crore. So, there was a gap of about Rs. 75,000 crore. Therefore, the Chief of Integrated Defence Staff and Chief of Staff were requested for giving their views. They recommended slightly reduced allocation of Rs. 4.61 lakh crore. In February 2003, in consonance with the recommendations, it was done. The matter was again taken up with the Finance Ministry in March 2003. But we did not have received any response from them thereafter.

We had to carry out a review of our projections. This was because if some scheme was supposed to be sanctioned in the first year of the Plan, it will involve expenditure in the first, second, third years and leading up to the fifth year. If, for the first two years, projected allocations are not utilized, there is no way the original amount, which was projected for the entire five years could be spent in the last three years. It is because in defence acquisition, we are not really buying things off the shelf and paying out for the whole thing. So, if you take a case of some scheme or project costing Rs. 5,000 crore in five years with simplistic allocation of expenditure of Rs. 1,000 crore each year, and if in the first two years, it is not sanctioned and in the third year it is sanctioned, we are not going to have anything in the first two years, but the expenditure will be Rs.3,000 crore in the remaining three years and not Rs. 5,000 crore. When we received the projects, we reviewed what would be and what would not be sanctioned. Then the revised figures came to something like Rs. 4,18,000 crore as indicated. But they did not give us any annual allocations, not capacity utilization, etc".

On the lessons learnt and the measures that are being implemented to overcome the nagging delays of Defence Planning, the Defence Secretary deposed that : "Presentation of the fourth year Budget is made to the Parliament. As has already been mentioned, there is the Ministry of Defence and there is the Ministry of Finance which are the players in this exercise. The exercise for preparing the plan is undertaken by us well in time, much before the start of the year in which the next Five Year Plan is going to start. For example, for the 11th Plan, to answer your question, we have already started the exercise. For doing that planning as to what would be needed, considering the gaps that is there in the Tenth Plan – if any exercise of this nature is to be undertaken – we might have a wish list; it might represent a large figure. But we still have to have some kind of an indicative figure from the Ministry of Finance saying that we have asked for this much amount, which may not be available, but we can have so much amount at the outer limit, beyond which we cannot go. This kind of an indication is no forthcoming. This is what happened in this current year. If you contrast it with the situation of the Ninth Plan, as the Chairman was enquiring, the Ninth Plan was approved on 1st January, 1998.

Therefore, it was approved in the first year. It was a very major achievement and they indicated a total allocation of Rs. 2,20,000 crore. The Annual Budget, as it took place during those five years if you total up those they came to Rs. 2,43,000 crore. That means the annual allocation was more than the indicative figure of the Plan. That was a situation which was quite in contrast to what is prevalent just now where, firstly, the figure itself was not known to us till December – finally what we wanted and how much they can give. This went till December of 2004. If we were to juxtapose the Tenth Plan indicative figure of Rs. 4,18,000 crore divided by four years, which are known, it is nowhere. There was no relation. Therefore, this figure becomes an academic figure. That is the point that we have been discussing, that is the outlays have to be finalized at the beginning of the plan and secondly Annual Allocation should be conforming to the overall outlay".

Adding further on the issue, the Defence Secretary has also stated that : "As has been mentioned earlier, how initial projections of Rs. 4,97,000 crore was done at the beginning of the Tenth Plan (2001-02).This was also communicated to the Finance Ministry with the break up. They needed it in a particular format. It was given in that format. Subsequently, they had indicated Rs. 4,97,000 crore is too much and we may plan within Rs. 4,21,000 crore. There was a gap of about Rs. 75,724 between the projection and what they had indicated. By that time certain time had elapsed. We were involved in an internal exercise of readjusting. In December 2004 they indicated Rs. 4,18,000 crore, which was what we had projected earlier".

Explaining the details of the ongoing measures to formulate the Eleventh Defence Plan and how these initiatives have a bearing on the implementation of annual plan programmes, the Defence Secretary has briefed the Committee : "As I just said, we have started our exercise of preparing the Eleventh Plan which means that the Integrated Defence Staff which gets inputs from all the three Headquarters puts together the long-term perspective plan requirements of each service and makes them into one composite plan called the Defence Plan. It sees whether there is any overlapping of capabilities or whether there is any repetition or commonalties. So, it does such modifications and vetting and then it is projecting that requirement to the Ministry where we see whether it is all right or whether it needs any change or not.. Accordingly, we pass it on to the Ministry of Finance for approval. Of course, we have discussions with the Ministry of Finance because they might also like to understand the details. So, that dialogue is there. Our request is, if the Ministry of Finance were to give its indications well before the start of the first year of the

Eleventh Plan, then that would help everybody to know what is going to be the situation during the five years of the Eleventh Plan. Secondly, we do need some kind of a figure to show that this is the total figure and whatever amount it might be would be divided in the five years in this fashion in the Annual Budget so that the Annual programmes can then be fine tuned to adjust to the availability. Otherwise, there is likely to be a mismatch between what we might project and the money availability".

When asked whether the Ministry of Finance had intimated the details of the 10th Plan allocations in time, the Defence Secretary has stated that : "It was towards the end of the third year. This was one part of the problem. The second part, as I said, is annual allocations are nowhere matching even this figure. Therefore, how do we do the Planning? We do not know what will be the figure for the fifth plan. Budget has been submitted for the fourth year. It totals up to Rs. 2 lakh something".

The Ministry of Defence in its written Action Taken Reply on the recommendation of the Committee on long term planning of three Services contained in the First Report on Demands for Grants of the Ministry of Defence for the year 2004-05, has stated as under : "A draft Long-Term Integrated Perspective Plan (LTIPP) covering the 15-year period from the Tenth to the Twelfth Plan (2002-2017) was formulated in June 2004 in consultation with the three Services. Since more than two years of the current Tenth Plan period have already elapsed, a new approach paper has been made formulating a Long Term Integrated Perspective Plan (LTIPP) covering the period from 2007-2022. This Plan is expected to be finalised by the Integrated Defence Staff by the last quarter of 2005."

The Committee are unhappy to note that the Ministry of Finance has failed to finalise the 10th Defence plan even after three years of the plan have passed. Non-finalisation of the 10th Defence Plan at its beginning by the Ministry of Finance has created a great deal of uncertainty about the availability of adequate finance for the acquisition of the vital equipment, modernization, etc. The Ministry of Defence had projected a demand of Rs. 4,97,000 crore in 2001 for the Tenth Plan. However, the Ministry of Finance has given indicative figure of Rs.4, 18,000 crore in December 2004,without any firm commitment. The total allocations in the first four years of Tenth Defence Plan just come to about Rs.2, 76,300 crore which is nowhere near their requirements. This gap between the demand and allocations, has adversely affected the defence planning and our preparedness. The Committee take a serious note of this and want the Government to finalise the Tenth Plan immediately and take steps to utilise the committed amount in full. The Committee would like to be apprised of the fmalisation of the Plan as well as the follow-up steps being taken to utilise the total allocation of the Tenth Plan.

The Committee also observe that due to non-finalisation of the Tenth Plan in time, the long term perspective plan of the Forces has got affected and is presently at the fmalisation stage with a revised plan schedule spanning from 2007-2022. The Committee, while expressing their displeasure over the present situation, recommend that the Ministry of Defence should reorient the plans and strive to adhere to the schedules envisaged. As regard the 11th Plan, the Committee desire that it should be finalised at least an year before the plan period starts. It is high time that the Government prepared a road map for self-reliance. The Committee strongly feels that India should not be taken as a weapons/arms market by the global suppliers and action in this direction should be visible by the end of Tenth Defence Plan and 11th Plan should entirely be devoted to self-reliance.

The Committee has also observed that the surveillance capabilities of our forces are in adequate. This is primarily due to non-availability of low-level radar systems with the three services. The Committee feel that all round effort should be undertaken by the Government to ensure that the entire country is covered. The Committee feel that the Ministry should explore all possibilities of acquiring the required radar systems in adequate numbers without any delay.

REGIONAL SECURITY CHALLENGES OF INDIA

Six of India's neighbours rank in the top 25 dysfunctional states in the world, as tabulated by the Failed States Index of the Fund for Peace. India is uniquely positioned to be a driver of interstate cooperation in South Asia, which is a 'predominantly Indocentric region' because, in terms of religion or culture, or both, 'India has something in common with [each of] its immediate neighbours but the neighbouring states of India do not share similarities of such magnitude or depth among themselves.'

Yet India has been unsuccessful in generating such cooperation. Despite the great strides it has made in economic growth, it remains mired in the security dilemmas of its own region. As Vikram Sood suggests, 'Globally, India is being recognised as a rising economic power but not in the region where economic development has become hostage to security issues.' Varun Sahni describes India's regional status as one of 'contested dominance'. The two types of regional security challenges for India. The first is a set of what might otherwise be classified as domestic law-andorder problems were it not for the involvement of India's neighbours. The second relates to bilateral disputes between India and its neighbours over resources, particularly land and water. Territorial disputes (prominently, Kashmir and Siachen with Pakistan, and Arunachal Pradesh and Aksai Chin with China) fall within this category.

Subnational Ethnic Movements

Indian populations in border regions tend to share common ethnic bonds with populations in adjacent countries. This is true, for example, of Tamils and Sri Lanka, Muslims in Kashmir, Punjabis with their cousins in Pakistan, Indian populations bordering the Tarai region of Nepal, and even Keralites and their ties to Gulf countries. The broad territorial division of ethnic groups within India and the strength of regional ethnic identities ensure that Indian policy towards the countries in question is often attentive to the preferences of domestic actors in these regions, as with Sri Lanka, where at one time the Indian government acquiesced in the brutal armed tactics of the Liberation Tigers of Tamil Eelam (LTTE). Similarly, there is 'widespread sympathy' in Indian border regions for the campaign for autonomy in the Tarai region of Nepal, for which 'most [Indian] politicians and bureaucrats do not hesitate to express moral support'. And Pakistan was widely believed to have supported Sikh separatist movements within India's state of Punjab during the 1980s.

Secessionist Movements and Insurgencies

Because of India's vast size and heterogeneous society and polity, it has been home to many (often armed) movements aiming for sovereign status separate from the union. Some of these secessionist movements have allowed neighbouring countries interested in destabilising India to interfere in its internal affairs. The separatist assertion of regional identities has sharply accentuated the importance attached by Delhi to the territorial integrity of the Indian Union ever since independence. Indeed, this theme first arose during the early months of independence, when Delhi made every effort (including the use of force) to integrate the 536 princely states of India into the Union. It was echoed in the military action taken by India to wrest control of Goa from the Portuguese in 1961; in India's integration of Sikkim into the Union in 1975; and ultimately in the lack of official support given to the LTTE, seen first and foremost as a secessionist movement. It is also reflected in India's longstanding policy of rejecting involvement in its neighbourhood by nations outside South Asia. Concern over territorial unity thus runs deep in Indian foreign policy.

New Ethnic Groups

The cross-border movement of large populations from neighbouring countries has resulted in the creation of new (or newly large) ethnic groups in India, thus complicating policy towards the originating countries. Two examples stand out—the migration of Tibetans escaping Chinese persecution, and the steady inflow of immigrants (legal and illegal) from

Bangladesh—with implications for Delhi's relationship with both countries. In the case of China, India has walked a tightrope between official recognition of Tibet as an integral part of China and granting asylum to the Dalai Lama and his followers on Indian territory. Tibetan migrants have integrated relatively well into Indian society. By contrast, the domestic response to Bangladeshi immigrants has been much less forgiving, possibly as a result of their purely economic motivation for migration, leading to riots in Assam against migrant Bengalis as far back as the 1960s and 1970s. This has produced a negative impact on Indo-Bangladeshi relations, with India in 1984 initiating construction of a still unfinished 4,000-kilometre concrete barrier along the Indo-Bangladeshi border.

Religious Conflict

Religion has a significant impact on social stratification and political mobilisation in India. The religious composition of Indian society influences social and economic policy, particularly with regard to minority rights. The frequent occurrence of violence between religious groups—predominantly between Hindus and Muslims—in various parts of the country, sometimes on a startling scale, has led to instances of radicalisation, for example through the Students' Islamic Movement of India (SIMI). Religiously inspired terrorism has also been attributed to Hindu activists following serial bomb attacks in the predominantly Muslim town of Malegaon in 2006. While the Bharatiya Janata Party (BJP) generally proved responsible when in power (1998–2004), its connections with radical Hindu organisations hostile to Islam and Christianity have at times stoked tension, which early on benefited the party politically, as in the case of the demolition of the Babri mosque in 1992 and the Gujarat riots of 2002.

In the former case the BJP's connections with these organisations tended to polarise public opinion further, while in both cases cadres from these organisations were involved in events on the ground. The BJP's current lack of traction is largely attributable to an ageing leadership and ideological fatigue, as well as a failure to build on limited breakthroughs into southern India. But it is likely to persist as a potentially volatile faction in Indian politics, and one that could complicate relations with Muslim countries.

Bilateral Issues: China

Increasingly, China is more worrying than Pakistan for India, whatever the provocations launched against India from within the latter's territory. While India has experienced significant economic success over the past 20 years, China initiated its economic reforms well before India did, and has consistently outstripped India's impressive growth by 2–3 percentage points every year since then. The result is that China's economy has expanded to nearly three times the size of India's, enabling Beijing to invest significantly in its military sector. Thus, while China and India are often grouped together as 'emerging' countries, China is well on the way to establishing itself as the principal global competitor of the US, while India, for all its recent economic achievements, lags well behind.

India's relationship with China has been a tense once since the mid-1950s, reaching its nadir with their border war of 1962, in which India suffered a humiliating defeat. The Sino-Indian border disputes continue to be a thorn in the side of bilateral relations. And mutual needling by the two capitals abounds (although it mostly does not involve Pakistan). The matter of Tibet looms over the bilateral relationship. After a tense decade in Lhasa following China's takeover in 1950, India gave asylum to the fleeing Dalai Lama in 1959, since when the Tibetan refugee population in India has grown steadily. Tibet is a hot-button issue for China, a nation at least as worried about territorial integrity as India. Beijing watches the Dalai Lama's activities in India keenly—and its anxieties about a seemingly powerless Dalai Lama living there may not be as irrational as they seem, in the light of history. In 1910 the 13th Dalai Lama, the immediate predecessor of the current incumbent, fled a Chinese Qing dynasty invasion of Tibet, establishing residence in India. Three years later, he reclaimed his throne and authority in Tibet triumphantly, the distant Qing regime having collapsed. India and China, while cooperating in a variety of multilateral processes ranging from trade negotiations to discussions on climate change, are increasingly competitors in a global race for wealth, energy and influence as emerging (or, in China's case, now emerged) powers.

Whether in commodity-rich Africa or the oil and gas fields of Central Asia, India and China are increasingly rubbing up against each other. To complicate matters, both nations espouse parallel nationalistic mythologies of civilizational greatness that breed a sense of entitlement to Great Power status and a tendency to be irritated by the pretensions of others. Indian analysts fear a Chinese strategy of encirclement in Asia. This refers to China's numerous investments in building up port facilities in the Indian Ocean, seen by some strategists as a 'string of pearls' strategy to constrain India's freedom of manoeuvre. China's booming exports and hunger for international markets have also led it to develop substantial trading relationships with India's neighbours.

China's penetration of India's neighbourhood presents a finely calibrated challenge to Indian foreign policy, seen by some as deriving from the following calculus: 'Restricting India to the Asian subcontinent remains Chinese policy. The tactics are simple: keep borders with India tranquil but do not solve the [border] dispute, trade with India but arm Pakistan and wean away Nepal, Bangladesh, and Myanmar.'

Bilateral issues: Pakistan

The last 60 years have witnessed two major wars (in 1965 and 1971) between India and Pakistan, and two major acts of aggression by Pakistan (in 1948 over Kashmir and 1999 in Kargil), in addition to numerous smallscale incidents across their borders. During the Cold War, Pakistan was the ally of choice for both the United States and China in South Asia, while India inclined towards, and eventually allied itself with, the Soviet Union. Pakistan received billions of dollars' worth of military aid and equipment over the years from its major patrons, much of which was employed in conflicts with India and to sponsor insurgency in Indian-occupied Kashmir. Pakistan's alliance with China, which has endured since the

1950s, is a much greater source of worry to India than Pakistan's erratic friendship of convenience with the US, particularly in respect of China's transfer of nuclear weapons technology and missile systems to Pakistan.

In recent years both China and the US have established a more balanced approach to the Indo-Pakistani rivalry, notably at the time of the Kargil war of 1999. Pakistan's nuclear tests of 1998, following those of India in the same year and establishing at least notional nuclear parity, promoted strategic stability of sorts in the volatile relationship. But peace initiatives involving Indian prime ministers Vajpayee (1998–2004) and Singh (since 2004) and their Pakistani counterparts have failed to yield meaningful results. The deadly terrorist attacks in Mumbai in November 2008 created fresh challenges in Indo-Pakistani relations.

However, international pressure eventually forced Islamabad to acknowledge Pakistani connections with the perpetrators, and after a long freeze bilateral high-level contacts resumed, albeit amid much mutual distrust, in 2009. Prime Minister Singh has been roundly criticised by many at home for his handling of the Mumbai attacks and his post-Mumbai overtures towards Pakistan. However, others have praised the resumption of dialogue with Pakistan. Siddharth Varadarajan suggested: 'Over time, India has realised the best way to deal with the threat of terror is by strengthening its internal capabilities while utilising engagement as a lever for influencing Pakistan's behaviour over the long run.' C. Raja Mohan, while supporting Dr Singh's overtures, nevertheless worries about Pakistan as a reliable interlocutor: 'Put simply, is Pakistan a country or a grievance? States negotiate with others on the basis of an enlightened self-interest and are open to give and take. But revanchists consumed by real and imagined grievances find it hard to split the difference in a negotiation.' Further significant terrorist attacks credibly linked to Pakistan would probably force targeted retaliation, and could produce wider escalation if not carefully managed, including by Washington and Beijing.

Bilateral Issues: Sri Lanka, Bangladesh, Nepal

India's relationships with other nations in its region are far from settled. India's hegemonic status—or at least its perceived aspiration to this status—creates threat perceptions among its smaller neighbours. They see India's varying military (and other) interventions with and in neighbouring countries in terms of 'the outward projection and demonstration of military might'. In the case of the Sri Lankan conflict, India's justifications for military intervention during the 1980s were based on the security imperatives associated with the influx of Tamil refugees, the purported risk to commerce, and the danger of external Great Powers involving themselves in the conflict; but India's peacekeeping action proved counterproductive, alienating the Tamil community, the LTTE and the Sri Lankan government. Similarly, India's action in 1971 in East Pakistan to relieve West Pakistan's military oppression, while justified in humanitarian terms and on the basis of massive refugee flows to India, was widely viewed internationally and in the region as primarily an attempt to dismember an archrival.

Moreover, contrary to India's expectations, the assistance it rendered to Bangladesh did not win it an ally but rather produced a neighbour that has often proved prickly and resentful. While some in India saw the hand of Maoists in Nepal behind the early success of India's own Naxalite movement, any such claim today is far-fetched. However high-handed India's past approach to Nepal has been, and however hostile Maoists in Nepal may have been towards India, the Naxalite movement in India is homegrown and driven by local factors.

Bilateral Issues: Afghanistan

Aside from smaller nations such as Bhutan and the Maldives, perhaps the one country in the region where India's involvement has not played against it to date is Afghanistan. Indians tend to see Delhi's Afghan policy as altruistic. But this assessment glosses over a simple calculus—the need to prevent Kabul from tilting excessively towards Pakistan and allowing itself to be subsumed by Islamabad into its security space. Delhi worries that when the US-led NATO forces begin to pull out, as the Netherlands and Canada have pledged to do in 2010 and 2011 respectively, Kabul could submit to the combined influence of Pakistan (supported by China) and the Taleban, leaving India as the loser in a geostrategic tug-of-war. As of mid-2010 Delhi's worries are not ill-founded: desperate for an exit strategy of its own, Washington appears to be encouraging a negotiated solution to the conflict that could only strengthen Pakistan's hand locally. India is rumoured to have opened up channels of its own with the Taleban, despite maintaining that there is no distinction between 'good' and 'bad' Taleban.

A western withdrawal from Afghanistan would leave numerous Indian assets there highly vulnerable. Even under present circumstances, with NATO troops thick on the ground, the Indian embassy in Kabul was attacked twice in 15 months in 2008–2009. Delhi's remaining option if NATO and President Karzai compromise with the Taleban, that of seeking (perhaps with Moscow, conceivably also with Tehran) to revive the Afghani Northern Alliance, would doubtless prove a disappointing and expensive consolation prize.

3

External and Internal Security Environment

The Line of Control (LoC) in Jammu and Kashmir (J&K) and the Actual Ground Position Line (AGPL) at Siachen Glacier, are perpetual flashpoints between India and Pakistan due to their active nature. Further violations of the LoC, such as the intrusions engineered by Pakistan in the Kargil district of J&K in the summer months of 1999, have the potential to lead to full-scale conventional conflict. With a hawkish military "chief executive" in power in Pakistan, the recurrence of such misadventures has gained credibility. India's unresolved territorial and boundary dispute with China and an un-demarcated Line of Actual Control (LAC) on the Indo-Tibetan border do not augur well for long-term peace and stability between these two Asian giants. There has been an almost unending influx of migrants from Bangladesh into India's northeastern states. Hence, good border management will remain a major security imperative for many decades to come.

Though there has been a gradual reduction in the enhanced levels of post-Pokhran II intrusions and patrolling activities by the People's Liberation Army's (PLA) border troops along the LAC with China, there has been virtually no progress on the resolution of the major territorial and boundary dispute. While the Border Peace and Tranquillity Agreement (BPTA) of 1993 remains in place, the confidence building measures (CBMs) agreed upon in 1996 are yet to be translated into practically viable ground level measures even though the stalled Joint Working Group meetings have since been resumed. The LAC continues to remain ill defined and ambiguous and its early 'clarification' on ground and map still appears to be a distant goal. The only conclusion that can reasonably be drawn is that China is apparently in no hurry for further progress on these substantive issues and that it suits China to put them on the back burner for some more time.

China's unjustifiable opposition to India's nuclear weapons programme, its continuing nuclear and missile collusion and defence cooperation with Pakistan, its support to the military regime in Myanmar, its assistance to the LTTE (Liberation Tigers of Tamil Eelam) in Sri Lanka and increasing activities in the Bay of Bengal, its attempts to isolate India in the ASEAN Regional Forum (ARF) and its relentless efforts to increase its influence in Nepal, Bhutan and Bangladesh, are all pointers to a carefully orchestrated plan aimed at the strategic encirclement of India. Clearly, China poses a long-term strategic challenge to India as a competing regional power in Asia. India needs to take this reality into account and distinguish between what China professes and what it actually does.

India has also been saddled with a long-drawn low intensity conflict (LIC) in J&K and the northeastern states where Pakistan is continuing to wage a 'proxy war' against India by actively aiding and abetting insurgencies. Militancy in Punjab, though dormant at present, could also come to the fore again if the state exhibits signs of being complacent. The ongoing People's War Group agitation in Telangana, the tensions simmering in the Ramnad coastal belt of Tamil Nadu, fuelled by the Liberation Tigers of Tamil Eelam (LTTE), are keeping the pot boiling in southern India. The occasional violent outbursts of the Jharkhand Mukti Morcha and the Ranvir Sena, among other such organisations in Bihar, the latent movements for autonomy in Uttarakhand in Uttar Pradesh and Gorkhaland in West Bengal and the increasing fundamentalist Islamic influence along Rajasthan's border with Pakistan, will ensure that India's internal security remains in a state of flux for decades to come, particularly when Pakistan loses no opportunity to provoke internal problems.

NUCLEAR NEIGHBOURHOOD

The future of nuclear deterrence constitutes a crucial facet of India's security. India has for long lived under the shadow of China's nuclear weapons. China is rapidly modernising its nuclear-tipped ballistic missiles and is "quite openly proud of its emerging MIRV (multiple, independently-targeted re-entry vehicle) capability for which it has coined the slogan 'one arrow, three stars'." Most of China's nuclear weapons are known to be short-range, battlefield or 'tactical' nuclear weapons and a large number of them are deployed in Tibet. China's Strategic Rocket Wing was formerly called the Second Artillery. Since China has already signed a de-targeting agreement with Russia and the United States (US), the nuclear weapons in Tibet, particularly the short-range ones, constitute a threat-in-being to India. It would be in India's interest to offer a mutual 'no first use' agreement to China as a confidence building measure (CBM).

Other Asian powers with nuclear weapons include the US (due to its forward military presence), Russia and Israel. India and Russia enjoy a good relationship based on a mutuality of interests. Neither India nor Russia sees the other's nuclear weapons as an existing or a likely threat. With Israel, India now has a burgeoning defence equipment procurement relationship. The growing menace of Islamic fundamentalist terrorism poses a common problem that requires a coordinated approach. Israel's nuclear weapons are primarily meant to underwrite its survivability as a nation-state in a perpetually hostile environment and are unlikely to ever pose a strategic challenge to India. After President Bill Clinton's Indian sojourn in March 2000, the US and India now have a relatively warmer strategic relationship than during the Cold War period when the US had seen India as leaning towards the Soviet Union and had itself tilted towards Pakistan. However, the US still sees India's nuclear weapons as an unacceptable violation of its non-proliferation agenda. Many Indian analysts have expressed the view that the continued presence of nuclear weapons at Diego Garcia, an Indian Ocean island only about 1,800 kilometres from Kanyakumari (Cape Comorin, India's southernmost tip), and on board ships and submarines of the US Navy's Indian Ocean Fleet, constitutes a threat-in-being to India. Such an impression has not gained currency without reason and the issue merits closer examination.

Since the end of the Cold War, the US has increasingly tended to see many new threats from diverse sources. Among these, India has often been cited as a potential source of security problems for the US. A Pentagon report entitled Proliferation: Threat and Response, released by Secretary of Defence William Cohen in November 1997, referred to "the threat perceptions posed by 'two nuclear powers' - India and Pakistan. It refers to their potential to use chemical and biological weapons if their 50-year old rivalry flares for the fourth time." In all fairness, it must be stated that the focus of the report was on Iraq; however, the reference to India stirred a hornet's nest. In another Rand Corporation report Sources of Conflict in the 21st Century: Regional Futures and US Strategy, a scenario prepared for the Pentagon predicts a nuclear conflagration over Kashmir in 2006 after "the insurgency in Indian Kashmir has become unmanageable" and Pakistan "launches major attacks all along the international border, accompanied by an intense air campaign." As Indian forces "continue to press forward, Pakistan detonates a small bomb on an Indian armoured formation in an unpopulated area of the desert border region... India's response is by destroying a Pakistani air base by a two-weapon nuclear attack. Pakistan then attacks Jodhpur with a 20-kiloton (kt) weapon and demands cessation of hostilities. But India strikes Hyderabad with a weapon assessed to be 200 kt and threatens 'ten times' more destruction if any more nuclear weapons are used. Pakistan then offers a cease-fire in place." The Rand report was intended to serve the long-range planning needs of the US Air Force and has visualised an inescapable role for it in a future Indo-Pak conflict. The report states: "For example, imagine a situation in which several densely populated South Asian cities have been struck by nuclear weapons by India and Pakistan in an ongoing regional conflict. The United States would surely be called upon to lead relief efforts and the US military would be at the leading edge of any response."

In a report entitled 1998 Strategic Assessment, prepared by the National Defence University's Institute for National Strategic Studies and presented to General Hugh Shelton, Chairman of the US Joint Chiefs of Staff in August 1998, shortly after the nuclear tests conducted by India and Pakistan, India, Russia and China were "dubbed as large transition nuclear states with economic potential, population size and technological capacity to challenge the US military might." The report characterised these three countries as US security strategy 'wild cards' and recommended "encouraging these countries to reform and become integrated into 'core' US alliances, while maintaining the capability to respond to dangers and 'destabilising behaviour' of these nations." The report painted a 'worst case scenario' in which the three states could "encourage instability, proliferation and challenge the US military supremacy." In the same month, Jim Ryan, a Republican Congressman, "clubbed India and Pakistan with China and the so-called rogue states like Iraq and Iran and said these countries pose long-term danger to the United States." He wrote in an article in The Washington Times that, "China, India, Pakistan, Iran and other rogue nations... are arming their war machines with missiles capable of hitting cities in the US."

There have also been reports of US war games in which India's western seaboard is targeted with Tomahawk cruise missiles, followed by US Marine landings, even as nuclear armed submarines patrol the Arabian Sea and bomber aircraft from Diego Garcia stand by. However, not all US think-tank reports visualise a threat to American interests and not all such reports predict an inevitable US intervention. In his much-discussed documented briefing Stability in South Asia, prepared for the US Army, while predicting "ugly stability" in South Asia in the decades ahead, Ashley Tellis has written that, "It is unlikely that the United States will intervene militarily in South Asia in the foreseeable future..." Indian defence analysts, who are normally more than willing to go the extra mile to accommodate US security interests, even though US analysts have always had great difficulty in comprehending Indian security concerns, find these reports alarming. What concerns them even more is that the US might miscalculate and that it may launch a cruise missile and even a nuclear attack occasioned entirely by misperceptions. K. Subrahmanyam has written: "... The weapons are a threat and that needs to be countered by India acquiring similar systems... There is also a need for India to acquire sea denial capabilities, both conventional and nuclear powered submarines, which will be a deterrent against navies with unfriendly intentions coming close enough to Indian coasts to pose threats to our cities and infrastructure." It is for these reasons that the US nuclear weapons and launch platforms in India's neighbourhood are perceived as a threat-in-being.

The transition of India and Pakistan to the status of states with nuclear weapons (SNWs) has led to many misgivings. In particular, the bogey of Kashmir as a nuclear flashpoint has been raised by vested Western interests and Southern Asia has been classified as an unstable region. The termination of the 1999 Kargil conflict through mutual agreement has conclusively proved that such views are merely hype and hoopla and have little substance.

Though nuclear weapons in Pakistan are under the control of the army that now also holds the reins of power, India has no reason to believe that the Pakistani Generals will act less responsibly than the political dispensations in power in other nuclear weapons states when they know clearly that unleashing the nuclear genie will certainly lead to the end of Pakistan as a nation-state, regardless of the damage that India might sustain. India's interests lie in actively pursuing universal nuclear disarmament even while developing a credible minimum nuclear deterrent to meet the country's security needs.

INTERNAL ARMED CONFLICT IN INDIA

Though the Indian Army has been committed to counterinsurgency operations for the past 60 years, Indian policymakers are yet to formulate a joint civil–military doctrine for resolution of internal armed conflicts. The lack of the same is evident from the internal security situation obtaining in the country. Rostum Nanavatty's *Internal Armed Conflict in India: Forging a Joint Civil–Military Approach* is based on his vast experience as a young regimental officer to an Army Commander, varying from the North-eastern region—Nagaland, Manipur, Mizoram, Tripura and south Assam—to Sri Lanka, and Jammu and Kashmir (J&K).

Nanavatty has correlated the views of experts and suggested ways in which the fundamental principles of counterinsurgency operations can be applied in the peculiar Indian context to create conditions necessary for the success of a campaign. The book is India-centric, based on the premise that internal armed conflict in India, irrespective of its causes or its goals, will persist and that the military will continue to play a significant role in its management and resolution.

The various terms relevant to internal armed conflict, followed by the influence of globalization on internal armed conflicts, its impact on national power and external involvement in internal armed conflict. He adroitly tabulates the evolution of fundamental principles of counterinsurgency and compares the same in the British, the US and Indian armies. He highlights the commonality in their doctrines; yet there are variations in perceptions and emphasis.

India has witnessed protracted nature of such conflicts, essentially due to the government's inability to capitalize on the successful conduct of operations by the security forces: to build civil counterinsurgency capacities within the state; to provide good governance; and to arrive at a mutually acceptable political solution to the problem.

He examines the current external environment, followed by an analysis of the current internal armed conflicts in India, aptly summarized in tabulated form. Indian Constitution related to internal security, highlighting the demarcation of responsibility: dealing with external threats is the job of the Union government, while internal threats to law and order are dealt with by the state, albeit with the former's assistance. However, there is some ambiguity regarding armed rebellion exceeding threat to public order as given in the Code of Criminal Procedure (CrPC). While the CrPC is precise in the manner in which armed forces are to be employed in aid to civil authorities, it does not cover their employment in internal armed conflict situations. These are contained in the Armed Forces (Special Powers) Act (AFSPA). The author has very rightly summated its necessity, correlating the existence of a similar act in the United Kingdom (UK) for Northern Ireland.

The apprehension about AFSPA is due to misinformation and lack of understanding—if there was no insurgency, there would be no requirement for the army in those areas; if there is no requirement for the army, then there is no requirement of AFSPA. He has illustrated some of the aberrations and how they have been dealt with as per the law.

Nanavatty then comments on the proliferation of the Central Armed Police Force (CAPF). He refers to their 'proliferation' because the government yields to temptation to establish a discrete force in response to each new operational requirement. The establishment of this 'type' force can prove to be inflexible, uneconomical and impractical—there is always the danger of having too much or too little of a type force. He has also covered, in detail, the organizational and functional deficiencies which impinge on effectiveness of CAPF in counterinsurgency.

He argues against the recommendations of the *Group of Ministers Report on National Security, 2000*, that the Central Reserve Police Force (CRPF) progressively take over a counterinsurgency role nationwide. He questions whether the CRPF will attain the status of an effective counterinsurgency force while retaining its other policing skills, and would it be able to do so devoid of military leadership and ethos. The Assam Rifles have proved their capability, more with less, of achieving success in their counterinsurgency role. However, organizational, management and operational changes have begun to impact this potent force. Recommendations for the Assam Rifles' assuming the exclusive responsibility of guarding Indo-Myanmar border based on the principle, 'one border, one force', is a retrograde step as it will preclude them from participating in counterinsurgency operations for which they are ideally suited. Similarly, suggestions to cease their affiliation with army will surely sound the death knell of an effective counterinsurgency force.

The need for a re-look at the role of the army as delineated by General K.M. Cariappa in 1952 and the Army Doctrine of 2004: 'defence of the country against external forces' being the primary aim and 'assisting government agencies to cope with proxy war and other internal threats and provide aid to civil authorities' as its secondary role.

He opines that the army views the latter as secondary, thus being less important, and does not favour involvement in internal security operations. By categorizing its internal role as secondary, it unwittingly downgrades the importance of this function, leading to less-than-appropriate levels of preparation in terms of organization, equipment profiling and training, thus forcing army to improvise and adapt for this role. The author suggests that the army re-define its role and also incorporate countering internal threat as its main role.

The evolution and development of village guards, 'I' battalions, Rashtriya Rifles and infantry battalions (Territorial Army) (Home and Hearth), and conduct of military operations in counterinsurgency campaigns. Commenting on special operations, Nanavatty emphasizes that the military in India is neither authorized nor responsible to execute special operations, particularly in operations other than war and internal armed conflict. Civil government officials lacking knowledge, skills and tools are entrusted with the authority and responsibility for special operations, while the military, which has the knowledge, skills and tools, is denied such authority and responsibility.

It suggests lack of confidence on the part of the political executive in the ability of the military to think in strategic terms. The author suggests that special operations in internal armed conflicts, being sensitive in nature, need politico-military sanction at the highest level, but once approved, the authority and responsibility for their execution should be delegated to senior military commander in the theatre.

India's response to insurgency as militarily stout, administratively weak, and politically absent. He emphasizes the near-total absence of civil counterinsurgency, a major lacuna in conducting an effective counterinsurgency campaign. Further, the absence of a joint civil–military national counterinsurgency doctrine prevents the government from fully exploiting its vast resources and responding to the security of the state in a coherent, cohesive and consistent manner.

It stems essentially from contradictions inherent in centre–state and civil–military relations. Even the Constitution is ambiguous on how the responsibilities for the 'defence of India against internal threats' are to be precisely shaped between governments at the centre and in the state. Nanavatty opines that it is imperative to formulate, articulate and adopt a joint civil–military doctrine involving the three key arms of the government—the civil administration, the police and the army—for the conduct of a counterinsurgency campaign. Equally important is the need for the political executive to understand, appreciate and approve of such a doctrine and demonstrate the will to apply it in practice.

Nanavatty examines various options and a way forward. He suggests revised fundamental principles for the government's counterinsurgency campaign. He argues that the government should not hesitate in introducing emergency legislations to deny insurgents taking advantage of existing rules. He recommends that punitive military operations should be an integral part of India's declared doctrine. The author further suggests revised fundamental principles for security forces operations with the aim of security forces operations being to 'secure the people'.

While advocating restructuring and reorganization of the security forces for counterinsurgency, Nanavatty emphasizes operational cost-effectiveness and not empire-building; intensifying the existing force structures to minimize turbulence and disruption; and resisting the temptation to raise type forces for every new exigency: the role of each type force must allow flexibility in its employment. He has suggested that state police forces should raise properly trained and equipped village defence committees over which they must exercise effective command and control. It is a very pertinent suggestion since the involvement of locals will facilitate better intelligence and denial of support base to the insurgents. The author has also suggested review of the composition of border-guarding force and functioning under the Ministry of Defence.

The suggested re-organization includes establishing an Internal Security (IS) force providing government a flexible and calibrated response, thereby diminishing dependence on the army for internal security operations. At the same time, the author cautions that this could lead to undesirable proliferation of forces. In order for the IS force to be capable of high-intensity counterinsurgency operations, it must possess the character and ethos of the army, be led by army officers, and function under command and control of the army.

The two possible models of Rashtriya Rifles and Assam Rifles have been analysed, though it could create division within the army—one force preparing for a conventional war which may never come and the other perpetually embroiled in low-intensity operations. Nanavatty recommends the re-organization of Headquarters Director General Assam Rifles (DGAR) into Headquarters Internal Security Command (ISCOM), headed by a general officer commanding-in-chief (GOC-in-C), and the establishment of an independent Headquarters General Officer Commanding Internal Security (GOC [IS]), under an officer of rank of Lieutenant General who will be responsible for advising the state government on the conduct of security forces operations. He then outlines two possible options for command and control.

The army may be a better option than establishing a dedicated force. Right-sizing the force needs deliberation since boots on ground are important, but technology needs to be incorporated more vigorously, and a greater focus is needed on small team operations instead of merely increasing force levels. Similarly, raising GOC (IS) and ISCOM and retaining the arrangement of command and control under the headquarters regional army command does not sound logical.

Nanavatty suggests the re-organization of the Ministry of Home Affairs; he also proposes a structure and organization for management of internal armed conflict at the national level. He follows it up by evaluating the existing structures and organizations for management of internal armed conflict at the state level, and proposes restructuring and reorganization at the same level for management and resolution of internal armed conflict in India as part of a joint civil– military doctrine.

Its proportional and dimensional spread, it merited much more elaborate coverage as well as suggestions for tackling the same, including the possible role of the armed forces. Overall, the book is an excellent treatise on internal armed conflict in India and is a comprehensive work. It is the product of rigorous research and decades of experience of the author. It is prescriptive and essential for practitioners—politicians, civil servants, policemen and soldiers—and should serve as a catalyst for formulation and articulation of a joint civil– military doctrine.

JAMMU & KASHMIR

The problem has been with us since independence even though Pakistan has no legal case. The ruler of this erstwhile princely state decided to accede to India. According to the Independence Act it was for the rulers of the princely states to decide to join India or Pakistan. Pakistan has been disputing the legality of the accession signed by the then J&K ruler, Maharaja Hari Singh. The initial hesitation of the Maharaja to accede to either India or Pakistan and the unilateral Indian offer to find out the wishes of the people of the state has given Pakistan an excuse to challenge the legality of the accession.

It has been doing everything for the last 56 years to grab this state. It has not been able to achieve its objective through wars with India. So, it has started a proxy war since 1989. Waging of a proxy war fits into the Pakistani designs of bleeding India.

Unfortunately, the weaknesses of the state and of the administrative systems have provided Pakistan with opportunities to fish in troubled waters. More interested in perpetuating their rule than governing the state, its rulers have been exploiting regional and religious differences.

Anti-national forces thrived in this environment and Pakistan has missed no opportunity to support and encourage them. Over the years it has succeeded in building a pro- Pakistan base in the state.

Frustrated in their efforts to gain power through democratic means, some politicians joined the anti-India front, more to put pressure on the Indian government than on ideological grounds. In a state, where the overwhelming population was against communal politics at the time of partition, the fundamentalist forces have managed to penetrate into the secular polity.

The many serious problems of the people have to be addressed. It is not a coincidence that Pakistan's efforts to destabilise the situation in the state received some success only when our own political mismanagement provided it with an opportunity to intervene, as in 1965 and again in 1989. One of Pakistan's main aims is to divide the polity on communal lines.

The attitude of the Pakistani military government is unlikely to change in the near future. But that does not mean that Pakistan should be allowed to set the Kashmir agenda. Moves will have to be made on all fronts to regain the initiative on both political and diplomatic fronts. The proposals made in the announcements by the Cabinet Committee on Security on October 22 are steps in the right direction, but the ground situation does not justify over-optimism. There are likely to be many ups and downs on this long torturous road to peace in Jammu and Kashmir.

Left Extremism

Making a beginning in Naxalbari in West Bengal and Telengana in Andhra Pradesh in the 1970s, the movement has since spread to many states: Bihar, Jharkhand, Madhya Pradesh, Chhattisgarh and Orissa. The root cause for the rise in Left extremism is the inability of the states to address the many genuine grievances of the people. The gap between the unrealistic expectations, fuelled by populist rhetoric, and their actual fulfilment has increased and not decreased over the years. The younger generation is no longer willing to put up passively with injustice and humiliation without a fight. The bitterness of the angry young man against the prevailing unjust socio-economic system is spilling over. The older generation is not unsympathetic to them. An educational system which produces unemployable young boys and girls has not helped. Pressure on land has made the task of survival on agriculture more difficult. A callous district administration, especially in the rural areas, a clogged judicial system and feudal attitudes have compounded the problem. The land disputes have multiplied, but the land records and the judicial system to settle them is in disarray. There is a sense of frustration and anger.

The most prominent among the groups, that have mushroomed in the recent years, are the People's War Group (PWG) and the Marxist Communist Centre (MCC). But it is not ideology and revolutionary zeal that is driving them. For many, joining these groups is the only way to survive. Their main activity is extortion. Huge funds amounting to hundreds of crores of rupees are being extorted by them. What they cannot get through legitimate means they obtain through arms and explosives. Their tactics are no different from the insurgents and terrorists. Create terror and extort money. They are, however, not secessionists. Their aim is to overthrow what they call an unjust socio-economic system. But they are in no hurry to achieve their ideological aims as long as they can extort enough money. Corrupt politicians, policemen and civil servants have made their own adjustments with these groups. A live-

and-let live attitude is mutually beneficial to all of them. Who knows how much money goes to the extremists and how much goes to the others. The real sufferers are the very people for whom the extremists are waging this war against the state.

In public perception a government that is unable to discharge all its responsibilities is more likely to respond when the demand is loud, organised and backed by acts of violence. The many progressive, well intentioned legislations are not being implemented effectively and sometimes have done more harm than good by creating more bitterness and frustration, e.g., the Minimum Wages Act. The marginal and deprived sections of the society are the worst hit.

Social and economic factors are important, but even more important are religion and identity. The secessionist movement in J&K is politically motivated, but its ideological base is built around religious fundamentalism. Fired by religious fervour, the young recruits have no hesitation in attacking ruthlessly what they consider the decayed political and moral order, which they perceive as hedonistic. Once the instruments of governance are discredited, it is not too difficult to justify their destruction as in J&K, the North-East or in the states afflicted by Left extremism. In another sense, however, the aim of all these movements is no different from the aim of legitimate political movements. They too seek to acquire power, measured in terms of exercising influence or control over the people and acquisition of wealth for them is the source of all power. Extortion, therefore, becomes an essential part of their strategy. Their goal and strategy could change during the course of the movement. In the initial stages some of them may only demand economic and political justice or more autonomy in the existing political system, like the Bodos in Assam, but they can take a more extremist stand and demand secession in the later stages.

Effective steps to reduce ethnic and social inequalities, disparities in educational and employment opportunities, and for creating an effective machinery for the redressal of public grievance, are absolutely essential to improve the environment in which extremist violence flourishes. Steps to reduce economic deprivation and improve the delivery of essential services can erode the base of public support on which the extremist movements survive. It is relatively easier to find solutions to seemingly intractable political problems, like in J&K, in an environment where people are by and large satisfied with the functioning of the government agencies and are not deprived of essential services. More than anything else, it is the economic policies that would ultimately determine the future of these movements. A thriving economy, which gives hope and opportunity to the people, is more likely to defeat all types of extremist movements than any other strategy.

The need for a well co-ordinated security apparatus can hardly be overemphasised. It should include the police, the paramilitary forces, the army and the intelligence agencies. A composite force on the lines of the National Security Guards (NSG) should be organised in all the states, even in those states where the internal security situation is not so serious. It is easier to deal with the problems at the initial stages, than later, when the state police is no longer able to cope with them.

But in the states where the situation has gone beyond their control, the Centre, as laid down in the Constitution, is duty-bound to intervene, notwithstanding the fact that law and order is under the State List. The Union government is charged with the responsibility of protecting the states from internal disturbances under Article 353 of the Constitution, even though law and order comes under List-II, the State List. The Union government can issue directions to the state under Articles 257-258. Action for non-compliance of the directions from the Union government can be taken under Article 365. A state government can be dismissed under Article 356, if a situation arises in which the administration of the state cannot be carried on in accordance with the provisions of the Constitution. A national emergency can be declared under Article 352.

But, even if the Centre decides to intervene, the state's role cannot be minimised. The primary responsibility to deal with the security challenges must rest with the state governments. A situation should not be allowed to develop where the state government washes its hands off, or its forces instead of cooperating with the central forces, actually work against them. The many internal security challenges can be met effectively only with full cooperation between the central and the state governments. The police, the paramilitary forces, the army and all the intelligence agencies must act in close co-ordination. The hostile foreign forces can and will take advantage of the internal situation to destabilise the country in pursuit of their own agenda. All serious internal security problems: communal and sectarian violence, organised crime, drug-trafficking, labour and students' unrest, political violence and even economic crimes, if not checked effectively can develop an external dimension. There is an urgent need to make the police and the paramilitary forces more professional. The emphasis has to shift from 'more numbers' to 'more professionally trained forces'.

The internal security problems should not be treated as merely law and order problems. They have to be dealt with comprehensively in all their dimensions and at all levels — political, economic and social. They are all interlinked. At times, the required measures will conflict with each other. Going too far in one direction could be counter-productive. The security requirements have to be met, but that does not mean giving the security agencies a free hand. Striking the right balance is the key to success in meeting these challenges effectively. We need a comprehensive security policy that will be implemented effectively at all levels.

KASHMIR: AN ARGUMENT FOR THE MULTI-SCALAR APPROACH

My central argument in this chapter will be that the militancy in Kashmir is best understood through both levels of analysis : the relationship of the terrorists to the Indian state and the ways in which terrorists operate on a transnational level. In demonstrating how both levels of analysis are relevant, this chapter will also begin to explore one way of constructing such a multi-scalar approach that will be further elaborated upon in subsequent portions of the paper. The chapter will be organized as follows: first, I explain the relevance of Kashmir to Islamist terrorism in India as a whole; second, I will provide a brief overview of the militancy; and third, I will apply the state-based and transnational approaches to the Kashmir conflict to demonstrate their limitations.

Relevance of Kashmir

The point of using Kashmir here is not to suggest that it is representative of Islamist terrorism in India as a whole. Rather, the use of Kashmir is two-fold. First, as the place which accounts for approximately 72% of attack attempts of Islamist terrorism in India (START 2011), it is worth understanding on its own merit. Second, Kashmir is increasingly becoming intertwined with terrorism in other parts of India, by virtue of the groups currently controlling the conflict and their broader ambitions (Swami 2003). Thus, being able to study Kashmir through the best approach gets us a long way toward understanding much of Islamist terrorism in India.

Overview of Conflict

Kashmir has been a source of tension between India and Pakistan at least since partition (Varshney 1991), as well as the reason for two of their three wars (Bhatt 2007). India and Pakistan's battle over Kashmir is linked to their fundamentally divergent ideas of nationhood (Bhatt 2007). Muhammad Ali Jinnah, leader of the Muslim League and founder of Pakistan, argued that India and Pakistan should be two nations on the basis of religion (Bhatt 2007). His two-nation theory suggests that Kashmir, as a Muslim-majority area, is rightfully part of Pakistan. By contrast, India's ideal nation is a secular democracy, and for India, having Kashmir would affirm its own model of statehood (Bhatt 2007).

The insurgency, which began in 1989 against this backdrop of a struggle between two nations, was the result of both long-term precipitous factors as well as more proximate causes (Ganguly 1997). The long-term factors were increasing political mobilization and institutional failure which no longer made a political solution viable (Ganguly 1997). When Sheikh

Mohammed Abdullah's Jammu and Kashmir National Conference took over, it had popular support but was not particularly democratic. The Conference's ability to govern was based on the personality of Abdullah, who was also the party's primary decision-maker (Ganguly 1997). The Indian government, for its part, was not concerned about the lack of democracy in Kashmir as long as its leaders didn't pursue secession (Ganguly 1997). There were only four elections in Kashmir in 54 years, three of which were tampered with in some way (Bhatt 2007). Despite the lack of democracy, however, economic development took place in Kashmir, consequently increasing political demands among citizens (Ganguly 1997).

While the failure of democratic institutions at the same time as political mobilization was already making Kashmir volatile (Ganguly 1997), the biggest proximate cause of the insurgency was the failure of the 1987 elections (Varshney 1991). The Congress-National Alliance won a significant majority of the seats even though it did not even get half of the popular vote (Ganguly 1997). The election demonstrated to Kashmiris that state was no longer a feasible means of expressing their frustration. By 1989, the situation had turned violent (Behera 2006).

Led mostly by the Jammu and Kashmir Liberation Front (JKLF), the insurgency at this point sought an independent and unified Kashmir (Behera 2006). Before proceeding, it is important to slightly expand our understanding of Islamism. Initially, a component of the definition of Islamism was that it sought to establish an Islamic state. Of course, relative to other Islamist organizations, JKLF stands apart from this goal as a more secular group which wanted an independent Kashmir (Behera 2006). However, in the case of Kashmir, this delineation of an organization as 'secular' proves far more difficult, as there are significant ideological continuities between different groups (Swami 2003). Even the JKLF was involved in the expulsion of the Pandit minority (Swami 2003) and in this way is more than just a separatist organization. For the remainder of the paper, therefore, we will classify the JKLF rather loosely as an Islamist terrorist organization.

The general populous in Kashmir valley supported the JKLF as an extension of Kashmiri identity, and being able to fight was seen as a form of honor (Behera 2006). These young militants also had the support of Pakistan with regard to training and financial assistance (Varshney 1991). Even years later, Pakistan has retained its hand in the conflict as approximately three quarters of the groups fighting in Kashmir are funded by the ISI and other Pakistani organizations (Jamwal 2003). However, the JKLF stopped being the dominant group in the 1990s because it was marginalized by the ISI in favor of other, more radical terrorist organizations:

Where Pakistan was concerned, the "Kashmiri card" had served its purpose and, if allowed to reach its logical conclusion, might back-fire, especially since the JKLF's goal was "independence and re-unification of the divided Kashmir and not accession to Pakistan." (Behera 2006: 151)

One of the most prominent groups to rise after the decline of JKLF was Hizb-ul-Mujahideen (HuM) (Behera 2006). HuM and several other right-wing Islamist groups changed the discourse of the Kashmir struggle from one of secession to one of accession with Pakistan. Their strategy followed the "Afghan model" (2006: 154)—they intended to make holding on to Kashmir expensive for India, and did so by calling for Jihad. For example, a popular HuM slogan translates as 'It is neither a guerrilla war nor a national war: it is a holy war' (2006: 154).

Not only did HuM and the groups that followed it change the rhetoric behind the struggle, but in so doing, they also lost the local support that was such a big part of the initial stages of the movement (Behera 2006). Consequently, these more extremist groups struggled to radicalize significant numbers of Kashmiris, causing Pakistan to increase the number of foreign terrorists (Behera 2006). Whereas until about 1996, the terrorists taking part in the insurgency were mostly ethnically Kashmir (Swami 2003), as of 2002, an estimated fifth of the militants were foreign, about 90 percent of whom were Pakistani (Trehan 2002).

Moreover, of the many active groups in Kashmir, only three are operating in Kashmir exclusively1—the vast majority are also operating elsewhere (Haleem 2004). Some of the largest terrorist organizations in the region are based out of Pakistan and simultaneously pursue objectives that are global in scope (Roy-Chaudhary 2003):

These groups are the JKLF, Harkat-ul-Ansar, and Al-Faran

In (the militants) world-view, the armed struggle in Kashmir is but one stage of a wider, indeed global, Jihad. Kashmir is not a territorial dispute between India and Pakistan, not even a clash between cultures, but nothing less than a war between two different and mutually opposed ideologies: Islam and kufr (disbelief). (Behera 2006: 157).

In addition to the more global goals of the organizations now dominating the violence in Kashmir, the conflict also has an international dimension because of the symbolic significance of Kashmir to groups like AQ (Rapoport 2006).

NAXALISM: NATIONAL SECURITY IMPLICATIONS

The first recorded incident of left wing insurrection in free India was in Telengana.[1946-1951]. The movement was launched by peasants in their struggle on economic issues against forced labor, illegal exaction and unauthorised evictions. The movement was directed by the Communists and soon developed into an uprising against the feudal rule of the Nizam. More than 4000 lives were lost before the communists finally withdrew the struggle.

Naxalbari 1967

A revolt took place in three police stations in the Naxalbari area in 1967. About 65 per cent of the population of those areas are Scheduled Castes and tribals. When the land reform act was passed in 1955, *jotedars* started malafide transfer of land. Tribals armed with bows and arrows forcibly occupied the land, lifted stocks of hoarded rice and killed an inspector of police.

Thereafter there were a number of similar incidents. The leadership of the movement was by communist cadres The CPI[M] government of West Bengal ordered a major deployment of police forces and after several operations the movement was squashed.

This culminated in the formation of the Communist Party of India, Marxist-Leninist [CPI-ML]. About 30 people were killed in this uprising. But the term Naxalite came to stay. Naxallites are followers of Che Guevara. They believe that once the masses are convinced that the social wrongs cannot be rectified by pacific action, it is possible to ignite the spark of revolution. Their aim it to create condition where the authorities are forced to break the peace. The resultant violence then gathers its own momentum. Naxalism had a far reaching impact on the entire agrarian scene in India.

Tribals of the Srikakulam district of the eastern ghats are mainly involved in the organistion and collection of minor forest products. The British had decreed that no land could be transferred from the tribal to a plainsman without a permit of the district collector. After independence, traders took full advantage of advantage of inexperienced Indian administrators and the poverty of the tribals. They gave them their daily requirements of tobacco, kerosene, salt and cloth on credit and also lent money for the purchase of seeds. Ignoring the British decrees, they forced those who owed them money to part with their land which was then sold to plainsmen who squeezed the tribals, paid them low wages and made them give up two-thirds of the produce. In 1967 a clash occurred between a group of tribals going to a meeting of the Marxist Party and a group of landlords armed with guns. Two tribals were killed. The movement became violent. There were a series of raids on houses of landlords and moneylenders, cash was looted and houses burnt down. Charu Mazumdar, the CPI-ML leader who had inspired the Naxalbari operations, visited the area and gave a fillip to the movement. From December 1968 to January 1969, 29 policemen were killed in action. During 1969 the Naxalities committed 23 murders and 40 dacoities before the situation was brought under control. The West Bengal districts of Midnapur and Birbhum bordering Bihar and Orissa have a sizeable tribal population. The majority are landless labourers. A few are cultivators. From 1967 to 1971 the area saw well planned and organised Naxalite movements fostered by CPI-LM workers and a host of students from Calcutta University who identified themselves wholeheartedly with the tribals. Groups armed with spears, bows and arrows attacked houses of landlords, killed some of them, looted cash and burnt all land deeds.

The Government deployed CRPF and state police and brought the area under control. Almost 150 CPI-LM supporters were arrested and the movement died down. From 1968 to 1970 tribal violence erupted in Muzaffarpur district of Bihar. This followed the usual pattern of blatant oppression of landlords and peasant reactions. These uprisings caused ripples and spread to other districts of Bihar and into Uttar Pradesh [UP]. These movements were coordinated by CPI-ML leaders who believed that there would be a mass uprising and that they could build a Peoples Liberation Army from peasants who had revolted against the atrocities of landlords and moneylenders.

A British girl, Mary Tyler, who was living in an *adivisasi* village, was rounded up during a police search operation. She later wrote about her experience. "The Naxalite crime was the crime of all those who cannot remain unmoved and inactive in an India where a child crawls in the dust with a begging bowl, where a poor girl can be sold as a rich man's plaything, where an old woman must half starve herself in order to buy social acceptance from the powers that be in her village; where countless people die of sheer neglect, where many are hungry while food is hoarded for profit, where usurers and tricksters extort the fruits of labour from those who do the work, where the honest suffer, while the villainous prosper, where justice is the exception and injustice the rule and where the total physical and mental energy of millions of people is spent on the struggle for mere survival." It is no wonder that the movement attracted idealistic students from major universities across India. They left their studies and went to live in forest villages and share the tribulations of the tribals. However the movement fizzled out when the Central Reserve Police Force [CRPF] and state police carried out well-planned raids and search operations.

Peoples War Group

In the 80s, the CPI-ML formed the Peoples War Group [PWG], which over the years grew into the most formidable Naxalite formation in the country. The first actions undertaken by the PWG was in Telenga, Andhra Pradesh [AP], where long suffering tribals were still being economically and socially exploited by landlords, traders, money lenders and indifferent government bureaucrats.

The crux of the unrest was that in AP, as in many other states, the land ceiling act was not being imposed. The PWG took the law into their hands and redistributed nearly half a million acres across AP. In the process, the PWG fought a running battle with the Telugu Desam government. When the Congress Party came into power in 1989, the government took a soft line with the Naxalites and released a number who were in detention. The government however did nothing to control the exploitation of tribals.

The PWG began running peoples' courts and giving the general impression of a parallel government. The Government was forced to adopt a hard line. However, by now the PWG had acquired AK 47 rifles and began stepping up their violence. They began attacking railway and electrical installations, police patrols and police stations.

Their influence spread to adjoining tribal areas in Maharashtra, Madhya Pradesh [MP], Bihar, Orrisa, Tamil Nadu [TN] and Karnataka. In 1992, the PWG was banned and central paramilitary forces and state police undertook coordinated operations against it. The results were good. About 3500 Naxalities were arrested and 8500 surrendered. The PWG lay low but in 1993 commenced operating in tribal districts of MP and Maharashtra. By now the Group had attained expertise in the making and detonation of improvised explosive devices [IED]. In 2001 the PWG announced that it would give sophisticated arms to its guerrillas and extend the war to as many other states as possible.

It is evident that the Naxalites operate in the tribal belt and are welcomed by tribals because of the administration's indifference to the persistent criminal activities of landlords, money lenders, forest officials and traders. There has been a response to this simple analysis in two states.

The CPI[M] in West Bengal carried out Operation Barga under which share croppers were registered and given permanent and inheritable rights on cultivation of their plots covering a total area of 11 lakhs acres.

Besides this, 1.37 lakh acres of ceiling surplus and *benami* lands were acquired by the state government and distributed among 25 lakh landless and marginal cultivators. This saw the emergence of a new class loosely termed rural rich, which weakened the social and political power enjoyed by landlords in the countryside, and resulted in the disappearance of moneylenders and Naxalites.

In Kerala the upper classes were generally landlords. They had tenant farmers on their land who deposited half the crop to their landlords. The landlords and their progeny were educated and took up white collar jobs in the cities. When the CPI[M] government was elected in the late 50s, it legislated tenancy laws that transferred ownership of tenant holdings to those having a tenancy for 12 years. At one stroke hundreds of landlords lost their holdings and tenant farmers got ownership rights of land they had tilled for long years. This is one of the reasons why the Naxalite movement did not grow roots in Kerala. It had no cause.

When the Chief Ministers of Chhattisgarh, Maharashtra, AP, Orrissa and Bihar ask how the Naxalite problem could be solved, they have to be told to impose the land ceiling. Many would admit in private that this is impossible as the upper caste landlords would never allow the land ceiling act to be enforced. Here then is the crux of the problem

Solving the Naxalite Problem

The main reason for the upsurge of Naxalism is exploitation of tribal and poor scheduled castes. Naxalites support the poor against exploitation by corrupt government official in collusion with landlords, contractors and moneylenders. In Naxalite infected areas the first step is to enforce land ceiling laws. This has to done despite the pressures of landlords, money lenders and influential castes. The CRPF and state police which are now being used in operations against the Naxalites should be used to enforce the land ceiling, evict landlords for excessive holdings, and ensure that surplus lands are cultivated by the lower castes and tribals. They should ensure that the crops grown by the new land holders are secure. In forest tracts, laws should be legislated that only forest dwelling tribals and scheduled casts should have access to forest lands. Others should be prevented from entering the forests. Cooperatives should be organised of tribals who can be trained to trade in forest produce. Para military forces should be used to enforce these new laws and keep the moneylenders out. They should guard the branches of the micro-credit banks that sanction loans to cooperatives. When this is done, the tribals and scheduled castes will know that the government is now with them and they will turn away form the CPI-M:L cadres and will befriend the police. But it is romantic to believe that this will result in a cessation of hostilities and that the Naxalite movement will wither away.

The PWG has become a well-armed force and will fight to try and retain power by targeting the para military forces and police. States will find it difficult to deal with this problem. Some states have attempted to mobilize the tribals and arm them against Naxalites. [The Salwa Judum organinsed in Chhattisgarh is an example of this.] This has been criticized as a dangerous practice, which leads to high handedness. Others condemn this move as a clever ploy by upper caste politicians and bureaucrats to avoid the main issue, which is land ceilings. Whatever that be, it should be evident that if the CRPF find it difficult to deal with the PWG and are often overwhelmed by them, it would be unreasonable to expect that untrained armed tribal will fare better.

Some suggest that the army should be given this task. The army could no doubt deal with the PWG but this a dangerous suggestion and not acceptable in a democracy. It is not the army's role to deal with such internal problems. The Soli Sorabjee Committee on police reforms, which is drafting a model Police Act, has told the Supreme Court that it strongly recommends the creation of a federal agency to combat terrorism, arms and drug trafficking, money laundering and even organised crime. As per the Constitution, "police" and "public order" are subjects in the State list of the Seventh Schedule. The Sorabjee Panel has made a strong case for handing over such operations against such crimes to this newly created force. "Such perilous activities cannot be left to be routinely dealt with as ordinary crime or law and order problems by state police who do not have knowledge of the inter-state and international dimension of the crimes in question. There is need for a specialized national level agency, other than the Central Bureau of Investigation [CBI], to be constituted by a statute of Parliament which can tackle these federal crimes. The proposed agency should not be confused with existing CBI, which is essentially an investigative agency. The prevention and control of national-security crime does not fall within the CBI's charter of duties."

Thus, the fight against Naxalism has to take place on two fronts: against Naxa;lites and against the causes of Naxalism. The latter will prove to be the more difficult task. The Prime Minister is right when he said that the greatest security threat facing India is the Naxalite movement. If the Government is serious about dealing with this threat, then the slogan for the coming decade should be ":get tough with the Naxalites but get tougher with the causes of Naxalism."

NORTH-EAST

The Naga leadership under Z.A. Phizo had challenged their integration into the Indian Union even before India became independent in 1947. The Naga insurgency started way back in the early 1950s. Since then the insurgencies in this region have multiplied and spread to many new areas. In this extremely diverse and strategically sensitive region, there are different reasons for the ethnic upsurges and insurgencies in different states. Some seek secession from the Indian Union, some others seek separate states and yet others greater autonomy within the existing state. The number of such insurgent groups could reach three-digit figures. In Manipur alone, more than twenty-five groups are operating. Thousands have died in the insurgency-related violence. Insurgencies have seriously affected the economic life of the region. The whole developmental process is seriously hampered because of this unending violence. One can imagine the plight of the people who are already living on the margin. What to talk of getting a share of the fruits of development, they are deprived even of the most basic services. Unfortunately, unlike Jammu & Kashmir, these violent movements do not stir much response in national consciousness. Even serious incidents of violence hardly find any mention in the so-called mainstream media. The geo-strategic importance of the North-East is not sufficiently appreciated even in the security establishment. All the states in the North-East share an international border with other countries and the seven North-Eastern states are linked to the rest of the country only by a narrow strip of land. The lack of physical, cultural and emotional links has encouraged a feeling of alienation, which is being exploited by the nottoo- friendly neighbours to pursue their own agenda. They are giving support and sanctuaries to many of these groups to use them as leverage against a much bigger and more powerful neighbour.

The roots of these many insurgencies in the North-East lie deep in its history and its geography. But, it would be wrong to treat it as one homogeneous region with common problems, or social systems and customs. Even physiographically, the region can be divided into three broad areas — hills, plateaus, and plains. The many ethnic groups, speaking many different languages and dialects, who inhabit this remote part of the country consider themselves as separate people with little in common with the people in the rest of the country. The lack of physical, cultural and emotional links has encouraged this feeling of separation.

The partition of the country seriously dislocated the old system of communications with serious demographic consequences. At the heart of the problem, however, is the new political consciousness and an urge for asserting their identity, especially among the fiercely independent tribal communities. The partition left the entire region land-locked, and even the old road, railway and river-waterway links with the rest of the country were severed, because they all passed through East Pakistan (now Bangladesh). The new rail link via North Bengal is circuitous and too long and expensive for easy access to the region. The air link is not only expensive, but also unreliable due to climatic conditions. The people have to bear enormous additional transport cost for all their supplies. Another intractable problem is created by the influx of migrants from East Pakistan and now continuing from Bangladesh. In the beginning it was confined to the Hindus leaving East Pakistan due to insecure conditions, but later, because of intense population pressure even Muslims started migrating. The fear that immigrant population will one day dominate them is keeping many of the insurgent and secessionist movements alive.

The terrain in this region is eminently suitable for insurgency. The hilly terrain and dense forests provide convenient hiding places to mount ambushes on the moving convoys of the security forces. Large parts of the interior areas have little or no police presence. The insurgent groups virtually control the administration in these areas. After attacking the security force they can easily disappear into the local population. Because of deprivation and alienation, a large section of the people tend to be sympathetic to the members of these groups. It is the alienation of the people that has sustained insurgency all these years, though logistic support and sanctuaries provided by the neighbouring states play a vital role in sustaining them. The dispersion of ethnic groups across the international boundaries has profoundly influenced the nature of political conflicts. However, it needs to be emphasised that internal-external linkages originate with the failure of the domestic political and administrative system in coping with the internal conflicts.

Secessionist leaders often adopt alternative strategies to achieve their goal. They keep on changing their tactics and demands according to the ground situation. The intensity of the conflict depends very much on how strong the public support is. Ethnicity can become an important dimension of internal conflict when it becomes intertwined with other social, political and economic issues.

As conflicting groups go from one crisis to the next, they learn by experience to raise their demands to increase their bargaining power. Political changes that offer new opportunities for personal gain and extending their influence can spark violent conflicts.

Even though most of them are conscious of the fact that secession is not a viable option, they keep on raising this demand to bring together the various contending conflicts on one platform. Making common cause against the Indian state is how many of these groups with conflicting ideologies cooperate with each other in their fight against the Indian state. The United Liberation Front of Assam (ULFA) was born out of the demand to throw out the migrants from Bangladesh, and yet its top leaders are today finding sanctuary in that country.

The South Asian countries have more in common with India than with other countries in the region. They do not even have a common boundary with each other. But this reality has not made them friendlier towards India. History and geography have encouraged negative sentiments rather than positive sentiments about India in these countries. The big powers too have not hesitated to fish in troubled waters. Till the 1970s, China was directly supporting the insurgencies in the North-East. Strategically, politically and economically the North-East is the most sensitive part of the country and should receive the serious attention it deserves.

The ongoing dialogue between the government and the NSCN (IM) is a positive development, but it is going to take a long and torturous route. The NSCN (IM)'s claim on the Naga-inhabited areas in the neighbouring states has created serious complications. The riots in Manipur in 2001 following the extension of the ceasefire to the areas beyond the boundaries of Nagaland are a pointer to the difficult road ahead. The situation in Assam has shown some signs of improvement, but large-scale extortion by the ULFA and other groups is posing serious problems. The NLFT and the ATTF continue to be active in Tripura. They have sanctuaries in Bangladesh. Mizoram is quiet, but there are problems between the Mizos and the Chakmas, and the Mizos and the Reangs. Thousands of Reang refugees from Mizoram are staying in camps in Tripura. In spite of many rounds of negotiations between the Mizoram government and the representatives of the Reangs, so far no solution appears to be in sight. The unending internecine feud between the NSCN (IM) and the NSCN (K) has spilled over from Nagaland to the neighbouring states and even to Myanmar. A number of Meitie and Kuki groups have sanctuaries in the Chin Hills in Myanmar. The ULFA and the Bodo groups have sanctuaries in the forests of Bhutan. There are unconfirmed reports of some sort of tie-up between the ULFA and the LTTE. A number of groups have also come up in Meghalaya and Arunachal Pradesh. Many experts have called the Naga insurgencies as the mother of all insurgencies in the North-East. The level of violence, however, in this explosive region continues to be high in spite of the fact that the ceasefire agreement with the NSCN (IM) has been in place since 1997. This only goes to show how difficult the road to peace is going to be in this trouble-torn region.

It is truism to say that it is not only a law and order problem. It has many other dimensions. No strategy will succeed unless it strikes a right balance between political, economic and security measures. There is need for closer co-ordination among the policymakers. Ideally, there is need for a consensus among the major political parties. The pursuit of narrow political agenda can be exploited by the subversive groups. Many political leaders in this region indulge in double-speak. They mouth nationalist slogans in Delhi but have no hesitation in making strong anti-national statements and collaborating with the insurgent groups in the state. Nor do they have any reservation in changing parties. They frequently hop from one political party to another. In Manipur some politicians have changed sides as many as six times in a year. A chief minister changed his party three times in one month, and his coalition partners three times in 48 hours. A party label has very little meaning. Money and muscle power with active support of the insurgent groups play a key role in the elections.

Most of these states are not financially viable. They hardly collect any revenue and depend almost entirely on the Union government for financial support. This has caused lack of responsibility in incurring public expenditure. For example, Manipur has created a huge bureaucratic structure with a workforce of almost 100,000 on its pay roll. Over 80% of its total revenue (both Plan and non-Plan) is spent on payment of salaries and pensions. Extortion by the insurgent groups, the leakage's of huge funds through corrupt practices leave very little for development. And they conveniently put the blame on the Centre for not giving them adequate funds. Through years of neglect this potentially rich region is today the most backward, almost primitive, part of our country. In these appalling conditions an alienated population becomes an easy target for the secessionist propaganda.

AN ANALYSIS OF INDIA'S 'NATIONAL ACTION PLAN ON CLIMATE CHANGE'

To deal with challenges of climate change, India's National Action Plan on Climate Change (NAPCC) was announced by the Government of India in 2008. The NAPCC includes eight national missions with separate mandate for each mission. Each national mission is formulated by its respective ministry which will also implement it for the remaining part of the current 11th Five Year Plan (2007-2012) and the 12th Five Year Plan (2012-2017). In the last three years, comprehensive documents have been prepared by the respective ministries of the Government of India. All of these missions have some relevance to gender because they all aim for adaptation and mitigation and have to work under overarching concerns for inclusive and sustainable development. The NAPCC recognizes the importance of gender in climate change and development discourse. It states "*with climate change there would be increasing scarcity of water, reductions in yields of biomass, and increased risks to human health with children, women and the elderly in a household becoming the most vulnerable. With the possibility of decline in the availability of food grains, the threat of malnutrition may also increase. All these would add to deprivations that women already encounter and so in each of the Adaptation programmes special attention should be paid to the aspects of gender*". But this understanding has not been translated into the NAPCC's assessment of the effects of climate change or its outlines of mechanisms that could support people to adapt. Partly, this has to do with the lack of gender/sex-disaggregated data on climate risks, and the relatively poor documentation of adaptation programmes, or the lessons they can provide, in terms of building resilient communities. Since all the eight national missions would be integrated with various flagship programmes for development, capacity building, and empowerment of central and state governments, inclusion of gender in the national missions will benefit women as well as lead to successful and efficient implementation of the missions.

National Solar Mission (NSM) notes that as a tropical country, India has immense potential for solar energy. Therefore, the mission aims to tap the potential of solar power and envisions routes for conversion of solar radiation into heat and electricity, namely solar thermal energy and solar photovoltaic system. Women can not only be beneficiaries but can also be involved in production, decision making and management of the energy cycle. Many gender issues can be associated with the mission by providing women access to energy and electricity, lighting for their households, and livelihoods. Street lighting can help to provide them a sense of security, and solar appliances " solar water heater, solar cookers, solar pumps and solar dryers " could reduce their workload. Access to adequate energy will ease the process of supplying water and help in irrigation, enhance food security through better crop productivity and income from agro-food processing and pollution-free fuel, for prevention of heart and lung diseases. It also helps to generate extra income from agri-waste processing and storage, diversification of crop production, or higher yields via modern farming tools/ techniques, ability to process materials locally, storage, diversification of off-farm activities like dairy products, and other small scale businesses.

National Mission for Enhanced Energy Efficiency (NMEEE) has a mandate to adopt a market-based mechanism to enhance cost effectiveness of improvements in energy efficiency in energy-intensive large industries and facilities, accelerating the shift to energy-efficient appliances to make them more affordable, providing energy-efficient financing platform and developing fiscal instruments to promote energy efficiency. The NMEEE should also consider gender measures for attaining its goals of energy efficiency. The household and residential sectors consume significant percentage of fossil fuel energy as well as electricity. Women empowered with knowledge and training of energy utilization can save energy in this sector. Capacity of women should be enhanced to optimize energy efficiency and the usage of domestic appliances.

The National Mission on Sustainable Habitat (NMSH) intends to make habitat sustainable through improvements in basic infrastructure and by providing basic services such as transportation, modern energy services, waste management, etc. Such initiatives would definitely empower women and contribute to their development. The mission can emphasize on gender issues by making special provisions for women for sustainable energy access; robust public health and transportation system, and increase women's participation in urban planning at the local level. In addition, there should be measures for building material for ensuring safety.

Water is linked to the crises of climate change, energy and food supplies and prices, and troubled financial markets. The

National Water Mission focuses on conservation, preservation, efficiency, integrated water resources management and equitable distribution.

India's per capita availability of water, on the basis of the 2011 population census, has fallen below the global threshold. The access to potable water is the primary concern of every household and mainly managed by women. In rural areas they travel far from their habitat to fetch water. Gender issues are related to this mission in multiple ways: to provide women easy access to potable water in their locality, a role in water management, in planning on the principle of integrated water resources development and management, in water conservation and water resource project management. Women can be the primary agent for promoting usage of water in a sustainable manner.

Himalayan ecosystem is fragile and diverse and includes over 51 million people who practice hill agriculture, and remains vulnerable to climate change. Sustainability of the Himalayan ecosystem is crucial for the livelihood of about 1.3 billion people in Asia.

Particularly, Himalayan ecosystem is critical for the Indian landmass for environmental sustainability and economic development. The National Mission for Sustaining the Himalayan Ecosystem focuses on national and institutional capacities, strengthening of existing institutions, standardization of observational systems, decoupling of changes from natural and anthropogenic causes, prediction/projection of future trends and assessment of possible impacts, governance for sustaining Himalayan ecosystem and building a state of the art institution in glaciology.

The Mission is quite comprehensive and covers almost every aspect of Himalayan ecosystem, and therefore, there is a need to include a concrete gender-oriented policy framework for women's empowerment and a greater role of women in the adaptation strategies. Specific programmes should be formulated for knowledge and capacity building of women. Women should be allowed greater participation in the decision making process of institutions, and in planning and implementation of developmental programmes. Since the National Mission talks about community participation in adaptation, mitigation and coping mechanisms inclusive of farming and traditional health care systems, it should be ensured that women get their due representation. Women can be more useful in increasing the growth of flora and fauna.

National Mission for a Green India aims to increase forest/ tree cover on 5 mha of forest/non-forest lands and improve quality of forest cover on another 5 mha (a total of 10 mha), and improve ecosystem services including biodiversity, hydrological services, carbon sequestration as a result of treatment of 10 mha and increase forest-based livelihood income of about 3 million households living in and around the forests and also enhance annual CO_2 sequestration by 50 to 60 million tonnes in the year 2020. The key innovations of the mission include focusing on the quality of forests, ecosystem services biodiversity, water and improved biomass, carbon sequestration, and addressing ecosystems like grasslands, wetlands, urban and peri-urban, and implementation aspects as well.

Women's role is crucial in forest management, food security, livelihood through non-timber forest products, and in preserving the entire ecosystem and biodiversity. Particularly in the context of energy, women manage the entire energy chain from collecting, transporting and managing cooking fuel in the rural and remote areas. Integrated Energy Policy (IEP, 2006) states to provide fuel within one kilometer of their habitat. Their role in social forestry and communities is also crucial. Unless women are factored in explicitly at all levels, the intended outcome may not materialize.

National Mission for Sustainable Agriculture (NMSA) has devised strategies to make Indian agriculture more resilient to climate change, and therefore, intends to identify and develop new varieties of crops, especially climate resistant ones, and alternative cropping patterns capable of withstanding extremes of weather, long dry spells, flooding, and variable moisture availability.

The Mission, therefore, seeks to transform Indian agriculture into a climate resilient production system through suitable adaptation and mitigation measures in the domain of crops and animal husbandry. The implementation of NMSA up to the end of the twelfth Five Year Plan would require additional budgetary support of INR 1080 billion. The Mission should have provisions for enhancing food and nutrition security for women and for providing them rights in land tenure, food processing and storage and post-harvest management. Information and knowledge dissemination are also crucial for reducing vulnerability of women in the agriculture sector.

National Mission on Strategic Knowledge for Climate Change aims to identi-fy the challenges of, and the responses to climate change. A strong and strategic knowledge system is essential for identifying, formulating, planning and implementing policy-driven actions while maintaining the necessary economic growth rate. The Mission should boost up applied research into various aspects of climate change as well as collect gender-specific data for formulating specific measures for the policies and programmes for women, particularly vulnerability assessments, health problems, energy and socio-economic implications.

To sum up, it has been shown that there is gender differentiation regarding the impact of climate change due to different roles that gender plays and its different capabilities and situations. To ensure well-being of women and promote their development, National Missions on climate change should address the concerns of women and incorporate gender-sensitive measures to make adaptation strategy more robust.

4

India's National Security and Defence Response

India has been subjected to wars in every decade of its Post – Independence existence and increased armed insurgencies, proxy wars and terrorism of the Islamic fundamentalist variety. India has been so subjected to aggression because in the last fifty years, it exhibited the propensity to be pacifist or defensive in nature. It shied away from the use of power despite its size and resources. The resultant effect was that India's adversaries perceived India as a "Soft State" incapable of strong military responses even when its national security interests were threatened and trampled upon both externally and internally.

INDIA'S SECURITY CHOICES

As we consider India's rise to power, there are two main scenarios that come to mind. According to the first and most commonly held, India's current trajectory will continue in a 'straight line'. Exponents of this view hold that India's underlying growth rate of 7-9 per cent and growing military capability mean that by 2030 it will join China and Japan as one of Asia's three great powers.

By 2030, India will have the world's largest population. It will have the world's third largest economy in purchasing power parity terms (PPP) after China and the US. It is likely to remain democratic and will have enormous 'soft' power potential, resulting from its large English speaking population, vociferous free press, innovative IT industries, vibrant civil society and widely influential Bollywood film industry. Its navy will be able to range at will over the Indian Ocean and beyond. It will have a fleet of nuclear submarines and an independent nuclear deterrent capable of deterring even China. It will be a major power in space, with the capacity to 'neutralise' enemy satellites.

According to the second and more pessimistic analysis, this new superpower will be expected to rise out of one of the most-troubled sub-regions of the globe – South Asia. South Asia will continue to have more people living in poverty than any other region in the world for the foreseeable future. It will be awash with economic and political refugees. Its great rivers and ground water will be under severe stress. Its regional association, the South Asian Association for Regional Cooperation (SAARC), will still be struggling to provide a viable forum, according to which all in the region can 'rise on the same tide' through enhanced trade, security, travel and cultural exchange. Pakistan, India's neighbour of 166 million and a long-term adversary, will have added another 85 million mouths to feed and jobs to find. It will be subjected to extreme environmental stress. Hundreds of thousands of its young men will have been educated in madrassas that provide inadequate modern education and extremely narrow interpretations of Islam. Bangladesh – another neighbour which has already despatched an estimated 10 million illegal immigrants to India – may well be struggling to accommodate the estimated 10-15 millions of its population currently living on and farming low lying areas, subject to ever-increasing inundation resulting from climate change.

Trapped within this region (or so this pessimistic scenario goes), India will confront its own demons. It will be ever more dependent on costly imported energy. Its mega cities will be struggling to provide sufficient fresh water, accommodation and sanitation. Riots over distribution of drinking water – as witnessed in 2009 in Mumbai – will be frequent events. Antiquated infrastructure and restrictive labour laws will constrain labour-intensive manufacturing that could provide jobs for the massive rural population seeking a better life. Corruption will continue to be a major burden on governance, as democratisation spreads to new classes who are hungry for its benefits but impatient with its norms. Maoists will continue to recruit those in the poorest states suffering from corruption and poor governance. Maoist-generated unrest will jeopardise India's extractive industries, which happen to lie within the regions most seriously affected. Criminality will continue to flourish under a creaking legal system that provides near impunity to the wealthy and powerful and no rapid legal punishment for the guilty. Criminals, corruption and terrorism together will continue to erode the security of citizens and tarnish India's investment reputation.

In many states, the massive police service, which today totals 1.5 million for India as a whole (not including paramilitary forces and un-filled police positions), will remain an ineffective, repressive, colonial-era relic, incapable of investigating crime, providing security to communities, supporting human rights or lifting intelligence from the grassroots to the strategic level. India's 150 million Muslims – 75 per cent of whom belong to underprivileged groups and occupations – will still not have the benefits of the Constitution provided for Dalits and tribals. As the community sinks further in comparative terms, its members will provide more people willing to engage in violent, home-grown Jihad, assisted from across the border in Pakistan.

According to this sombre view of the future, these difficulties in India's polity will continue to resonate across borders in South Asia, just as the domestic difficulties of India's large neighbours will resonate in India. They will be transmitted by a brand of democratic politics, which seeks to blame the neighbour for local ills, by refugees and economic migrants, by sharpening religious misunderstanding as the region's traditional syncretic values erode in a world of globalisation and by ever-deepening cross-border environmental problems, particularly relating to the sharing of the diminishing river waters upon which hundreds of millions depend. Thus, South Asia will continue to be caught in a vicious circle of local and national troubles that wash back and forward across borders like so much political 'flotsam and jetsam'.

These two scenarios are at the outer extremes of what is likely to occur. Reality will likely be somewhat closer to the middle. But it will nevertheless veer towards one end or the other of the spectrum. Governments of the region will make choices that will have a role in shaping reality. This is particularly true of Indian governments – India being the giant of the region and having greater capability of influencing outcomes.

This chapter is especially concerned with Indian choices around the problem of security. The concept of security can range from the traditional, realist idea of security as constituting freedom from threats to the existence of the nation state, to the concept of 'comprehensive' or 'human' security. The latter involves a focus on the security of individuals within the state and surrounding countries, rather than on the existential security of an individual state. It includes all aspects of the welfare of individuals, including their human rights, gender rights, environmental rights, health, nutrition, education, employment, security from violence (whether from state or non-state actors), and so on.

In this chapter, we will be concerned with security from existential threats to the nation (as an important basis for the security of individuals within the nation) along with threats of physical violence and property threats to governments and individuals. Such threats can come from other nations, state actors such as security personnel and police, corrupt politicians and officials, terrorists, criminals and insurgents. We will not be considering directly some of the broader aspects of human security, encompassed by issues such as lack of water or food or work, environmental problems, or pandemic diseases – serious though they may be. But we do consider such factors indirectly because of their role in triggering violence, terrorism, insurgency and social dislocation. This relationship between deprivation and security is present throughout India, but is most noticeable as it applies to the tribal, Maoist-affected belt that covers east-central India. Here, environmental degradation, poor governance, poverty, human rights abuses and corruption have each played major roles in triggering the discontent that lies at the heart of the Maoist revolt.

Our primary concern is to demonstrate that there is a 'seamless web' between security of communities at the grassroots and security of nations and sub-regions (in this case India and South Asia). Such a line of analysis requires linking mechanisms between lower and higher order security issues. It needs to be explained, for example, why an attack on a police contingent in Chhattisgarh can be relevant to India's higher order security and even to its rise as a power. It is this linking process, we argue, which means that it is as important for governments successfully to address lower order security issues as it is to tackle higher order issues.

This approach to security is by no means unique or new: many recent Indian commentaries have covered similar ground. This chapter does, however, bring the added perspective of an Australian security analyst. Australia, as a Westminster-style democracy with a federal structure similar to India's, has experienced similar difficulties with establishing its internal security architecture. Australia's experience with internal security and terrorism is, however, obviously of a much less intensive nature than India's. And as a small, resource-rich nation, it also has many more available resources with which to deal with the problem.

POST-26/11 SECURITY REFORMS

In common with many countries, India's internal security architecture has evolved in an ad hoc way. The National Security Guard (NSG) was founded in 1986 in the aftermath of the 1984 Operation Blue Star. The Multi-Agency Centre (MAC), an intelligence 'fusion centre' within the Intelligence Bureau (IB), was first mooted in the aftermath of the intelligence failure associated with Kargil in 1999 and re-furbished in the aftermath of the 26/11 attacks. Due to this ad hoc process and because of India's federal structure, the current security architecture is characterised, in the words of Home Minister Chidambaram, by the fact that "there is no single authority to which these organisations report and there is no single or unified command which can issue directions to these agencies and bodies." It is also plagued by 'turfdom', fragmentation and careerism.

According to its status as a Westminster-style democracy, the apex of India's security architecture is the Prime Minister and the Cabinet and various offices attached to them. The Cabinet Committee on Security (CCS) consists of ex-officio ministers (the Prime Minister, Minister of Home Affairs, Minister of Defence, Minister of External Affairs and Minister of Finance). It is supported by a National Security Council (NSC), with representatives from the above ministries and the Deputy Chairman of the Planning Commission and National Security Adviser (NSA-who answers to the Prime Minister). The NSC, in turn, is serviced by a secretariat of officials. The NSA is responsible for the Joint Intelligence Committee (which brings together the heads of various intelligence agencies), the Aviation Research Centre (ARC) and the National Technical Research Office (NTRO). The Cabinet Secretariat is responsible for the external intelligence agency, the Research and Analysis Wing (RAW). The Ministry of Finance hosts the Financial Intelligence Unit (FIU). The Ministry of Defence hosts the Defence Intelligence Agency (DIA) and the respective arms of the defence forces host their own intelligence agencies. The Ministry of Home Affairs (MHA) hosts the major domestic security intelligence agency, the Intelligence Bureau (IB), which in turn hosts the MAC. The MHA also hosts the various central government police and paramilitary services, such as the Indian Police Service (IPS), central paramilitary forces (which in turn hosts the NSG), various border paramilitary forces such as the Border Security Force (BSF), the Central Reserve Police Force (CRPF – used to support states in crisis), the Central Bureau of Investigation (CBI), and recently formed National Investigation Agency (NIA).

The major connectivity in terms of intelligence between the Centre and states comes about through the state offices of the

IB, through the fact that the Centre can insert its various agencies into the states at the request of the states, through the newly created Subsidiary Multi-Agency Centres (SMACS) and through the connectivity between the SMACS and state police Special Branches. Under the Constitution, except in the case of President's Rule, intelligence relating to national security or investigations relating to the central government's jurisdiction (such as fraud in a central government agency or those relating to the newly created NIA), these relationships all exist according to the invitations and goodwill of the states. Thus if a state does not wish to call in the central government agencies, it need not do so.

As with other federal structures, such as Australia and the US, the artificial bifurcation of intelligence between state and central authorities constitutes a major impediment to the flow of intelligence between the grassroots and the central agencies. This natural tendency of federations is greatly exacerbated in India because of the vast size of the country. Further, intelligence agencies everywhere are extremely poor at sharing intelligence, and India is no exception. They are restricted in doing so by different 'intelligence cultures', the existence of multiple agencies essentially doing the same thing ('stove-piping'), lack of trust and the natural desire to protect sensitive sources. Unfortunately, the police are particularly prone not to share intelligence for all the above reasons and because of a police culture that can often be sceptical of the intelligence function.

The hallmark of sound intelligence in the age of terrorism is the ability to fuse the intelligence gathered at the grassroots with that gathered and analysed at intermediate, national and international levels – what has become known in the US as 'connecting the dots'. Intrinsically, this demands that police and the intelligence agencies work closely together at all levels and develop the capability to share intelligence. It requires that intelligence be 'sucked up' from operations to the analytical and strategic levels. In turn, it requires a sound relationship between the police and the communities they are policing. It also involves trust, compatible data sharing arrangements and adequate security for information and intelligence. Ideally, it requires that all this happens in as near as possible to real time, which in turn implies sound data sharing and analytical systems. But however sophisticated the systems, the sharing of intelligence always Under Section 356 of the Constitution, the central government may dismiss a state government and govern the state directly if the state is deemed to exhibit a failure of the constitutional machinery. If, after six months, no workable majority has emerged, fresh elections must be held.

Since he took over the Ministry of Home Affairs portfolio in December 2008 in the aftermath of the 26/11 attacks, Mr Chidambaram has already conducted a series of reforms and has outlined further major reforms. Reforms, either anticipated or accomplished, include the following (compiled from press reporting and from Chidambaram's speech in December 2009):

Re-vitalisation of the Intelligence Agencies and Counter-Terrorism Mechanisms

- The Multi-Agency Centre (MAC), within the Intelligence Bureau (IB), has been re-furbished and strengthened. The IB has been given an additional Rs 147 crore for the purpose. So-called 'Subsidiary Multi-Agency Centres' (SMACs) have now also been established in the states.
- The MAC and SMACs are to be linked by a dedicated, secure network. In all, 30 locations (including the MAC, the SMACs and a number of police Special Branches) are to be linked by this network.
- • A new, over-arching counter-terrorism organisation is to be created by end 2010, to be called the National Counter-Terrorism Centre (NCTC)
- To incorporate the MAC, NIA, NTRO, JIC, NCRB and National Security Guard (NSG)
- To have an operations division (presumably to include the NSG)
- And thus to minimise the current bifurcation between agencies currently controlled by the NSA and the Ministry of Home Affairs.

- To enable a more rapid response to major terror attacks than was achieved on 26/11, NSG hubs have been established in Hyderabad, Bengaluru, Chennai and Kolkata and two additional regional response groups have been located in Hyderabad and Kolkata. Each hub is staffed by 250 people.
- The Border Security Force (BSF) has been significantly upgraded and re-equipped and 29 additional battalions are to be raised. The Central Reserve Police Force (CRPF) and other central paramilitary forces have also been significantly upgraded.
- In the next 12-18 months, 21 existing, standalone databases will be networked through NATGRID. According to Chidambaram, NATGRID will provide "quick, seamless and secure access to desired information for intelligence/enforcement agencies".
- In a recent development, the National Security Adviser has resigned, possibly opening the way for an integrated security architecture, one more fully reflecting the objectives laid out by Chidambaram.

Strengthening of Coastal and Border Defences

- Coordination has been strengthened between the Coast Guard, Navy and coastal police.
- 64 coastal police stations have been operationalised.
- 56 interceptor boats have been purchased (of 204 scheduled).
- A vessel tracking and monitoring system is being considered.
- Intensified patrolling is in place.
- ID cards are to be issued to fishermen and possibly also coastal residents.
- Following the exposure of serious gaps in the visa system by the Headley case, the Mission Mode Project (MMP) will be implemented. This will provide for online visa and foreigners' registration and tracking with the objective of creating a secure and integrated service

delivery framework for facilitating legitimate travellers and strengthening security. It is estimated to cost Rs 1,011 crore and will be implemented over a period of four-and-a-half years.

Policing and Legal Reform

- The National Investigations Agency (NIA) has been established and is now staffed by a small number of investigators and analysts
- The remit of the NIA is to investigate terrorism crimes under the Unlawful Activities (Prevention) Act and other crimes, such as drug-related crimes, counterfeiting, and major organised crime and money laundering, that have international or multi-state implications.
- The Union government has assisted with funds for the recruitment of 400,000 additional state police
- It has promulgated guidelines for non-corrupt recruitment and developed an electronic system to ensure 'hands free' and non-corrupt recruitment. This system has already been implemented for central recruitment.
- The Union government is to assist with connectivity between police stations and the establishment of a system for police called Crime and Criminal Tracking Network System (CCTNS) "to facilitate collection, storage, retrieval, analysis, transfer and sharing of data and information at the police station and between the police station and the state headquarters and the central police organisations".
- The Home Minister has admonished states to implement 'community policing'.
- He has also requested that "to organise and analyse information derived from the community, the state police Special Branches should be restructured as a specialised and self-sufficient cadre of the State police in terms of personnel, funds and equipment." To this end, on January 7, 2009, the central government circulated a

proposal to restructure the Special Branch in the State police forces. The implementation of the proposal will mark the beginning of a long-haul effort to restructure the intelligence-gathering machinery at the district and state levels.

- The Union Government will assist state police to establish 24x7 command and control posts and quick response teams (QRTs), properly equipped and trained.
- States are admonished to establish (where they don't have them) antiterrorism units (ATUs) to pre-empt and investigate terrorist attacks.

Analysis

The collective changes outlined above, if fully implemented, would amount to an internal security 'revolution' in India. The idea of a NCTC, to bring a number of important agencies under one umbrella, act as a 'fusion centre' for terrorist related intelligence, minimise 'stove-piping', and provide operational coordination, closely reflects changes introduced in the US following 9/11, especially the establishment of the umbrella NCTC there, under the auspices of the Director of National Intelligence (DNI). This mimicry of the US architecture in part arises from the early assistance provided by the Federal Bureau of Investigation (FBI) in the aftermath of 26/11 and a subsequent series of visits to the US by senior Indian politicians and officials, including the Home Minister and Prime Minister.

But do the changes go far enough? Do they 'press the right buttons', and are they likely to be successful in providing better governance throughout the Indian Union – a prime consideration of this chapter in its approach to counter-terrorism and counter-insurgency?

In all such architecture relating to federations like India, Australia, Canada and the US, there are five major heuristic 'gaps to be bridged':

- between overseas and domestic intelligence;
- between military and non-military intelligence;

- between central and state intelligence;
- between the intelligence agencies and police intelligence; and
- between intelligence and the operational counter-terrorism role (response), which is in turn divided into:
- investigations;
- operational coordination in event of an attack; and
- consequence management.

These five major 'gaps' are heuristic in the sense that each and every inter-agency relationship also needs to be bridged. But they represent the major conceptual divides and provide a useful point of departure for the analysis. We will now briefly critique the proposed Indian architecture in light of each of these five main areas.

CHALLENGES IN DEFENCE PLANNING

Defence planning is essentially a subset of overall national level planning in the political, economic and social spheres and has to be evolved in the context of global and proximate factors affecting the nation.. It has also to take into account the philosophy and ethos animating the national psyche; in other words the historical and cultural forces which have shaped the collective memory and outlook of the people over the centuries. The Cold War, was a classic example of the factors stated above. There were fundamental philosophical differences between the adversaries – the western bloc, advocating the virtues of free enterprise and its own interpretations of democracy, and the Soviet bloc, equally strongly asserting the merits of the socialist system as the only one genuinely meeting democratic aspirations and assuring social equality and economic well-being of the people as a whole, rather than for a few. Fifty years of the Cold War could not conclude the capitalism-socialism debate, though, in the end, it did push the socialist forces into, perhaps temporary, retreat. This was because the struggle was really for power and domination. "The evil empire" of Ronald Reagan's description may have withered away, but the necessity for the US to target the so called "rogue states" has not disappeared.

Many examples can be found of philosophical differences leading to stand-offs, usually with the USA as one of the parties. The USA-Cuba divide is a long-standing one. USA-Venezuela stand-off is just developing and resonating in other Latin American countries. Sometimes the differences are couched in the language of anticipated threats, such as in US-North Korea, or US-Iran relations. The true reasons and underlying causes are buried in verbiage and obfuscation. A more serious rift has developed over the selective and poorly conceptualised US war on terrorism, launched for spurious reasons in Iraq, when the real source of terror was elsewhere and far more complex. Differing religious beliefs and rigidities are often cited as causes but do not sufficiently explain conflicts within the same religion, as between Protestants and Catholics in Northern Ireland or the Shias and Sunnis in Iraq and elsewhere.

Planning for the security and defence of a vast country like India with its particular geographic location, historical experiences and associations, social, ethnic, religious and cultural diversity, political and economic structure and a large, relatively poor, democratically governed population, is a complex and challenging task. It is rendered more so in the context of the national and international situation in the last sixty years or so, embracing post-World War II de-colonisation, partition, the creation of Pakistan and later Bangladesh, conflicts with Pakistan and China, the Cold War and its aftermath, the disintegration of the Soviet Union, the re-definition of NATO's role, and of most recent and decisive significance, the September 11, 2001 terror attack on the United States mainland. This last factor is significant because it resulted in a major re-orientation in US foreign policy.

Strategic Overview

Planning for defence pre-supposes identification of threats and contingencies. Until about five years ago, the strategic situation for India was difficult but relatively clear. Pakistan was a definite threat, conventional, clandestine and nuclear. China was a strategically reducing threat, though its international power, influence and economy were growing. Uncertainties in Bangladesh and Nepal required us to be vigilant for fall-out effects. There were problems in the north-east of insurgent groups exploiting the ethnic ties and jungles in Myanmar, and the destabilising spill-over effects of the activities of the Liberation Tigers for Tamil Eelam(LTTE) in Sri Lanka. The presence in our proximate waters, of non-littoral naval forces in substantial numbers, such as those of the US, which has been traditionally supportive of Pakistan, had to be taken cognisance of. Also the fact that warfare at sea, because of its distinctive characteristics of rapidity of concentration and dispersal of forces, mobility, flexibility and speed of execution, requires a different, longer term approach to threat assessment. Strategically the global situation is now evolving in a manner less inimical to India's interests than in the preceding fifty years. Yet the end of the Cold War did not see any easing of pressures on India. On the contrary, economic sanctions and technology denials were increased so as to coerce India to conform to norms of international behaviour prescribed by dominant world powers, led by the US and the European Union on the one hand and China on the other. The reason was the desire of the P-5, the five permanent members of the UN Security Council, who are also the N-5, the self-certified nuclear powers, to preserve their monopoly power status in the face of India's challenge through the nuclear tests of 1998. Yet, the re-evaluation of foreign policies by leading powers set off by the September 11, 2001 terrorist attack on the USA, has initiated processes that are, by and large, beneficial to India. An indication of this is the US declaration of seeing India as a strategic partner for the 21st century, and its efforts to legislate exceptions to its domestic laws to allow supply of nuclear materials for peaceful civilian use to India by the cartel operated by the Nuclear Suppliers Group (NSG).

Nearer home, the pathological hostility of the Pakistanis establishment towards India is rooted in its quest for a national identity, which no novel interpretations, distortions or reinventions of sub-continental history seem able to provide. It will be a long time before there can be normal relations with Pakistan because they are influenced more by the internal contradictions and dynamics of the Pakistani state rather than considerations of mutual benefits through good relations. Since the Pakistan army is the self-appointed guardian of the undefined "ideology of Pakistan", normalcy will come when the Army decides it should be so; or the cost-benefit equation alters.

With China, there is perceptible progress on resolving disputes and fostering economic and cultural relations. As for Nepal, Bangladesh, Myanmar and Sri Lanka, there is no significant positive change, and because of shared borders, internal problems in those countries will continue to spill over into India. Instability in Afghanistan remains a cause of concern, especially because of Pakistan's dubious role, and this will have its impact on the pursuit of India's energy and strategic interests in Central Asia.

Non-littoral naval forces in significant numbers are still present in the Indian Ocean, but there is no coercive or inimical intent as in the past. Indeed, the Indian Navy holds regular friendly exercises with them on a routine basis. China's long term plans for a naval presence in the region have to be taken note of. There are ample signs of Chinese maritime interest, starting from building and operating communications facilities in Myanmar to financing and building Pakistan's Gwadar Port on the Makran coast, collaboration in building warships for the Pakistan navy at Karachi shipyard, as well as port building in Sri Lanka. On the western rim of the Indian Ocean, China is vigorously pursuing options in Africa, underlined by the meeting of 49 heads of state/government in Beijing in early November this year.

National Objectives in the Long Term

Planning for defence has to be in the framework of national objectives over a period of decades ahead, even if these are not publicly articulated. USA does not hesitate to state its intention to remain the dominant global technological, space and military power for the foreseeable future and tailors strategic policies accordingly. China has, by its actions, investments and developments over the years, demonstrated that it intends to be at least the equal of the USA, though with "Chinese characteristics". Pakistan makes no secret of its intention to be "different" from India, and to compete with and undermine India at every opportunity.

India too has shown in various ways that it intends to be in the forefront of nations in every sphere: economic, technological, industrial and human development. What about military capability? Does it wish to have only a capacity to ward off aggression by land and sea? Or does it aspire to play a larger role in the region? If it emerges as the world's third or fourth largest economy in a few years, would a commensurate military role follow? Or are national objectives to be largely achieved by a combination of diplomacy and economic policies? If it aspires for a permanent seat in the UN Security Council, is it prepared for the increased diplomatic and military responsibilities attached? Many of these seemingly philosophical issues require to be debated to facilitate meaningful defence planning for the future.

INDIA'S DRAFT NUCLEAR DOCTRINE

In April 1998, the Indian government had constituted a Task Force to recommend the establishment of a National Security Council (NSC). The Task Force submitted its report in June 1998 and, in November 1998, the government constituted a three-tier NSC with a full time National Security Advisor and a National Security Advisory Board (NSAB). Although the first task that was planned to be originally entrusted to the NSAB was to conduct a strategic defence review, because of post-Pokhran II compulsions, the NSAB was asked to first formulate India's nuclear doctrine. The NSAB submitted a draft nuclear doctrine paper to the government that was released to the public for wider debate on August 17, 1999. The key features of the proposed nuclear doctrine are reproduced below:

India shall pursue a doctrine of credible minimum deterrence. In this policy of 'retaliation only', the survivability of our arsenal is critical. This is a dynamic concept related to our strategic environment, technological imperatives and the needs of national security. The actual size, components, deployment and employment of nuclear forces will be decided in the light of these factors. India's peacetime posture aims at convincing any potential aggressor that:

- Any threat of use of nuclear weapons against India shall invoke measures to counter the threat; and
- Any nuclear attack on India and its forces shall result in punitive retaliation with nuclear weapons to inflict damage unacceptable to the aggressor.

The fundamental purpose of Indian nuclear weapons is to deter the use and threat of use of nuclear weapons by any state or entity against India and its forces. India will not be the first to initiate a nuclear strike but will respond with punitive retaliation should deterrence fail. India will not resort to the use or threat of use of nuclear weapons against states that do not possess nuclear weapons, or are not aligned with nuclear weapons powers.

The draft nuclear doctrine, while generally following the policy guidelines enunciated by the Prime Minister in Parliament, fleshed out his pronouncements and "provides a broad framework for the development, deployment and employment of India's nuclear forces." The draft paper proposes that India should establish a credible, minimum nuclear deterrent capability comprising sufficient, survivable and operationally ready nuclear forces based on the principle of no first use of nuclear weapons. It emphasises that the level of India's nuclear capability should be consistent with maximum credibility, survivability, effectiveness, safety and security. It provides for the establishment of effective intelligence and early warning systems. It recommends that India's nuclear forces be based on a triad of strategic bombers, land-based ballistic missiles and submarine launched ballistic missiles (SLBMs). Though a sea-based nuclear capability will take many decades to develop, the requirement of SLBMs is considered inescapable due to their relatively lower vulnerability. Nuclear forces that need to survive a first strike have no option but to ensure that at least 50 to 60 per cent of the arsenal is made comparatively invulnerable by being maintained as SLBMs. The draft paper proposes that India's nuclear strike capability be configured to inflict punitive retaliation the consequences of which would be unacceptable to a potential adversary who will therefore be deterred from doing the unthinkable. The doctrine highlights the cardinal supremacy of civilian control over India's nuclear weapons and proposes that the final authority for the release of nuclear weapons must vest with the Prime Minister or his designated successor(s).

The proposed doctrine also rejects the concept of nuclear warfighting and does not, hence, consider it necessary for India to match its nuclear warheads and delivery systems with those of its potential nuclear adversaries. A small number of survivable nuclear warheads and delivery systems that can inflict damage which would be unacceptable to the adversary are considered adequate for the purposes of deterrence. Although the paper has left some ambiguity by not clearly rejecting the need for tactical or battlefield nuclear weapons in India's context, the tenor of the paper and its emphasis on a retaliatory policy appear to rule out any thinking towards tactical nuclear weapons. However, the real distinguishing feature of India's nuclear doctrine is that it is "... anchored in India's continued commitment to global, verifiable and non-discriminating nuclear disarmament..." that has been described as India's national security objective. The use of nuclear weapons is considered "the gravest threat to humanity and to peace and stability in the international system." The doctrine paper clearly points out India's desire to see the world completely rid of nuclear weapons.

As expected, the draft doctrine initiated a major debate in the country about its nuclear policies. Amitabh Mattoo called it "an unapologetic realpolitik articulation of the principal raison d'être of India's nuclear weapons and the requirements needed to lend credibility to the country's deterrent posture." While agreeing with the thrust of India's nuclear policy, he wrote that India's primary quest appeared to be to acquire the strategic autonomy necessary for making independent decisions in an often unfriendly world and to pursue economic and political development without fear of external threats. R. Prasannan called the draft doctrine a wish list attached to the collective speeches of the Prime Minister and his Cabinet colleagues. Bharat Wariavwalla criticised the draft doctrine on the grounds that the definition of minimum deterrence would be very different vis a vis China and Pakistan and, hence, the term is much too loose to pass off as doctrine.

Many analysts and even foreign governments have sought to raise doubts about India's draft nuclear doctrine. It did not help matters that the doctrine was unveiled the week after the Indian Air Force had shot down a Pakistani Atlantique reconnaissance aircraft that had intruded into Indian territory. The US government rejected the Indian desire to develop a nuclear arsenal." The Indian tests also spurred fears of a new Middle East arms race. However, not all Western powers denounced India's attempts to establish a credible weaponised nuclear deterrent. France welcomed the release of India's draft nuclear doctrine as a "logical and indeed wanted step". The most surprising criticism of the draft doctrine is that it conjures up dark visions of a nuclear arms race in Southern Asia. If all nuclear weapons states were to follow a no first use policy, it would be logical to assume that there would gradually be a net reduction in the size of nuclear arsenals - an arms race in reverse! Jasjit Singh offers the following explanation:

The concerns about a potential arms race reflect a perception arising out of the prism of Cold War mind-sets where first strike (and even "launch on warning") was the order of the day. This necessitated large arsenals and potentially pre-emptive strikes with nuclear weapons. The result was the peak of 67,000 nuclear warheads. But China did not follow the same route and relied on minimum deterrence concept with a no first use commitment. There is no evidence that China's nuclear posture led to any arms race. Even in future, China's nuclear arsenal is likely to be dictated by the size of US/Russian arsenals and issues like ballistic missile defences etc. rather than the defensive doctrine of India.

The worst criticism of the draft doctrine has been that opting for a triad of nuclear forces is not indicative of a minimalist posture but of a maximalist one, particularly as sea-based nuclear weapons have been envisaged to form part of the nuclear force. This criticism fails to take into account the fact that the credibility of a nuclear deterrent that is limited to retaliatory strikes only hinges around the ability of the nuclear force to survive a first strike in sufficient numbers to inflict unacceptable punishment in retaliation. Since submarines offer the best survival potential, India has to rely on a small number of SLBMs for credible deterrence. Raja Menon has also criticised the proposed doctrine: "...There is a serious dysfunction between 'minimum deterrence' and a tri-Service arsenal. The two cannot go together, and is (sic) akin to yoking a horse and camel together." However, surprisingly, he finds no use for aircraft-delivered nuclear bombs and states that "to even consider the role of the army in nuclear deterrence, minimum at that, is truly distressing." His hypothesis is that an arsenal for minimum deterrence requires only second-strike weapons, which can only be based on SSBNs.

Some critics have averred that the nuclear threats have not been enunciated and that the draft document does not define the nuclear force levels that India considers "minimum". Others have protested that the costs of India's nuclear deterrent have not been spelt out. The critics of the draft document forget that doctrine defines only a set of beliefs and guidelines on which policy and strategy is based. In the Preamble of the draft paper it is clearly stated in Para 1.6 that "this document outlines the broad principles for the development, deployment and employment of India's nuclear forces." Details regarding the targeting philosophy, nuclear force structures and the finer nuances of command and control cannot be expected to appear in a paper on nuclear doctrine.

The exception in the draft doctrine that India's non-use of nuclear weapons policy against countries that are not nuclear weapons states does not apply if they are militarily aligned with nuclear weapons states, has also been criticised. This exception would include non-nuclear members of NATO and the military allies of the US such as Japan. Rajesh Rajagopalan explains the reasons behind such exceptions:

Two reasons could be suggested for this exception, one practical and the other strategic. The practical reason is that the Negative Security Assurance (NSA) of various nuclear weapons states, around which this non-use policy is based, makes similar exceptions. In fact, the exceptions there are broader and the NSA does not apply to countries that have refused to sign the NPT or are suspected of nuclear weapons ambitions...

The strategic reason... (is that) a good number of non-nuclear countries still host the nuclear arms of nuclear weapons states and share in the command and control infrastructure of nuclear powers. Theoretically, a nuclear attack on India could be mounted by the nuclear forces hosted in third countries. Excluding these countries would mean that no retaliation could be mounted on the bases from where such attacks are launched...

Rajesh Rajagopalan points out that 'minimum deterrence' is mistakenly characterised as doctrine whereas it actually refers to the nuclear force structure. He states that the Indian doctrine is one of 'assured retaliation' and this is to be given effect by a minimalist nuclear force as "an assured retaliation posture is premised on the belief that no one will start a nuclear war if they are assured of a nuclear retaliation, even if it is a weak retaliation. In other words, for an Indian nuclear deterrent to work effectively against China or Pakistan, it is not necessary to threaten them with complete destruction: even retaliating with a few nuclear warheads will create unacceptable costs to both." While the interpretation is no doubt technically correct, it is also true that a policy of assured retaliation, combined with a small nuclear force built on the principle of sufficiency, could overall be characterised as minimum deterrence. However, it is a finely nuanced distinction that must be noted.

Pakistani government spokesmen and scholars have been particularly critical of India's no first use doctrine on the grounds that it is only a declaratory policy and can be easily changed when the need arises. They have failed to take note of the fact that a country's nuclear force structure, command and control system, alert status and its deployment posture are based on its nuclear doctrine. First use doctrines require hair trigger alerts, launch-on-warning and launch-through-attack strategies and elaborate surveillance, early warning and intelligence systems with nuclear warheads loaded on launchers and ready to fire. Nuclear armed aircraft would need to be ready on runway alert, if not constantly airborne as in the case of the erstwhile US Strategic Air Command. India cannot ever resort to any of these measures without Pakistan learning about them almost immediately. What the Pakistanis also forget, or deliberately ignore, is that India has offered to negotiate a mutual no first use treaty with Pakistan that would be binding and verifiable. India's track record of adherence to international treaties has been exemplary. Unfortunately, the same cannot be said of India's neighbours who have violated numerous treaties with impunity, including the NPT and the MTCR.

The charge that India's nuclear doctrine would initiate an arms race in the Southern Asian region is specious and unjustified. China's gradual moves towards a nuclear triad over a period of three and a half decades have not forced India to play "catch up". Even now India does not feel it necessary to match China's 400-plus nuclear warheads, or to follow China and develop multiple independently targetable re-entry vehicles (MIRVs). India has decided to base its deterrent on a small force of survivable nuclear warheads and delivery systems for a retaliatory strike that can inflict punitive damage on a handful of value targets. There is no reason why Pakistan should feel compelled to match India's nuclear warheads and missiles, particularly as it has opted for a first strike doctrine and does not have to worry about the survival of its nuclear forces. With a first use doctrine, even for deterring conventional war Pakistan does not need to match India warhead for warhead and missile for missile. Kenneth Waltz has argued that the distinction between nuclear forces designed for war fighting, that need to be compared with one another, and those designed to deter the use of nuclear weapons, must be clearly understood. Forces designed for deterrence need not match the adversary's nuclear forces as long as they can do unacceptable damage to the adversary with unacceptable damage sensibly defined. Putting it most appropriately, he has said that "more is not better, if less is enough." Hence, those who are raising the bogey of a nuclear arms race in Southern Asia need to review their alarmist views.

It emerges quite clearly that most of the criticism of the proposed nuclear doctrine stems not from any genuine disagreement with India's no first use doctrine and its professed need to establish a credible minimum nuclear deterrent, but from the desire of many Western countries that India should "cap, reduce and eliminate" its nuclear capability and sign the NPT and the CTBT as a non-nuclear weapons state. Since India's nuclear tests and its declaration of the weaponisation of its nuclear deterrent were based on substantial national security interests, the cap, reduce, eliminate mantra is unlikely to now get anywhere.

Efficacy of No First Use

The concept of no first use logically flows out of the current conventional wisdom that the sole purpose of nuclear weapons, if they have a purpose at all, is to deter the use of nuclear weapons. As is well known in nuclear theology, Bernard Brodie had argued many decades ago that the advent of nuclear weapons had fundamentally altered the relationship between war and national policy and that nuclear weapons were so destructive that their only real purpose could be the avoidance of war itself. On the other hand, many other strategists saw nuclear weapons as simply one more addition to a nation's or even a military commander's arsenal, though a very destructive one, and convinced themselves that the use of nuclear weapons could be incorporated into warfighting strategies. Those who saw nuclear weapons as serving a military purpose in real combat naturally opted for first use and pre-emptive nuclear strategies and developed complex warfighting doctrines while the others saw no real purpose except that of deterrence and adopted deterrence strategies, including no first use.

India's declaration of its no first use doctrine has once again focussed international debate on the efficacy of no first use policies, even though India has repeatedly re-iterated that it is willing to negotiate no first use treaties bilaterally or multilaterally with all nuclear weapons states including China and Pakistan. It is often mistakenly believed that the concept of no first use is China's contribution to international peace and stability.

In fact, the no first use formulation goes back to 1925 when the international community concluded a no first use treaty on chemical weapons and toxins in the Geneva Protocol. Though enormous stockpiles of chemical weapons were produced during the Second World War, neither side used them. This was because mutual deterrence continued to operate among the nations that had chemical weapons stockpiles till these were finally delegitimised by the 1993 Chemical Weapons Convention. However, in situations of asymmetry, deterrence did not operate and chemical weapons were used on several occasions: "By the Italians in Ethiopia, by the Japanese against the Chinese and finally by Saddam Hussain against the Iranians." It could be concluded that a no first use policy works best during conditions of mutual deterrence.

A no first use commitment is not merely a verbal or even a negotiated assurance, it can and must be seen to be reflected in the nuclear force structure, the deployment patterns, the types of surveillance assets in place and the state of readiness of a country's nuclear forces. China announced a no first use commitment immediately after its nuclear test in October 1964. In recent years it has diluted this policy by emphasising that such a declaration does not apply to territories that belong to

China. While Taiwan falls in this category, so does Arunachal Pradesh in India which China still claims as its own territory. Hence, it can be plausibly stated that China could contemplate the use of nuclear weapons during a war over Taiwan or a border conflict with India in Arunachal Pradesh. The former Soviet Union had also subscribed to the no first use policy. As far back as 1955, the Soviet Union had proposed a no first use pledge by all nuclear weapons states. However, Russia's recently declared military doctrine has withdrawn that pledge and Russia is now committed to a first use nuclear policy even against conventional military threats. Several US thinkers, some of them important former members of the US military establishment such as Robert McNamara and George Kennan, have repeatedly called for a no first use pledge. Despite the end of the Cold War, the US and its NATO allies and friends, including the United Kingdom and France have refused to heed such wise counsel. In fact, the US has said that it would consider the use of its nuclear weapons against chemical and biological weapons and NATO, under US leadership, has developed an "out of area" strategic concept that undermines peace and stability in the international order.

Rooted in its strategic culture as it is, India's no first use doctrine is not a hastily formulated policy designed to win brownie points from the international community after upsetting the non-proliferation apple cart. It is a carefully thought through policy that has taken decades to mature, even if it was not publicly well articulated. Jaswant Singh has written: "No other country has debated so carefully and, at times, torturously over the dichotomy between its sovereign security needs and global disarmament instincts, between a moralistic approach and a realistic one, and between a covert nuclear policy and an overt one." K. Subrahmanyam had written in 1986: "Today the international system is dominated by nuclear dacoits who are refusing to disarm and there is nothing unethical if India were to secure for itself necessary self-protection capabilities to ward off coercive use of nuclear diplomacy... If India is to make a serious intervention in the disarmament debate and contribute to nuclear disarmament, acquiring nuclear capability is a fee that has to be paid." Even during the mid-1980s, defence analysts like General K. Sundarji and K. Subrahmanyam were advocating a minimum deterrent capability for India and had ruled out the need for tactical nuclear weapons as these were meant for nuclear warfighting - a concept that India did not subscribe to. Hence, minimum deterrence is not a new concept in the Indian context that has been thrust on an unsuspecting nation by the government and the NSAB.

The No First Use Dilemma

Ever since the May 1998 nuclear explosions and the Indian government's advocacy of the doctrine of no first use and a minimum credible deterrent, a major debate has been raging in the strategic community in India on the issue of no first use of nuclear weapons. Many analysts have averred that India has gained nothing and has unnecessarily elected to bear the horrendous costs of a nuclear strike by choosing to adopt a purely retaliatory nuclear policy. Rear Admiral Raja Menon asks: "Will India... be committed to absorbing a nuclear strike in case deterrence fails?" And answers: "Hardly, because in the event that an intelligence warning of a 'definite' nuclear strike is received, the NCP (National Command Post) will have to consider, among other options, a first launch." To advocate no first use and then consider first use as soon as the alarm bells are sounded would be duplicitous and worthy of the strongest possible condemnation. It is argued that after all India's no first use doctrine is only a declaratory doctrine and if other nuclear powers are not willing to accept India's offer of a negotiated no first use treaty, why should India subject itself to the ravages of nuclear destruction? It is likely that eventually one or more NWS (including Pakistan) will come around to accepting India's offer of a negotiated bilateral or multilateral no-first-use treaty. Given the groundswell of public opinion against the continuation of nuclear weapons almost all over the world, it may happen sooner rather than later. Meanwhile, some hard questions need to be asked. Is India likely to be faced by situations occasioned by operational realities when it might become necessary for the Indian political leadership to order the first use of nuclear weapons? When will the situation become operationally so critical that India might be forced to do the unthinkable? So, is India's no first use doctrine merely rhetorical nonsense or is it based on sound operational reasoning? These issues pose a strategic dilemma and present a complex challenge that is not at all easy to rationalise.

It is now universally accepted that nuclear weapons are political weapons and not weapons of 'warfighting'. However, the close link between nuclear weapons and a nation's conventional military capabilities is undeniable. If a nation's conventional capability is extremely low vis a vis a nuclear armed adversary, it may be necessary for that nation to adopt an in extremis 'first use' strategy to thwart a conventional military offensive that may threaten to undermine its territorial integrity and lead to its break up. This is the situation that Pakistan finds itself in at present. While India may have no intentions of launching a major conventional offensive into Pakistan, given India's conventional superiority (no matter how slender the edge may be), Pakistan has based its national security strategy on the first use of nuclear weapons to prevent its comprehensive military defeat like in 1971 and, consequently, its disintegration as a nation. It is for this reason that Pakistan does not accept India's offer of a bilateral no first use treaty as a nuclear confidence building and risk reduction measure.

Though overall China's conventional military forces far outnumber India's, due to China's problems in inducting, deploying and logistically sustaining large forces in Tibet, India enjoys a reasonable defensive capability at present and therefore does not need a 'first use' nuclear strategy to deter a conventional Chinese offensive backed by nuclear-tipped ballistic missiles deployed in Tibet. However, India's existing defensive capability is being quickly eroded as China is rapidly modernising its armed forces, raising rapid deployment divisions and improving the logistics infrastructure in Tibet while exhibiting extreme intransigence in resolving the outstanding territorial and boundary dispute with India. If India continues to neglect the upgradation of its conventional military capability and military modernisation by investing the grossly inadequate sum of less than 2.5 percent of its GDP for defence, as it is doing at present, the nation may again have to suffer the ignominy of large-scale military reverses, should China choose to fight even a limited border war after completing its military modernisation by 2005-2010.

While nuclear doctrine must undoubtedly be based on sound theoretical underpinnings, it has to be ultimately tested in the crucible of operational reality. The proponents of a first use strategy for India need to more deliberately ponder the threat scenarios that might justify the unthinkable. Some plausible scenarios are worth considering in this context.

Starting at the lower end of conventional conflict with low intensity conflict (LIC) and Pakistan's ongoing proxy war with India, would the use of a Stinger or Unza surface-to-air (SAM) missile by Pakistan-supported mercenary Islamists to bring down an Indian Airlines aircraft over Kashmir Valley justify an Indian nuclear strike?

Or, would a pro-active punitive response across the Line of Control (LoC) with massive artillery and air power sustained over a few weeks be more desirable? In another scenario, would a battalion or even a brigade size attack by the Pakistan army across the LoC, or even Kargil-type intrusions on the Indian side of the LoC, that result in major gains for Pakistan, justify the first use of nuclear weapons by India when their retaliatory use by Pakistan would be a certainty?

Or, would a punitive ground and air forces conventional response across the LoC (and perhaps across the international boundary by the IAF) in another sector yield better dividends? After all, it is well known that there are areas on the LoC where Indian forces could be heading for key value objectives in Pakistan Occupied Kashmir (POK) within days of the outbreak of hostilities in Jammu and Kashmir (J&K).

In case such exchanges across the LoC escalate to a larger conventional conflict, as they well might, Pakistan may launch its Army Reserve North (ARN) through the Shakargarh Bulge in the Sialkot sector and threaten to cut off Kashmir's lifeline NH-1A between Pathankot and Jammu.

If Pakistan achieved initial success, such an offensive would pose a grave danger to the security of J&K. Would the first use of nuclear weapons be a rational choice for India under such circumstances? Or would it perhaps be more prudent to launch one or more Indian Strike Corps counter-offensives across the International Boundary in Punjab, Rajasthan and Gujarat, as General Harbaksh Singh did in 1965 with Lal Bahadur Shastri as Prime Minister, to make the Pakistanis recoil from their offensive in the Jammu sector? Surely, the launching of sizeable counter offensives into Pakistan's heartland would be a better way to relieve pressure on J&K.

Another option favoured by military analysts is the "zero warning" option in which Pakistan is given the credible capability of launching what may be termed as a "cold start" conventional war due to the proximity of its cantonments to the International Boundary, or by concentrating strike formations under the garb of training exercises.

While there may be some merit in the initial military viability of such an option, unless India strengthens its technological intelligence and humint capabilities, what needs to be considered is the "day after" impact of India's counter moves to checkmate such a Pakistani offensive.

With the IAF in full flow within hours and army formations closing in rapidly on the ingressing Pakistani units, while also simultaneously sealing the border behind them, the invaders would be hard pressed to ensure their own security and would eventually be destroyed in detail.

International opinion would also be firmly on India's side. Any well prepared army or air force can achieve tactical surprise, as the Egyptians did during the Yom Kippur war against the Israelis in 1973; the acme of military skill lies in being able to sustain the offensive logistically beyond 48 hours and holding on to the initial gains in the face of the adversary's reaction.

It should be clear to perceptive observers that Pakistan has learnt the right lessons from its strategic blunder in Kargil during the summer months of 1999 and is unlikely to repeat such hara-kiri in a hurry.

Inherent in an Indian nuclear first strike option, as advocated by the opponents of no first use, is the Pakistani nuclear retaliation that would inevitably follow on Indian cities and military targets. Cities like Jodhpur, Bikaner, Ahmedabad, Jalandhar, Ludhiana and perhaps even New Delhi and Mumbai would be the likely targets of a retaliatory Pakistani nuclear strike.

The limited gains that an Indian first strike may achieve and the real possibility of successful Pakistani nuclear retaliation, the resounding answer to the first use nuclear option by India is no. An Indian nuclear first strike would not be justified as the costs of Pakistani retaliation would be prohibitive. Nor would it be operationally expedient. In none of the above scenarios India's survival as a nation-state is likely to be seriously threatened. Various other even more pessimistic scenarios could be considered but the result would be the same.

It clearly emerges that across the entire spectrum of conventional conflict, the first use of nuclear weapons by India does not make sound strategic sense. Besides, a first use doctrine would invite international opprobrium, seriously undermine India's efforts towards total nuclear disarmament and be prohibitively costly to implement.

It is not generally well appreciated that a first use doctrine requires a massive investment in surveillance and target acquisition infrastructure by way of satellite and aerial reconnaissance and human intelligence to execute 'launch on warning' and 'launch through attack' strategies, with the nuclear forces being maintained on permanent hair trigger alerts. A first use doctrine also requires quick political decision-making and decentralisation of the control of nuclear weapons to theatre commanders in the armed forces. Hence, such a doctrine is inherently more risky and more likely to lead to the accidental, even unauthorised, use of nuclear weapons.

It would, of course, be far better to mutually negotiate a no first use treaty with adversarial nuclear armed states as that would be the best nuclear risk reduction measure. Russia and China have signed a mutual no first use treaty. In case India's nuclear-armed adversaries continue to be recalcitrant in signing a binding no first use pact, it would be worthwhile for India to consider some essential qualifications to India's unilateral no first use doctrine. The first is to clearly spell out that a nuclear strike on Indian soldiers even within Pakistani territory would be deemed to be a nuclear strike on India and would invite massive punitive nuclear retaliation. The absence of this rider would negate India's conventional edge over Pakistan as the army would be forced to plan on launching only shallow limited objective offensives to avoid risking nuclear strikes on the mechanised spearheads leading India's advance. Only the capability of executing deep offensive strikes can ensure conventional deterrence and present viable policy options to prevent Pakistan's predilection for attempting salami slicing in J&K. The second caveat should be that even a conventional bombing or missile attack on India's nuclear establishments and nuclear weapons storage sites during war, that results in casualties due to a nuclear explosion or even radiation leaks, would invite a nuclear response.

Though India and Pakistan have signed an agreement on not targeting each other's nuclear facilities, such agreements have little value when war is declared. Also, state-sponsored acts of terrorism or sabotage of India's nuclear establishments and storage sites should also result in nuclear retribution against the sponsoring country. With better surveillance systems and improvements in the intelligence gathering apparatus, it should be possible to accurately determine the identity of the originator of such heinous crimes. Without these inescapable qualifications, with others to be added when necessary, it would be extremely difficult for India to implement a credible no first use doctrine.

Key Features

Even though the draft nuclear doctrine formulated by the NSAB is yet to be formally debated in Parliament, there is a broad national consensus on its central facets. According to Jasjit Singh, the following essential elements constitute the key features of India's nuclear doctrine:

Firstly, India's nuclear weapons are meant to deter the use and threat of use of nuclear weapons against India. "But unlike most their nuclear weapon states, India's nuclear weapons are not meant to deter the use and threat of use of conventional weapons, chemical weapons, biological weapons or a generalised formulation of protecting national interests any time anywhere. The doctrine requires that the nuclear policy should seek to deter rather than fight a war with nuclear weapons. The orientation of the doctrine is thus quite narrowly focused on the need to defend India through deterrence against nuclear weapons threat." However, India recognises that nuclear weapons cannot provide deterrence in all circumstances and limited conventional conflict remains possible even under the overhang of nuclear weapons. This was borne out by the 1999 Kargil conflict between India and Pakistan.

Secondly, India's nuclear doctrine is firmly anchored on the principle of "no first use" even against nuclear threat or use. "India's use of its nuclear weapons would be predicated on failure of deterrence, that is, if and when an adversary uses nuclear weapons against India. This severely circumscribes the potential development, deployment and employment of the nuclear arsenal."

Thirdly, India's no first use doctrine is a defensive doctrine that limits the use of nuclear weapons to retaliation only. Hence, it is only a precaution against the use of nuclear weapons against India and is in total harmony with the UN Charter. "Article 51 of the Charter under Chapter VII clearly endorses 'the inherent right of individual or collective self-defence if an armed attack occurs against a Member of the United Nations' (emphasis added)... In fact, UN Security Council Resolution 1172 is a gross violation of the UN Charter since it seeks to deny India the right enshrined in the Charter (by seeking) elimination of the capabilities that the permanent members of the Security Council themselves possess and jealously guard by disregarding their treaty obligations of nuclear disarmament." Fourthly, the doctrine is based on the concept of minimum deterrence that implies that India's nuclear policy, strategy and posture would be guided by the minimalist principle.

"The emphasis on "minimum" deterrence clearly defines this principle in relation to the capability sought, the size of the arsenal, costs involved, the level of retaliation required and the nuclear posture in peace time and in times of crisis and active threat."

Finally, "India's nuclear doctrine emphasises that global, verifiable and non-discriminatory nuclear disarmament is a national security objective. This is to be expected from a country that has pursued the goal of complete abolition of nuclear weapons for decades in order to remove its own security dilemma as well as ensure greater prospects for international peace and security."

India's desire to develop a credible minimum nuclear deterrent against nuclear blackmail and the threat of use of nuclear weapons, is an eminently justifiable national security imperative. India's no first use, retaliation-only nuclear doctrine is not only morally befitting and worthy of India's civilisational heritage, it is also operationally sound strategy. However, deterrence hinges on credibility and India is still far from demonstrating strong political resolve to execute a massive retaliatory nuclear strike. Only when India's adversaries are convinced that India has both the necessary political and military will and the hardware wherewithal to respond to a nuclear strike with punitive retaliation that will inflict unacceptable loss of human life and unprecedented material damage, will they be deterred. Only then will the nuclear monster remain tightly leashed in and around India's neighbourhood.

The adoption of graduated or flexible response strategies will weaken the quality of India's deterrence and may tempt its adversaries to test India's resolve and capabilities. As long as offensive nuclear deterrence continues to be so unabashedly practised by most of the other NWS, India's defensive nuclear deterrence policies are totally justified.

INDIA'S INTERNAL SECURITY REFORMS UNION GOVERNMENT CHOICES IN SECURITY REFORM

Given India's limited resources, New Delhi's increasing re-allocation of its overall security resources towards internal and border security, and 'continental' defence against near neighbours like Pakistan tends to detract from military modernisation and development of force projection capability. One way of illustrating this is to show that the share of defence spending on the 'blue water navy', the classic tool of force projection, has remained in percentage terms fairly constant over the last few decades, shifting only from 13 per cent of the defence budget in 1994 to 14.5 per cent today.

This percentage share is low for a power seeking a force projection capability. For example, it compares with a percentage share for the US Navy of 26 per cent. Against this, concentration on close-in coastal defence and security has risen dramatically following 26/11.

Another way of measuring the costs of internal security is to look at the rising cost of police and paramilitary forces in relation to military forces. State police numbers have been rising at well above the rate of the population increase, from 1.37 million in 1997 to 1.75 million in 2007 (available positions – there are about 1.5 million police in situ.) This rise reflects the position of the Union Government that India is under-policed. As well as this rise in police numbers, the Union Government's burden of expenditure on homeland security has also risen significantly. Since 9/11, the percentage share of homeland security (not including the Coast Guard or state police) in relation to defence spending has risen from 11.76 per cent in 2000-01 to 18.5 per cent in 2009-10 (budget estimate). The Union Government now supports police forces costing Rs 12,817 crore (US$2.27 billion), up from Rs 5,677 crore (US$ 1.2 billion) in 1999-2000 – or a rise of 126 per cent in nominal terms.

The data suggest that there has been a proportional shift within India's security spending between power accretion spending and internal security spending. This is not to say that conventional defence spending has not been rising handsomely, but rather that internal security has become an urgent focus of the Union Government.

Internationally, however, this proportional shift has been overshadowed by the far greater global interest on India's rise as a military power. Although there has been a shift in emphasis in favour of internal and border security spending, the focus of that shift is still in favour of 'hard' (or some might say 'repressive') use of power and against other instruments for achieving better governance outcomes.

In this equation, the various paramilitary forces, the armed constabulary (numbering nearly half the state police), the Coast Guard and the various intelligence agencies might be considered as 'hard' power.

'Soft' elements, on their part, might be said to consist of the police working to protect the community from crime, the legal structure, various measures to ensure governance, justice and accountability, and approaches that seek to alleviate the lot of those with grievances, such as economic support for tribal and Muslim populations or granting greater autonomy to separatist regions. Diplomatic, economic and aid efforts designed to create a more robust regional grouping in South Asia also fall within this 'soft' category.

This chapter focuses only on India's security choices in relation to its internal security mechanisms rather than its diplomatic, trade and aid activities in the South Asian region or the needs of national defence against attack by another country.

But it is worth noting that, although regional security building is an extremely difficult area of activity for India as the regional 'giant', it is a crucial activity in terms of India's wider security, not least in achieving cooperative regional outcomes against transnational terrorism and crime. Nor do we deal with the various attempts of the government to meet the needs of disaffected minorities such as tribals, Muslims or those in other areas, seeking separation or greater autonomy.

Equally, these are absolutely vital areas of activity for balanced approaches to counter-terrorism and counter-insurgency. Due to the magnitude of these topics, however, they cannot be covered in this chapter.

Given the reality of India's federal structure, it will be natural to expect the Union Government to be most active in areas of its jurisdiction such as defence, federally funded paramilitary forces, the national intelligence agencies, central police and centrally administered laws.

State and local level activities will tend to get a lesser emphasis, at least from the Union Government. Thus, many of the activities at the 'soft' end of the spectrum, such as policing reform and 'community policing', will not fall directly within the jurisdiction of the Union Government.

As for state governments, while some may have an incentive to improve these aspects of security in their jurisdictions, others will be less active in the pursuit of reform. A state political class that has the police under its influence, for example, will be far less willing to conduct meaningful police reforms than one that is not. And it is because of this that many states have resisted efforts to reform the police, including the efforts of the Supreme Court and various police reform commissions.

It is a central tenet of this chapter that the Union Government should develop ways of providing additional focus on so-called 'lower order' issues of security, such as anti-corruption measures, the rights of individuals and modernisation of the police and judiciary, even though they fall predominantly within state government jurisdictions. Without leadership from the centre in these areas, the current drive for greater internal security – especially as it has been developed since the attacks of 26/11 – is unlikely to prove sustainable. Although the Union government is clearly restrained in the level of its activity in respect of these areas by the Constitution, there are a number of ways it can become more active and activist and these areas.

5

Cyber Security Challenge of India

The evolution of technology impacts the nature of conflict and war. Amongst the recent aspects of involving in conflict is "no contact war" (NCW) wherein there is no "physical" or "kinetic" action across borders. Operations are conducted in a covert manner using resources such as agents in the information domain to weaken or strike at an adversary to achieve political objectives. These are clouded in ambiguity and deniability. The enemy is unseen and the victim unsure of how and where to react.

Several states are on the way to achieving this capability. Historically speaking, China studied Gulf War I in detail and analysed that it could not defeat the USA with numbers or in technology. It therefore adopted the concept of asymmetric war based on vulnerabilities of the USA in the cyber domain. This was structured around the concept of " Wangluohua" – networkisation as a part of unrestricted and asymmetric warfare. Amongst others, a Task Force was created for Information War (IW), four universities set up, hacker groups supported, regular exercises held and IW units raised in 2003. Through a process of cyber espionage, reverse engineering, source-code sharing, manufacture of hardware, supported by a huge human resource (HR) base, China has greatly developed its capacity in this regard to formidable proportions. Unlike any other forms of warfare, there is no convention or ban on sharing of information with respect to the cyber domain. Thus countries which are inimical could put together resources. Additionally, this capability could be shared with terrorist and fundamentalist groups to wreak mayhem on an intended adversary.

As India progresses, its reliance on the Internet will increase at a rapid pace. Globalisation and governance require a wired society. Along with this India's vulnerability to the threat of IW will become greater. This danger must be foreseen and planned for. Failure to do so can result in a catastrophe and severely affect the country's status and international partnerships, especially in the financial sector. To understand the impact of IW a hypothetical situation at the end of this decade is presented here.

CYBER SECURITY - AN OVERVIEW

Cyber security is a complex issue that cuts across multiple domains and calls for multi-dimensional, multilayered initiatives and responses. It has proved a challenge for governments because different domains are typically administered through siloed ministries and departments. The task is made all the more difficult by the inchoate and diffuse nature of the threats and the inability to frame an adequate response in the absence of tangible perpetrators.

The rapidity in the development of information technology (IT) and the relative ease with which applications can be commercialised has seen the use of cyberspace expand dramatically in its brief existence. From its initial avatar as an NW created by academics for the use of the military, it has now become a global social and economic and communications platform.

The increasing centrality of cyberspace to human existence is exemplified by facts and figures brought out recently by the International Telecommunications Union (ITU), according to which the number of Internet users has doubled between 2005 and 2010 and surpasses two billion. Users are connecting through a range of devices from the personal computer (PC) to the mobile phone, and using the Internet for a variety of purposes from communication to e-commerce, to data storage.

The rise in the Internet population has meant that while the threats and vulnerabilities inherent to the Internet and cyberspace might have remained more or less the same as before, the probability of disruption has grown apace with the rise in the number of users. While such disruptions are yet to cause permanent or grievous damage worldwide, they serve as a wake-up call to the authorities concerned to initiate measures to improve the security and stability of cyberspace in terms of their own security. Governments are constrained in their responses by pressures exerted by politico-military-national security actors at one end and economic-civil society actors at the other.

Internet Governance - Challenges And Constraints

The success of the Internet has partly been attributed to its relative openness and low barriers (including minimal security features) to entry. However, the same openness, while allowing companies to flourish, has also facilitated those with malicious intent to operate with relative ease.

The origins of the Internet can be traced back to the attempts by the Defence Advanced Research Projects Agency (DARPA) of the US Department of Defence to create a communications NW that would survive a nuclear exchange between the two superpowers of the time. It was subsequently used by academia as a means of communicating and collaborating on research projects. The uniqueness of the Internet in being an open structure with few barriers to entry is the outcome of the circumstances in which it was conceptualised and a result of the worldview of its initial champions. Though a military project, its very nature of being a communications project plus the fact that it was quickly adopted by academics as a means of collaboration led to a quick crossover to the civilian domain. The fact that the technology did not belong to any one company saw the implementation of standards for its various protocols, which was responsible for continuing innovation and improvements of its capabilities.

In the early stages of development of the Internet, much of the task of developing cyberspace was in the hands of line organisations such as the Department of Information Technology (DIT) at the national level or the ITU at the international level, and other expert bodies. While these organisations were competent in their own right, they were unable to bring a holistic perspective to the issue, given their domain-specific focus on issues.

This also resulted in fragmented approaches to cyber security, dictated by different requirements and priorities at different points in time.

Among the many institutions that came up and have endured are the Internet Engineering Task Force (IETF), set up in 1986. It comprised a number of experts on various aspects of the Internet who worked through a cooperative consensus-based decision-making process. The Internet Corporation for Assigned Names and Numbers (ICANN) was created in 1998 on similar principles to manage the Domain Name System (DNS), another key infrastructure of the Internet. Most of the ICANN's powers and functions were devolved to it by the US government, which hitherto controlled DNS. The multi-stakeholder approach to discussing the development of the Internet that was institutionalised though these organisations was further carried forward in the UN-sponsored series of conferences beginning with the World Summits on the Information Society held in 2003 and 2005, and ultimately resulting in the Internet Governance Forum (IGF), convened by and reporting to the UN Secretary General.

The US has had a major influence on the development of cyberspace by virtue of the fact that much of the initial infrastructure and use was centred in that country and it continues to be a major force in its development and use. The US has thus been in a position to fend off periodic attempts to challenge its supremacy, and those times when it has been forced to shed some of its control, as in the case of ICANN, it has done so very reluctantly. Though it has been a participant in multilateral fora, the United States' agenda invariably has been to ensure that its dominant position is not disturbed. More recently, approaches to cyberspace have taken on ideological hues, with countries ultimately seeking to gain effective control over deciding the form and shape of cyberspace within their national boundaries.

The jockeying for influence to impact Internet governance issues has seen increased activity in recent times. Most of these have taken place at the multilateral level, with countries forming coalitions and introducing resolutions at multilateral fora.

While Russia has been introducing resolutions on cyber security at the United Nations since 1998, it recently joined hands with China, Tajikistan and Uzbekistan to introduce an "International Code of Conduct for Information Security" (ICCIS).

Some of the clauses within this resolution have been criticised as an attempt to increase control over content and information in the guise of securing cyberspace. Proposals by the IBSA forum (India, Brazil, South Africa) have also been seen with similar scepticism. One of the unstated goals of the recent Cyber Security Summit held by the British government would be seen as an effort on the part of the advanced economies to regain the initiative in drawing up norms for cyberspace that highlight core Western values.

The Indian Cyberspace

The National Informatics Centre (NIC) was set up as early as 1975 with the goal of providing IT solutions to the government. Between 1986 and 1988, three NWs were set up: INDONET, connecting the IBM mainframe installations that made up India's computer infrastructure; NICNET (the NIC Network), being a nationwide very small aperture terminal (VSAT) NW for public sector organisations as well as to connect the central government with the state governments and district administrations; and the Education and Research Network (ERNET), to serve the academic and research communities.

Policies such as the New Internet Policy of 1998 paved the way for multiple Internet service providers (ISPs) and saw the Internet user base grow from 1.4 million in 1999 to over 15 million by 2003. Though the rate of growth has slowed subsequently, with Internet users now approximately numbering 100 million, exponential growth is again expected as Internet access increasingly shifts to mobile phones and tablets, with the government making a determined push to increase broadband penetration from its present level of about 6%. The target for broadband is 160 million households by 2016 under the National Broadband Plan.

According to the Report for 2010 of the Telecom Regulatory Authority of India (TRAI), over 381 million mobile subscribers possessed the ability to access the Internet through their mobiles, with 35 million having accessed at least once. of the Internet across various segments.

The two top email providers, Gmail and Yahoo, had over 34 million users registered from India. Similar figures have also been seen in the social networking arena, which is the most recent entrant to the cyber platform. India currently has the fastest growing user base for Facebook and Twitter, the two top social networking sites. An indication of the rapid pace of adaptation to the Internet in India is that Indian Railways, India's top e-commerce retailer, saw its online sales go up from 19 million tickets in 2008 to 44 million in 2009, with a value of Rs. 3800 crore ($875 million).

Even though the Indian government was a late convert to computerisation, there has been an increasing thrust on e-governance, seen as a cost-effective way of taking public services to the masses across the country. Critical sectors such as Defence, Energy, Finance, Space, Telecommunications, Transport, Land Records, Public Essential Services and Utilities, Law Enforcement and Security all increasingly depend on NWs to relay data, for communication purposes and for commercial transactions. The National e-governance Program (NeGP) is one of the most ambitious in the world and seeks to provide more than 1200 governmental services online.

Looking to the future, the Cisco Visual Networking Index estimates that India's Internet traffic will grow nine-fold between now and 2015, topping out at 13.2 Exabytes in 2015, from 1.6 Exabytes in 2010. That will be the equivalent of the data contained in 374,372 DVDs being carried every hour through these NWs.

In terms of contribution to the economy, the ICT sector has grown at an annual compounded rate of 33% over the last decade. The contribution of the IT-ITeS industry to GDP increased from 5.2% in 2006-7 to 6.4% in 2010-11. Much of the activities of the IT/BPO sector, which was responsible for putting India on the services export map, would not have been possible but for the cost-efficiencies provided through the expansion of global data NWs.

The government has ambitious plans to raise cyber connectivity. There has been a boom in e-commerce, and many activities related to e-governance are now being carried out over the Internet. As we grow more dependent on the Internet for our daily activities, we also become more vulnerable to any disruptions caused in and through cyberspace. The rapidity with which this sector has grown has meant that governments and private companies are still trying to figure out both the scope and meaning of security in cyberspace and apportioning responsibility. As in other countries, much of the infrastructure related to cyberspace is with the private sector, which also provides many of the critical services, ranging from banking, to electricity to running airports and other key transportation infrastructure. Taking telecommunications as a case in point, CII in India comprises around 150 Internet and telecom service providers, offering Internet, mobile and wireless connectivity to a user base of nearly 800 million. A major portion of data communication is facilitated by submarine cables. India has landing points for major submarine cable systems which are minimally protected. A preview of what could happen by way of these cables being disabled took place in 2008 when a series of outages and cable cuts in undersea cables running through the Suez Canal, in the Persian Gulf and Malaysia caused massive communications disruptions to India and West Asia. Other sectors that could be subject to serious threats include the financial sector, which has largely transferred operations online. Stock exchanges in the United States and Hong Kong have reportedly been subject to cyber attacks. The electricity grid is also vulnerable with the inevitable move towards a smart grid, given the economic and efficiency factors. The protection of critical infrastructure is a complex task requiring forethought, planning, strong laws, technologies, PPP and resources. For all these reasons it needs to be given top priority by the government. The country cannot afford to wait indefinitely for a robust policy to protect this critical infrastructure. Above all, the political will needs to be mustered to take the challenge head on.

The government would necessarily have to work closely with the private sector, particularly in promoting cyber security practices and hygiene.

Cyber Threats

Cyber threats can be disaggregated, based on the perpetrators and their motives, into four baskets: cyber espionage, cyber warfare, cyberterrorism, and cyber crime. Cyber attackers use numerous vulnerabilities in cyberspace to commit these acts. They exploit the weaknesses in software and hardware design through the use of malware. DOSS attacks are used to overwhelm the targeted websites. Hacking is a common way of piercing the defences of protected computer systems and interfering with their functioning. Identity theft is also common. The scope and nature of threats and vulnerabilities is multiplying with every passing day.

NATIONAL CYBER SECURITY POLICY

The NCSP essentially speaks of a framework for the protection of information in cyberspace by eliminating vulnerabilities. Major clauses include greater emphasis on research and development of indigenous security technology, and their effective testing and deployment. The policy also calls for enhanced public and private partnership vis-à-vis technical and operational cooperation, aimed at encouraging organizations to adopt individually tailored IT regulations and infrastructure, in conformity with international best practices. Development of human resources through training programs and other capacity-building measures is another crucial priority. The policy envisions creating a workforce of 500,000 cyber specialists in the next five years. Auxiliary services like the protection of private information in process, transit and storage; the creation of a well-defined legislative framework to deal with criminal investigations and prosecution; and the promotion of individual responsibility in dealing with cyber security also find a mention in the policy.

The policy has also facilitated the creation of a new agency called the National Critical Information Infrastructure Protection Centre (NCIIPC), charged with protecting assets in sensitive sectors such as defence, finance, energy, and telecommunications. The Indian Computer Emergency Response Team (CERT-In), which was previously tasked with security of national assets, now protects cyber assets in non-critical areas, and also acts as the nodal agency for all cyber security emergencies with round-the-clock functionality.

Despite being a positive step towards securing India's cyber assets, the NCSP is far from answering all nuances of the cyber threat, as they exist today.

The most critical factor is the lack of details, along with a feasible nationwide strategy to achieve the objectives set out in the policy. Unlike statutes, policies passed by the Indian legislature are neither binding nor enforceable, but merely provide guidelines for a standard operating procedure. In this regard, the NCSP does not maximize its potential for optimum benefit. The text of the policy is easy to comprehend, as it basically outlines the perceived requirement to amend the existing framework and make it better suited to countering the threat of cyber attacks today. Yet the NCSP fails to comment on any political, economic or legal measure it intends to implement to achieve this objective. The Indian government budgeted just $7.76 million for cyber security in 2013, compared with at least $751 million spent by the U.S. government on its cyberspace programs.

"Indian agencies don't have enough resources. Their budget should be at least 10 times bigger if they have to function properly," says Subimal Bhattacharjee, a cyber security expert and former India head of the U.S. information systems giant General Dynamics.

A crucial point missing entirely from the NCSP is the security concerns in the telecom industry. Today, telecommunications are fully integrated into cyberspace, since the advent of internet protocols on mobile devices, and this has been identified as one of the primary factors for the increase in the number of attacks. Russian cyber security solutions firm Kaspersky Lab placed India second on its 2013 list of those countries must vulnerable to attacks on mobile phones.

For its telecom industry, India incorporates equipment and infrastructure from global telecom companies, primarily Huawei Technologies Co.,Ltd., a leading Chinese telecommunications and networking equipment company, founded by Ren Zhengfei. It should be noted that Ren Zhengfei, an ex-major with the PLA, enjoys extensive ties with the Chinese military and the Communist Party, having been elected a member of the 12th National Congress of the Communist Party of China. For their part, the U.S. and U.K. have severely curbed Huawei's foray into their respective markets.

Another notable point on which the NCSP maintains an ambiguous silence are the deliberations presently underway on setting up a fully fledged Indian Cyber Command, under the aegis of the defence services, to engage in network-centric warfare. Should this actually happen, a question of jurisdiction will arise, one that could easily become a quagmire.

Even though the NCSP was released over a year ago, any benefits are yet to materialize. In the meantime, Indian companies and government organizations continue to defend themselves against unconventional warfare, which they do not understand in its entirety. Still, as the Dell Software Global Security Survey reports, companies in the Asia-Pacific have at least begun to prioritize their IT policies, to be in a better position to counter threats.

CERT-In's recent survey labels the *.in* domain as the most frequently attacked, which is alarming as this address is primarily used by government agencies and a few major private companies. Full statistics of the survey can be found here.

Meanwhile, the Indian government seems to have realized the urgency of the need to develop cyber security training. In January 2013, the University Grants Commission directed technical universities and institutions to add Cyber Security and Information Security as subjects for higher studies. Premier institutes like the Institute for Information Security and Indian School of Ethical Hacking now offer these technical courses, as do a few major private universities in India. The key to cyber security in India lies in the effective operationalization of the NCSP. Workshops, seminars and courses aimed at informing the general public about the issue of cyber security, coupled with feasible public-private partnerships will work to offset the threat to India's online assets in the long run.

INDIA'S ICT INFRASTRUCTURE

The growth of IT sector in India has been fuelled by equally impressive growth in telecommunication infrastructure. The world is moving towards converged networks being referred as 'Next Generation Networks (NGN)'. In the coming decade the NGN is likely to replace the legacy networks. This upcoming national information infrastructure would be marriage of IT and telecommunication infrastructure with various regulatory and security challenges that need careful scrutiny.

Regulatory issues concerning regulators around the world:

The deployment of NGN throws up many regulatory challenges. License conditions and regulations need to be revisited with a light touch regulatory approach with participation of all stakeholders to ensure smooth transition.

In case of legacy networks the business model, network and competition were already in place before establishment of formal regulatory framework. NGN permits us a window of opportunity to review regulatory framework by proactive consultation process and spirit of accommodation amongst all stakeholders. Regulators in many developing countries including India (TRAI, 2008) have begun process of firming up broad principles for NGN deployment ahead of actual transition.

Telecom sector in India is on a growth profile, and time is ripe to examine regulatory and licensing approaches for NGN deployment. New competitive networks are just being established and consumer's take-up of IP services and Broadband is at a nascent stage.

The recommendation on the security of NGN by expert committee on NGN vide para 3.4.2.2 (TRAI,2008) states:

"NGN-eCO acknowledged that security is of paramount importance to any network. Therefore, TEC may be asked to work on various aspects of security for the country keeping in view the global trends".

Imperatives for India's response to Cyber Threats

If one looks at the challenges India faces in the backdrop of the task of steering our ICT infrastructure on a sustainable and safe trajectory various factors emerge which suggest a synergetic approach. The ICT infrastructure should support diverse social objectives of empowering our rural masses, E–Governance, E-Commerce and disaster warning/relief. The details of India's initiative to secure her cyber infrastructure as available through open source is in stark contrast to the initiatives taken by the USA in the aftermath of attacks in September 2001. While it is true that each country should initiate measures as suitable for its needs and at a pace that is viable in its context, India with her aspiration to be IT superpower in the coming decade can ill afford to lag behind. Various lead agencies in USA to protect her critical Infrastructure as described in 'The national strategy to secure cyber space' document (DHS, 2008).

The Homeland Security Act of 2002 in USA provides the basis for Department of Homeland Security (DHS) responsibilities in the protection of the Nation's Critical Infrastructure and Key Resources (CI/KR). The act assigns DHS the responsibility to develop a comprehensive national plan for securing CI/KR and for recommending "measures necessary to protect the key resources and critical infrastructure of the United States in coordination with other agencies of the Federal Government and in cooperation with State and local government agencies and authorities, the private sector, and other entities."

USA has National Infrastructure Protection Plan (NIPP) in place under Department of Homeland Security (DHS,2008) with following goal:

"Build a safer, more secure, and more resilient America by enhancing protection of the Nation's Critical Infrastructure and Key Resources (CI/KR) to prevent, deter, neutralize, or mitigate the effects of deliberate efforts by terrorists to destroy, incapacitate, or exploit them; and to strengthen national preparedness, timely response, and rapid recovery in the event of an attack, natural disaster, or other emergency."

The NIPP provides the unifying structure for the integration of existing and future CI/KR protection efforts into a single national program to achieve this goal. The NIPP framework will enable the prioritization of protection initiatives and investments across sectors to ensure that government and private sector resources are applied where they offer the most benefit for mitigating risk by lessening vulnerabilities, deterring threats, and minimizing the consequences of terrorist attacks and other manmade and natural disasters. The NIPP risk management framework recognizes and builds on existing protective programs and initiatives.

Protection includes actions to mitigate the overall risk to CI/KR assets, systems, networks, functions, or their interconnecting links resulting from exposure, injury, destruction, incapacitation, or exploitation. In the context of the NIPP, this includes actions to deter the threat, mitigate vulnerabilities, or minimize consequences associated with a terrorist attack or other incident. Protection can include a wide range of activities, such as hardening facilities, building resiliency and redundancy, incorporating hazard resistance into initial facility design, initiating active or passive countermeasures, installing security systems, promoting workforce surety programs, and implementing cyber security measures, among various others.

The White House issued 'The National Strategy to Secure Cyberspace' in February 2003. The Department of Homeland Security (DHS) established the National Cyber Security Division (NCSD) in June 2003 to serve as a national focal point for addressing cyber security issues and to coordinate implementation of the cyber security strategy in the United States. NCSD's mission is to work collaboratively with public, private, and international entities to secure cyberspace and cyber assets, and to implement the actions and recommendations of 'The National Strategy to Secure Cyberspace'.

According to audit report submitted by Office of Inspector General (OIG) U.S. Department of Homeland Security in June 2007, there are still challenges in securing the cyber space in USA (OIG, 2007). While the National Cyber Security Division has made progress in meeting its mission, according to OIG report it can improve its efforts to secure the nation's cyber infrastructure in following areas:

- Establish priorities to ensure that its mission-critical tasks supporting its programs are completed timely.
- Develop enhanced performance measures that can be used to evaluate the effectiveness in meeting its mission.
- Fully develop its information sharing and communications programs with the private sector.
- Develop and implement enhanced procedures to ensure that all known cyber incidents from across the federal government are being reported.
- Ensure that its support systems comply with all 'Federal Information Security Management Act' requirements, including testing of contingency plans.

In Indian context creation of National Disaster Management Authority (NDMA) under an act of parliament was motivated by similar concerns for mitigating and managing national disasters from natural and manmade causes.

"To build a safer and disaster resilient India by developing a holistic, pro-active, multi-disaster and technology-driven strategy for disaster management through collective efforts of all Government Agencies and Non-Governmental Organizations"

In order to translate this Vision into policy and plans, the NDMA which appears to be nearest to USA's Department of Homeland Security, has adopted a mission-mode approach involving a number of initiatives with the help of various institutions operating at national, state and local levels. The central ministries, states and other stakeholders have been involved in the participatory and consultative process of evolving policies and guidelines.

This Policy framework is also in conformity with the International Strategy for Disaster Reduction, the Rio Declaration, the Millennium Development Goals and the Hyogo Framework 2005-2015. The themes underpinning this policy are:

- Community-based disaster management, including last mile integration of the policy, plans and execution.
- Capacity development in all related areas.
- Consolidation of past initiatives and best practices.
- Cooperation with agencies at national, regional and international levels.
- Compliance and coordination to generate a multi-sectoral synergy.
- From the national vision and aforementioned theme, the objectives guiding the policy formulation have evolved to include:
- Promoting a culture of prevention and preparedness – by centre-staging DM as an overriding priority at all levels and at all times.

- Encouraging mitigation measures based on state-of-the-art technology and environmental sustainability.
- Mainstreaming DM concerns into the development planning process.
- Putting in place a streamlined institutional techno-legal framework in order to create and preserve the integrity of an enabling regulatory environment and a compliance regime.
- Developing contemporary forecasting and early warning systems backed by responsive and fail- safe communications and Information Technology (IT) support.
- Promoting a productive partnership with the Media, NGOs and the Corporate Sector in the areas of awareness generation and capacity development.
- Ensuring efficient response and relief with a caring humane approach towards the vulnerable sections of the society.
- Making reconstruction an opportunity to build back better and construct disaster-resilient structures and habitats.

A quick tour of the NDMA's portal gives a feeling that unless NDMA is unwilling to share its plans with public, a lot needs to be done to achieve same coherence as being practiced by most of the developed world with USA being just an illustrative case. There seems to be no division equivalent to the National Cyber Security Division (NCSD) under DHS in USA. NCSD like organization would formalize our steps towards holistic cyber security.

INDIA'S CHALLENGE

Post liberalization, Information Technology (IT), electricity and telecom sector has witnessed large investments by private sector. Infrastructure development using private investment is being pursued in many developing countries including India. However, inadequate focus to disaster preparedness and recovery in regulatory frameworks is a cause of concern. No single operator controls the IT, Telecom or Power sectors and, therefore, responsibility to prepare for, and recover from, disasters is diffused. All operators are driven by the "bottom line," and cannot expend resources on activities that do not contribute to profit (Srivastava, Samarajiva, 2001).

Enterprise level customers value reliable service, including adequate levels of disaster preparedness and recovery. They would be willing to pay for the reliability and survivability of business critical ICT infrastructure. However, in the absence of institutionalized vulnerability analysis and benchmarking of ICT infrastructure, status quo is maintained.

In view of the grave repercussions of infrastructure failure in core sectors like power and telecom, government driven regulatory initiative would be justified even after liberalization. Pragmatic regulation would achieve twin objectives of attracting and retaining private investment to the infrastructure sector; and, efficacy in terms of disaster preparedness and recovery. Government agencies, business houses and common citizen alike are embracing the fast evolving ICT infrastructure to facilitate India's march towards e-governance and e-commerce. However, vulnerability of this infrastructure to natural and man made disaster and consequent cascading effect on our national security remains unarticulated.

National Telecom Policy (NTP, 1999) while emphasizing the need for growth of our communication infrastructure, does not specifically address vulnerabilities and action plan. National Disaster Management Authority has highlighted the need for reliable and robust communication support for disaster management and expected performance objectives are being firmed up (NDMA, 2008). Objectives enunciated on official web site of India's Department of Telecommunication (DOT, 2008) do not make any specific mention on this subject. It is surmised that policy makers know these vulnerabilities and suitable remedial measures are being taken. It would be prudent to bring these issues in the open through government–industry dialogue to evolve mutually beneficial arrangements

Initiatives taken in Indian Context

India started a process of economic liberalization in the 1990s. One of the main features of this process has been to simplify rules and regulations to attract foreign investment. As a result of this, India is becoming easier to enter from a regulatory and commercial point of view but there are still issues to overcome, one of them being Indian privacy standards for the outsourcing company. India lacks specific laws on privacy and data protection, how ever, there are proxy laws and other indirect safeguards, which provide adequate protection to companies off shoring work. Indian IT act in conjunction with other related acts.

As outsourcing becomes more widespread and competition in the marketplace grows, the ability to illustrate the existence and continued use of powerful safeguards will increasingly become one of the significant factors for companies that are deciding which provider to link up with. The Ministry of Information Technology, on August 29, 2005, proposed certain amendments to the Indian IT Act 2000. These amendments have been incorporated vide Information Technology (Amendment) Act, 2006.

In 1975, during fifth five year plan (1972-77), Govt of India strategically decided to take effective steps for development of information systems and information resources to overcome 'digital divide' National Informatics Centre (NIC) created towards this objective has been instrumental in steering information and communication technology (ICT) applications in government departments at centre, states and districts facilitating improvement in government services, wider transparency in government functions and improvements in decentralized planning and management.

In 1999 central government created a new ministry of information technology (MIT) by merging the department of electronics (DOE), national informatics centre (NIC) and electronics and software export promotion council. New Telecom Policy (NTP) announced in same year provided the much needed policy framework. In recognition of the convergence of IT and telecommunication, Department of Telecommunication (DOT) was later merged with MIT to give birth to ministry of communication and IT. Creation of Telecom Regulatory Authority of India (TRAI) in 1997 and Telecom Dispute Settlement and Appellate Tribunal (TDSAT) in 2000 gave regulatory framework to India's fast evolving telecommunication infrastructure.

To customize applications for facilitating decision support in development and responsive administration NIC has established its project centre at National Informatics Centre Network (NICNET) nodes. NIC implements IT projects in collaboration with central and state governments in the area of E-governance. The cyber security of the ICT infrastructure being created for E-governance is responsibility of cyber security group in NIC. However NIC website does not provide any details (NIC, 2008).

STQC under Dept of Information Technology (DIT), Govt of India, (MIT,2008) provides assurance services for Software Quality testing, Information Security and IT Service Management by conducting testing, training, audit and certifications. Based on this concept a Conformity Assessment Framework (CAF) for e-Governance project has also been developed and is in operation.

CERT-In functioning under DIT is India's response to cyber threats and has following charter, mission and constituency.

CYBER SECURITY CHALLENGES

Cyberspace comprises IT networks, computer resources, and all the fixed and mobile devices connected to the global Internet. A nation's cyberspace is part of the global cyberspace; it cannot be isolated to define its boundaries since cyberspace is borderless. This is what makes cyberspace unique. Unlike the physical world that is limited by geographical boundaries in space—land, sea, river waters, and air—cyberspace can and is continuing to expand. Increased Internet penetration is leading to growth of cyberspace, since its size is proportional to the activities that are carried through it.

Nations are investing heavily in their ICT infrastructures with a view to providing higher bandwidths, integrate national economies with the global marketplace, and to enable citizens or "netizens" to access more and more e-services.

Given the security problems, there is increased emphasis on, and investment in, the security of cyber infrastructure. Core Internet protocols are insecure, and an explosion of mobile devices continues to be based on the same insecure systems. This is adding up to increased usage of the Internet in more vulnerable cyberspace.

Protection of critical infrastructure operations has emerged as a major challenge. This is because trillions of dollars move through the networks every day involving a broad range of activities, including e-commerce, e-governance, travel, hospitality, health care, and general communications. Electricity distribution, water distribution, and several other utility services are based on ICT infrastructures. The defence sector relies heavily on electronic systems.

Ownership and Responsibility

Critical infrastructure is largely owned and operated by the private sector. But is security only the private sector's responsibility? Does this mean that government has a lesser role? These are some of the important cyber security issues that nations are grappling with. At an organizational level, too, cyber security is not merely a technology issue, but a management issue. This is grounded in enterprise risk management, which calls for an understanding of the human, process, legal, network, and ICT security aspects.

It is obvious that multiple agencies are involved in securing ICT infrastructure. These include private operators for their respective pieces of the infrastructure. Their efforts need to be firmly coordinated through an integrated command-and-control entity, which should serve as a unifying structure that is accountable for cyber security.

Roles and responsibilities of each of the parties need to be clearly defined. At the same time, governments need to establish the appropriate policy and legal structures. Nations, such as the United States, have advocated for a market-based, voluntary approach to industry cyber security as part of the National Strategy to Secure Cyberspace. But this has not worked entirely, because security investments made by industry, as per their corporate needs, are not found to be commensurate with the broader national interest. How will the additional private investments be generated? Is there a case for government incentives, as part of an incentive program to bridge the gap between those security investments already made and those additional ones that are needed to secure critical infrastructure?

Several security surveys point to this need. They reveal a lack of adequate knowledge among executives about security policy and incidents, the latest technological solutions, data leakage, financial loss, and the training that is needed for their employees.

Since cyberspace is relatively new, legal concepts for "standards of care" do not exist. Is there a case for governments to offer incentives to generate collective action? For example, they could provide reduced liability or tax incentives as a trade off for improved security, new regulatory requirements, and compliance mechanisms. Governments need to provide incentives for industry to invest in security at a level that is not justified by corporate business plans.

THE FIGHT AGAINST CRIMINAL CYBER NETWORKS

Security firms have battled botnets for many years, but only in the last 18 months, with takedowns of rogue ISPs (especially McColo), has the security community been more aware of opportunities to disrupt botnets, and grown more confident that this online menace can be successfully fought.

Botnets are distributed networks of 'zombie' or 'bot' PCs, infected by malware which enables them to be marshalled by cyber criminals primarily to distribute enormous volumes of spam and other malware and launch phishing attacks via e-mail.

Botnets have been around for years. Back in 2003–ancient history in internet terms–security firms often saw thousands of PCs infected with the Sobig mass-mailing virus, and later in that same year, when the Fizzer malware logged thousands of computers into internet relay chat (IRC) rooms. At that time this was perceived only as a problem for IRC admins. In fact, the infected PCs were being connected to chat rooms by their human bot-masters, waiting to receive command and control (C&C) instructions. It was only when MessageLabs Intelligence correlated the malware and spam traffic from each spam sending IP address, that the bigger picture was later revealed.

Over the years security firms kept botnets under observation, doing their best to inhibit their ever-increasing output of spam, but not knowing how to tackle their C&C infrastructure. Then in October 2008, the security community stepped up efforts to disrupt the botnets and start to pursue the ISPs that hosted them.

The first high profile ISP to go at the end of September 2008 was Intercage (aka Atrivo), linked to the infamous Russian Business Network. However, the most widely publicised was McColo, a San Jose-based ISP, which was found to deal almost exclusively with cyber gangs. McColo, set up by a 19 year-old Russian, was host to a botnet called Srizbi controlling 1.3 million IP addresses, as well as the Mega-D, Rustock, Asprox, Bobax and Gheg botnets.

In November 2008, community action resulted in McColo's peering ISPs disconnecting it from the internet, largely because of an article written by Brian Krebs in the Washington Post. Taking down McColo came as a shock to the botnet gangs and spam levels dropped instantly by as much as 80 per cent, which represented an enormous victory against the spammers.

Srizbi was crippled, never to return and the other botnets were badly disrupted. Over the following two months, spam gradually recovered to previous levels, as the surviving botnets relocated their command and control channels, the criminals spawned several new botnets as well.

The operations behind many of these botnets were forced to re-evaluate how they functioned and sought to put more protection in place to prevent a repeat of the huge disruption caused by the take-down of a single ISP. Take-downs like McColo must cost bot herders and spammers hundreds of thousands of dollars-perhaps millions-in lost revenues.

When Srizbi disappeared, activity from the surviving botnets increased dramatically, seeking to fill the huge gap in the market left behind. At that time, Srizbi had been responsible for as much as 50 percent of all spam. After losing their botnet of choice, spammers rented capacity from other botnet operators in order to keep up their spam campaigns.

However, when the next major take-down of a dubious ISP took place, it was clear that the cyber criminals had already learned from the strike against McColo.

This time the security community's target was another California-based ISP called 3FN (aka APS Telecom and Pricewert) which was hosting command and control channels for Cutwail (aka Pandex), one of the oldest botnets which had been spewing out malware since January 2007. By June 2009 Cutwail had swollen to more than 1.5 million active IP addresses in an aggressive recruitment drive.

3FN was put under a preliminary injunction by the FTC on Friday 5 June 2009 and Cutwail went with it. But within a couple of days, by Monday morning, Cutwail was back online and as strong as before.

Botnet gangs had made many refinements to their creations in the six months since the McColo take-down. Thus the organisations behind Cutwail were able to quickly reorganise after losing an important part of their botnet infrastructure. The fact that the technology was now much more flexible and robust allowed them to review the status of the botnet and return to business as usual in just a few days. It was clear that botnets now had a business continuity or disaster recovery plan of their own. The botnet C&C mechanisms had shifted away from IRC towards HTTP. Instead of receiving instructions from one place, algorithms were built into the bots so they would look for random-looking domain names, which are purchased by the botnet gang each day, and from which the bots receive their commands. This ensures that the botnets aren't so reliant on one ISP.

But as the botnet controllers evolved their tactics, so did the security firms. One botnet in particular had grown significantly in the wake of the McColo take-down; a botnet called Mega-D (aka Ozdok). By November 2009, the algorithms behind the C&C mechanism used to issue the botnet with new instructions were broken by FireEye, a security company that specializes in combating botnets. It was now possible to predict which domain names were to be used by the botnet and to register them in advance of the botnet controllers. It was almost like cracking the Enigma code; and for the first time it was possible to know the botnet's next move and to register these domains faster than the botnet controllers.

Mega-D appeared to be crippled, its spam-sending days seemed to be over, until a few days later, MessageLabs Intelligence identified large volumes of Mega-D spam being distributed from IP addresses that had not been used to send spam previously. This suggested that the botnet controllers had enacted their business continuity plan, seemingly with inactive sleeper bots or perhaps even a whole parallel backup botnet.

Disaster Recovery isn't the only tenet that botnet controllers have borrowed from the world of corporate IT; they also use a technique called "fast-flux" hosting, which dynamically distributes resources across a number of continually changing IP addresses using a form of "round-robin" DNS. In the hands of a botnet controller, fast-flux can hide the true location of websites used to host malware, spam and phishing content, by hiding them behind the IP addresses of compromised, botnet-controlled computers, each acting as a web server or proxy.

Another technique that botnet controllers use to hide their botnets from the prying eyes of security firms is to expose only a small proportion of their zombies at any one time, cycling their use over a period of several days and limiting the amount of spam sent from each to minimise the risk of them appearing in backlists of known spam-sending IP addresses.

Until recently, botnet controllers had to recruit one PC at a time. But with the advent of "generic droppers" like Bredolab, and perhaps Conficker, larger botnets can be assembled to order, whether for a spam campaign or something even more sinister.

Cyber criminals can now purchase the control of thousands– even tens of thousands-of ready-compromised PCs, recruited en masse to their own botnet. For example, cyber criminals may pay for malware, spyware or botnet Trojans to be installed by the Bredolab operators who would then instruct the Bredolab botnet to "drop" the malware onto however many computers were needed, using computers that were already under their control. This takes botnet recruitment from a random, scattergun approach where PCs are infected at random, to a more commoditized recruitment campaign. The only limitation to the size of the botnet is how much the criminals are prepared to spend.

Now cyber criminals with enough cash can set up a botnet operation and be in business virtually overnight.

As botnets grow in sophistication and number, there is a danger of them becoming an extension of the hidden world of international and industrial espionage. The authorities in many countries are now concerned that attacks on government and business resources will become the next battleground in cyber warfare. The botnet could become the weapon of choice to disrupt infrastructure, and a lot less expensive-or traceable- than a ballistic missile.

6

India's National Security Policy and Strategy

The concept of national security rests mainly on the proposition that many foreign and domestic political, economic and military issues are inter-related, each with implications on the other. In India's case, this has been highlighted by insurgencies and other political events, particularly in border-states, and other outside pressures, which are brought to bear on the country's economy and technological progress from time to time.

A response to this type of environment calls for a highly focussed national security policy and strategy. Effective guidance on national security and defence policy objectives is fundamental to the defence planning process. National security is a relative matter without a firm criteria but unless firm national security objectives are set and a defence policy evolved, there can be no military doctrine or balancing of defence effort with other national objectives and priorities such as maintaining a viable economy and supporting development of society.

The lack of a cohesive national security strategy and defence policy has many implications. First, it results in the absence of clear political direction regarding politico-military objectives, which is the very basis of sound defence planning. Secondly, there is inadequate coordination of defence plans and economic development. Finally, science and technology policies for defence, general industrialisation and other development programmes are not coordinated properly to achieve security goals and objectives.

Perspective Planning

A Defence Plan has to be prepared on the basis of a 15-year long perspective planning system, such that the first five years of the plan are very firm (Definitive Plan), the second five years less firm (Indicative Plan) and the third five-year term tentative (Vision Plan). There has to be a reasonably firm allocation of financial resources for the first five years and an indicative allocation for the subsequent period. Perspective planning needs to be done in the Integrated Defence Headquarters, where military, technical and R&D experts take an integrated view of future threats and challenges. This has to be based on future battlefield scenarios, and array of forecasts, evaluation of strategic options and force mixes, and analysis of potential technical and industrial capabilities. Based on this, the respective Service should work on their perspective plans and the R&D and Defence Production/Supplies experts should spell out their requirements in terms of effort, technology and indigenous production.

Integrated Planning

As stated earlier, the CDS, who would be the cornerstone of integrated operational planning for defence, has not been appointed. India's defence planning, therefore, continues to be Service based. Often, the threat perception of one Service is at variance with that of another Service. What emerges is essentially a sum of total of Service or department wise programmes. The focus is not on overall goals or priorities but on what is required by a particular Service. In its endeavour to lay the groundwork for an increased share of the budget, each Service tends to exercise its own priorities, favouring its own plans to the detriment of joint plans.

Subjects like surveillance, air defence, electronic warfare, and amphibious operations, which relate to more than one Service, do not get adequate attention. Integrated planning for defence is essential for creating balanced force structures and for the successful execution of all military missions. In fact, it is the most effective manner of ensuring effective defence. According to Charles Hitch, "the revolution in military technology has not only changed the character of our military programmes, it has also to a significant degree blurred the lines of demarcation among various Services". Most major military missions today require the participation of more than one military service. Therefore, the principal concern now must be centred on what is required by the defence establishment as a whole to perform a particular mission—not what is required by a particular Service to perform its individual part of that 'mission'. The areas of commonality in modern weapon systems are immense and growing rapidly. Communications, guidance systems, missiles, radars, lasers—even traditional equipment such as guns, fuses, ammunition and vehicles are common. Integrated defence planning is necessary in view of escalating costs of these weapons and equipment.

Self-reliance in Defence Technology

The DRDO has a network of 51 laboratories and establishments. The Scientific Advisor (SA) to the Raksha Mantri (RM) is the Secretary of this Department. The DRDO has a staff of 30,000, including 6,800 scientists and engineers. It receives approximately four to six per cent of the defence budget annually.

The DRDO is engaged in the pursuit of self-reliance in critical technologies relevant to defence. It formulates and executes a programme of scientific research, design and development for the induction into the Armed Forces of state-of-the-art weapons and other equipments. In April 1984, the DRDO envisaged a programme "to transform the Department into a leader of international class with the mission to capture and retain commanding heights in critical technologies". A 'mission mode' organisational structure and approach was approved by the Government with a view to increasing the element of self-reliance from the current 30 per cent to 70 per cent by 2005. This goal, however, is nowhere in sight.

The Department has developed more than 1,100 items of weapon systems and equipment with a production value of over Rs 6,000 crore. But it has not been able to make any major contribution to the state-of-art weapons and equipment. Most of its programmes, like Prithvi (sea borne version), Trishul (short-range surface to air missile), Akash (medium-range surface to air missile), Nag (anti-tank missile), Light Combat Aircraft with Kaveri engine, Pinaka (multiple-barrel rocket system), MBT Arjun, Electronic Warfare equipment, new radio sets for the Army, Sonar system for Navy, and many other items, are way behind schedule.

Despite the media hype, the costs have been heavy. MBT Arjun, when it goes into production mode, will have more than 60 per cent imported components, including several crucial components like the engine and gun control system. It will cost over Rs 25 crore a piece whereas the cost of a T-90 tank, which is as superior (if not more), is less than Rs 10 crore along with technology transfer. Matters have come to such a pass that the Armed Forces have stopped believing media reports about the so-called 'successful trials' of weapons and equipment.

Because of the failure to deliver the required weapons and equipment, defence planning and Force structuring by the Services has suffered continuously. The DRDO's inability to deliver in time has caused a crisis of confidence and constant dissatisfaction in the Services. In order to ensure smooth progress towards self-reliance in defence technology, the Government must undertake a periodic performance audit of DRDO projects to reinforce efforts in areas of success and weed out projects that are unproductive.

POLICE AND INTELLIGENCE AGENCIES

The main police body within the NCTC will be the NIA. The NIA is, however, a strictly limited agency that will not have the capacity according to its current legislation to provide the link between the intelligence agencies and state police. The NIA will need to be properly resourced and staffed, which is still not the case. The NIA Act is seemingly generous in providing agency officers with India-wide powers in respect of scheduled offences. The Act states at 3(3):

Any officer of the Agency of, or above, the rank of Sub-Inspector may ... exercise throughout India, any of the powers of the officer-in-charge of a police station in the area in which he is present for the time being and when so exercising such powers shall, subject to any such orders [of the Central government] as aforesaid, be deemed to be an officer-in-charge of a police station discharging the functions of such an officer within the limits of his station.

The procedures for putting an investigation in motion. Unfortunately, they are somewhat ambiguous and bear some of the hallmarks of hasty drafting. For example, Section 8 allows the investigator to investigate any other offence of the 'accused' related to the original offence scheduled under the Act. It is not clear whether this can only happen after an arrest, but presumably the reference to the 'accused' signifies that this is the case.

If so, then that will be a serious limiting factor in the scope of the investigations. Another limiting factor comes about through the system of notification.

This stipulates that any scheduled offence reported to any police station in India will be brought to the attention of the 'state' authorities, who will bring it to the attention of the Union Government authorities, who will in turn determine if it is a subject of the Act and bring it to the NIA for investigation. The relevant words of Section 6(1) are: "On receipt of information and recording there of under section 154 of the (Criminal) Code relating to any Scheduled Offence the officer-in-charge of the police station shall forward the report to the State Government forthwith."

Offences scheduled under the Act are: terrorism, counterfeiting of currency, human trafficking, illicit drugs trafficking, organised crime, plane hijacking, violations of the Atomic Energy Act and Weapons of Mass Destruction Act. In addition, all offences alleged against the accused under these scheduled offences may also be investigated.

This seemingly unambiguous stipulation has a myriad of practical implications. The system for involving the NIA in an investigation is extremely cumbersome and could take months. Anyone who has any practical knowledge of investigations knows that it is a virtually impossible situation to be brought into an investigation in the latter stages, when one has no control over the crime scene, collection and maintenance of evidence, or early interrogation processes (which are the most crucial).

But our main issue with the NIA Act is that it does not support the intelligence collection process – which is in turn essential for prevention. It is essentially concerned with an 'offence' reported as a FIR. But intelligence is not about offences or evidence as such (although it can include evidence) but the analysed information surrounding offences and potential offences. It is this information surrounding potential offences that will need to be collected by local-level police and passed upward through the intelligence process. Thus, the NIA Act is not an ideal vehicle for either investigations or intelligence and could prove very difficult to operate. That is not to say, however, that such intelligence will not be passed between Special Branches, the SMACs and the MAC, but rather that, if it is, it will continue to be a 'hit and miss' process. Moreover, and crucially, the intelligence feed from the grassroots will only be as good as the police providing it: and as mentioned above, nothing in the present reform process indicates that the process of state-level policing will be progressed from the present paramilitary thrust under the 1861 Police Act.

INDIA'S SECURITY CHALLENGES: PERSPECTIVES AND PROSPECTS

The profound changes in the world wrought about by the end of the Cold War have made for a fundamental restructuring of international relations. The end of ideological rivalry provided an objective opportunity for evolving a better security environment. However, there is a great deal of uncertainty and fluidity all around, as the new global equilibrium gets in place.

Two or three factors would deserve attention in this regard. The Cold War bipolar structure has been replaced by a "polycentric" world with the United States, Japan, China, the European Union and Russia emerging as the main partners in power. Technology and economic power has moved to the forefront of international relations, emerging as a crucial factor in global realignments in the new setting.

The near symmetry in power capabilities and global reach between the two superpowers in a tightly bipolar world has given way to a certain disaggregation in the levels of power and capabilities among the new centres of power, given their uneven spread of techno-economic power, military capabilities and political influence. Even the United States, the most powerful nation today, has neither the will nor the capability to play a global role of the earlier order and magnitude. China, Japan, the European Union and Russia are in a process of defining their role in the new world order. Relationships between and among these centres of power are increasingly marked by elements of both engagement and containment.

Notwithstanding a broad shift from confrontation to conciliation at the global and regional levels, new points of pressures are unfolding themselves even as some old conflicts remain unresolved. For the developing countries, there is also evidence of new concerted pressures in economic, security and nuclear fields. It is clear that there are manifold pressures emanating from the international environment which make for a complex and multilayered set of challenges and opportunities for India in the changed world order. India would have to respond to, if not anticipate, the new challenges and maximise its strategic political options, drawing essentially from its own power potential and bargaining leverages. This would at the least call for proactive strategies in terms of both restructuring old ties and forging new relationships at the regional and global levels.

India's security perspectives would inevitably be governed by the interplay of its domestic imperatives, regional balance of forces and the global challenges which impinge on its role and capabilities. India with its size, resource potential and strategic location is being increasingly seen as a regional influential poised on the threshold of emerging as a centre of power in the new international order. This is as much a recognition of its credible democratic functioning as the potential of its vast economic resources and political clout. India is a large multiplural society which has been able to successfully manage the challenges emanating from regional, linguistic and religious diversities without damaging its national cohesiveness. The remarkable resilience of its democratic functioning in a secular federal framework, despite some distortions, has continued to bely the scepticism of its worst critics. India's democracy remains fundamentally secure, underpinned as it is by an active judiciary, free media and a functioning and vigilant Opposition. India's economic development has also remained steady over the years. In the last couple of years, the Indian economy has registered an impressive growth rate of 7 per cent. The expansion and diversification of its industrial capacity have made important strides. Currently India ranks among the topmost industrialised nations of the world. It has the distinction of having the third largest pool of trained and scientific manpower in the world. Agricultural production has also shown substantial growth resulting in not only self-sufficiency in food grains but also reserves of impressive buffer stocks. Today with its burgeoning middle class, huge untapped markets for trade and industry, and large scale foreign investments, India has emerged as an economic power of some significance on the global scene. India has also built an impressive level defence capability. It has the fourth largest Army in the world with an impeccable professional record. It has a credible and self-reliant defence structure which has been built assiduously over the past three decades. India's missile development programme has also grown apace underlining its indigenous technological capabilities.

It is clear that India is slated to play an increasingly larger role in the coming decades. Its future as a credible power would, however, depend as much on its ability to manage the present stage of transition as on the projection of its strategic perspectives and policy options for the future. Two or three points deserve mention in this regard. First, India's status and power projections remain essentially contingent on its national security in terms of political stability, economic development and military strength. Second, although the asymmetrical power structure in South Asia ensures India's centrality, its regional power and influence tends to get circumscribed by the neighbouring countries' sustained pressure to counter its pre-eminence. In particular, Pakistan's unceasing search for parity with India makes for a deep-rooted strategic dissonance in the region which effectively reduces its capacity to shape or influence events in its neighbourhood. Third, continued involvement of external powers in the region remains an integral part of South Asian geo-political realities. The end of the Cold War has weakened the inevitable link up between regional conflict and Great Power rivalry. However, the inability of the states of the region to evolve a credible bilateral and regional framework for cooperation would continue to play an important role in reinforcing the pattern of external involvement—primarily in pursuance of their own stategic interests—in the region. This is bound to impinge on India's security perspectives, both short-term and long-term.

An overarching framework of India's national security has to take cognisance of military and non-military dimensions in terms of both external threats and internal challenges to its territorial integrity and national unity. Threats to a nation emanate as much from external aggression as from internal strife but at times internal factors can erode national security more critically than any external danger. National power based on political stability, societal cohesion and economic development would thus remain central to the future of India's national security.

India is passing though a crucial period of its post-independence history. Successively fragile coalition governments at both the central and state levels are affecting India's political, social and economic stability at a time when it is facing major challenges to its unity and integrity as a nation. The Indian political system is being subjected to manifold pressures from the progressive collapse of political and public institutions; incipient erosion of democratic norms; social unrest and corruption underlining a growing malaise in Indian polity. Increasing demands for power by more and more socio-economic groups, on the one hand, and limited resources and capabilities for redistribution of wealth, on the other, make for growing political and social turmoil. Widening economic disparities and growing rate of unemployment pose a major challenge for India's economic development notwithstanding a credible economic performance. It is estimated that by the year 2000, the total number of people living below the poverty line will more than the entire Indian population at the time of independence.

India's growing inability to manage political and economic challenges on the domestic front is a cause of deep concern. Although India's national integrity remains fundamentally secure, pressures from fissiparous cleavages in growing challenges of communalism and religious fanaticism have acquired disturbing dimensions. Political manipulation of religious sentiments for narrow political ends has long-term implications for the future of India's secular federal framework. The incipient threats to Indian federal polity in many parts of the country are putting growing strains on the political structure. Although India has been so far able to manage these challenges with a certain skill and patience, there is growing anxiety about the pressures getting intensified at a time when there is a steady erosion in the state's role in resolving conflict and bringing about social transformation. This is accompanied by a decline in the mediating role of the governing elite and party system. Decline in the state's order and authority has led to greater violence outside the established political channels, compounding the general law and order situation.

Continuing civil strife and incipient secessionism poses a major problem for India's national security. The northeast continues to be characterised by an uneasy peace. Although there is no full scale armed insurrection for secessionism as resorted to by the Nagas and Mizos in the Sixties, the problem of insurgency in Tripura, Manipur and Nagaland continues. Assam which had settled to a period of normal political functioning after the volatile agitation on the influx of foreign nationals in the early Eighties, is once again going although the fire of violence perpetrated by the United Liberation Front of Assam (ULFA) which is committed to armed struggle for the formation of a sovereign "ASOM". Punjab went through the unfortunate agony of sustained armed violence for over a decade before normal political processes were restored after heavy-handed crushing of Khalistan terrorists. The people of the state have, however, paid a heavy price for the then government's short-sighted policies for narrow political ends which changed what was essentially a party agitation to a Sikh movement encompassing divergent orientation and rationales. This has important lessons for the future of Indian federal polity which can only be ignored at one's own peril.

The situation in Kashmir remains a cause for deep and continuing concern. Mishandling of a brewing political crisis brought about by the state government's dismal performance, marked by rampant corruption and inefficiency, led to an explosive situation in the sensitive valley. The eruption of violence in 1990 served to underline the appalling failure of the intelligence agencies and the complete isolation of the political and administrative machinery from the ground realities. In the event, alienation of large sections of the civil population and their growing sympathy for the militants left little meeting ground between the people and the government. The recent restoration of political processes in the state following Parliamentary and Assembly elections and the increased weariness of the people with economic dislocation and high-handed intrusion of outside militants is leading to a slow change in the equation of forces on the ground. But the overall situation remains precarious. The process of rebuilding the sundered economic and political fabric in the state and winning over the confidence of its people for any worthwhile and lasting solution continues to remain in uphill task. There is no gainsaying that the problems facing Indian polity are enormous as evidenced by the persistence of insurgency and slow entrenchment of terrorism in several parts of the country. If left unresolved, these could critically jeopardise India's national sovereignty and territorial integrity from within.

It is self-evident that the foremost task for India is to overcome the challenge to its nation building and national security. India's real autonomy in working out its destiny as an independent centre of power would lie in its internal strength and cohesion. There is no getting away from the urgent task of upholding its unity and integrity as a nation state through a credible framework of secular federal democracy. The need for reinvigorating its democratic functioning and strengthening the role and efficiency of the state remains imperative in this regard. India would also have make sustained efforts to vitalise its economy through optimisation of its vast resources, manpower and technical know-how. The need for redefining the role of the state in terms of eradication of poverty and greater economic equity remains self-evident. At the same time, India would have to raise itself to a new level of efficiency and competitiveness to acquire necessary leverages to stand up to growing global pressures and to hold its own in a friendly competitive world.

India can also not afford to drop its guard on building an adequate defence capability to counter any vulnerabilities which can be manipulated by external forces. There is some concern regarding growing deficiencies in India's conventional capability due to reduced defence expenditure in recent years. The need for adequate defence expenditure and defence allocation, constant modernisation and updating of its defence acquisitions for its defence preparedness remains imperative in this regard. A credible defence capability would provide an effective guarantee for maintaining its territorial integrity in the face of both external aggression and also externally engineered internal subversion that has emerged as a primary threat in recent years.

In the final analysis, it is only a politically stable, economically prosperous and militarily strong India which can seek to play its legitimate role in the world community, commensurate with its size and vast power potential. Issues of regional peace and stability continue to loom large on India's strategic horizon. South Asia is today on the threshold of a new era of democratisation as the process of evolving democratic structure is under way in almost all the countries of the region. The peaceful electoral transfer of power in Pakistan four times in a brief span of nine years reflects a growing commitment to democratic norms in that country. Bangladesh is firmly back on the track of democratic functioning after a long paralytic spell of negative agitational politics. Notwithstanding ups and downs, Nepal also continues to manage its democratic experiment credibly. At the same time, there are vested and deeply entrenched authoritarian interests in all these states, particularly the ones which have been under military rule for long years. For instance, the continued dominance of bureaucratic military oligarchy in the political set-up in Pakistan makes for a fundamental dysjunctive in its policy. Given the fragile democratic institutions in all these countries, the democratic process itself is releasing new pressures. It is thus that the domestic environment in South Asia continues to remain generally characterised by political unrest and regime instability.

Pressures from ethno-sectarian conflicts and religious fundamentalism are also rising in all countries of South Asia. Pakistan is sitting atop an ethnic cauldron as pressures simmer, threatening to tear apart the fabric of Islamic identity from below. The challenge in Sindh underscores the disturbing dimensions of large scale violence between ethnic groups. The continued Punjabi domination in the power structure spells a certain uncertainty for the future of Pakistani federal polity. Running feuds between Shias and Sunnis in various parts of Pakistan have become a common feature on the Pakistani scene. Sri Lanka remains mired in prolonged ethnic conflict as the continued intransigence of the Liberation Tigers of Tamil Eelam (LTTE) makes for a virtual civil war in the strife-torn island. Sinhalese resistance to grant of effective and substantive devolution power to the Tamils only queers the pitch of ethnic politics in the multi-ethnic society of Sri Lanka. Even Bangladesh which has a relatively homogeneous society is facing problems in overcoming difficulties in integrating its small tribal minority. The likelihood of the region remaining in a state of crisis due to rising scale of political and social discontent is thus going to be a part of South Asian realities for quite some time. This not only poses a threat to state structures within these countries but also has an adverse impact on the matrix of inter-state relationships in the region.

The overlap of a large number of ethnic, linguistic and religious groups across essentially porous borders in South Asia makes for a cross-border spill-over movement of refugees, guns and drugs which generates inter-state tensions. The steady movement of refugees, following prolonged domestic conflict in the countries of origin, has emerged as a multi-dimensional problem which affects regional security. Refugees who tend to settle down in the host countries, given the intractable nature of ethnic conflict, put an intolerable burden on the demographic, financial and social sectors which has long-term implications for national security of the host country. Pakistan is still reeling under the impact of 3.5 million Afghan refugees who sought refuge following the Afghanistan crisis in the Eighties. Thousands of refugees are living in camps in Nepal as a result of ethnic conflict in Bhutan. Bangladesh has also had to cope with the Rohingyyas fleeing from Myanmar.

For India particularly, which has been the host to the largest inflow of refugees with practically no outflow, the magnitude and frequency of refugee movement has been a vexing problem. This has particularly grave implications for the social, economic and political stability of the sensitive northeast. The presence of a large number of Chakmas in Tripura is intensifying tensions among the local inhabitants who are resenting encroachment on limited jobs and resources and scarce land. Thousands of Sri Lankans who sought refuge in Tamil Nadu in the Eighties are continuing to stay on, creating pressures with the attendant problem of anti-social and criminal activities. Induction of arms and anarchy with refugees is becoming a growing political liability. Internecine conflict among militant refugees groups and their continued links with trans-border militant groups intensifies social unrest and level of violence with grave implications for the future of civil society in these regions.

Growing linkages between drug trafficking and organised violence and the magnitude of the proliferation of small arms are also becoming major sources of instability in the region. In India there is growing concern regarding inter-state linkages between militant organisations, on the one hand, and between states and militant organisations on the other, adding to the complexity of secessionist movements. The crucial link-up between hostile external forces and domestic forces of political subversion poses a serious challenge to India's national security by giving impetus to secessionist forces. Terrorism in Kashmir since the Nineties, and earlier in Punjab in the Eighties, has acquired disturbing proportions with Pakistan's unabashed manipulation and support through planning and coordination, training of militants, and unlimited supply of arms and finances. The supply of sophisticated weaponry in particular—including rockets and explosive devices—has undeniably helped to raise the level of conflict to a new high.

By some accounts, the number of men lost in combatting the low intensity conflict in the sensitive state of Kashmir has outstripped the number of casualties in all the full scale Indo-Pak Wars put together. It may be mentioned here that internal political dynamics in Pakistan would continue to make for increasing domestic compulsions to keep the pot boiling in Kashmir, both in terms of diverting attention from pressing domestic problems as well as the inherent stakes of the military establishment in retaining the primacy of calling the shots in Pakistan.

In the strategic northeast ringed as it is by Myanmar, China and Bangladesh, incipient secessionism remains vulnerable to external manipulation. Although China which had offered arms and sanctuaries in the Sixties is no longer doing so, its unchanged stand on recognising the grant of statehood to Arunachal Pradesh and its military presence in Myanmar underscores its potential to foment trouble at a time of its own choosing. Bangladesh's involvement—albeit low key—is well-documented. Pakistan's Inter-Services Intelligence (ISI) is also carrying out anti-India activities from Nepal and Bangladesh adding to India's security concerns in view of persistently unsettled conditions in the northeast. Today the growing incidence of insurgency, fomented and abetted by hostile external forces has in some way emerged as a major problem for India's security establishment. The statement of the former Chief of Army, terming the low-intensity conflict as the foremost challenge for India's national security only serves to underline the growing intensity of the problem.

Proliferation of small arms in the region is yet another disturbing dimension of cross-border terrorism. The inflow of weapons is a direct fall-out of the Afghan conflict and the siphoning of major chunks of arms sent by the US, China and Saudi Arabia for onward transmission to the Afghan Mujahideen.

It bears pointing out that "small" arms is a mere euphemism for progressively more sophisticated and lethal weapons. The weapons circulating in the region include automatic rifles, machine guns as also landmines, sophisticated explosive devices, and communication systems.

Even more worrisome in the fact that these lethal devices are finding their way to non-state actors and terrorist groups. This has significantly altered the level of internal conflict in India's troubled regions, making for deep concern for the inevitably long-drawn and prolonged conflict in sensitive border states with major implications for the deployment and engagement of security forces.

Unwholesome linkages between the drug barons and arms dealers comprise yet another cause for concern. The enormous funds generated by drug sales are being increasingly used to finance purchase of sophisticated weaponry by terrorist groups in South Asia. South Asia is abutted by two of the largest drug producing areas on its western and eastern flanks.

The growth of narcotics trade has been exponential in Pakistan, with the presence of a reported 1.5 to 2 billion heroin addicts. Infiltration of drug money into the Pakistan economy and political system is now well documented. There are also growing reports of significant penetration by the narcotics network in Pakistan's law enforcement agencies and military intelligence.

The widespread Kalashnikov culture in Pakistan is a function of the mutually supportive phenomenon of drugs and weapons. Vast quantities of these arms have found their way to Punjab and Kashmir. These weapons have also been used to create internal unrest in urban centres as evident by the vicious bomb blasts in Bombay in 1993. India is also fast emerging as a transit route for the narcotics trade, given its strategic location between two major narcotics producing areas. Drugs from Pakistan and Myanmar are being transmited from India for onward transmission to European markets. It is no mere coincidence that the most critical challenges of insurgency in India are located in the sensitive border states in the northwest and northeast which adjoin the drug generating regions. More important, the growth of a flourishing criminal underworld underpinned by a nexus between illegal traders, drug peddlars, and gun dealers in tandem with internal security forces and law enforcement agencies is a cause for increasing concern. The enormous toll in human and economic terms as a consequence of mindless violence and narco-terrorism getting entrenched in civil society has implications which have yet to be comprehended fully.

The complexity of these transnational problems defies strictly national solutions. The urgency for building bilateral cooperative relationships and promoting a coordinated regional perspective on these critical developments which are cutting across the sanctity of national borders, remains, if anything, self-evident. The South Asian Association for Regional Cooperation (SAARC) Conventions on curbing drug trafficking and terrorism in the region are important steps forward in evolving suitable regional mechanisms to tackle the twin menace. The conventions, however, remain presently at odds with the ground realities. The political push to add substance to declarations of intent obviously awaits a qualitative improvement in the political climate in South Asia. Till such time, the challenges of narco-terrorism would call for sustained vigilance on India's part to counter the insidious threat to its national security.

South Asia has been generally characterised by a great deal of political and strategic complexity. To understand the complex South Asian phenomenon, one or two factors deserve special attention. First, India with its undeniably greater power potential and centrality looms large on the South Asian scene. Second, the legacy of common civilisational heritage has lent a sharper edge to neighbouring countries' sensitivities regarding their national identity in a clearly uneven setting. India with its looming presence and power potential is often projected as a core threat by these countries.

India's relations with practically all its neighbours have been strained over a whole range of issues be they of trade, or water sharing or migration or ethnic sensitivities. At the same time, there have been no even patterns of relationships in the region. India's relations with Bhutan and Maldives have been generally smooth and rancour-free. India's relations with Bangladesh, Nepal and Sri Lanka have witnessed significant ups and downs over the years but have never been allowed to dip to an unmanageable low. Indo-Bangladesh relations which had become extremely strained over the Farakka issue and the Tin Bigha controversy have witnessed a dramatic improvement with the signing of the historic agreement on sharing of Ganga waters. India and Nepal have also been able to put the unfortunate events of the Eighties behind them. Today they are set for a qualitatively improved relationship with closer economic ties and better political understanding. The signing of the Mahakali Treaty and grant of overland transit route for its trade with Bangladesh by India underlines the positive shift. The Indo-Sri Lankan relationship today is a far cry from the palpable antagonism of the Eighties.

However, the Indo-Pak relationship has been characterised by a virtually unbroken record of sustained hostility. Indo-Pak discord which to some extent has been rooted in the bitter legacy of partition became more sharp with the conflicting national interests and ideologies of the two states. Pakistan's inability to work out a viable form of nationalism and its eternal quest for achieving parity with its larger neighbour remains at the core of Pakistan's hostility towards India.

The three Indo-Pak Wars—the only intra-regional wars in South Asia—were all motivated by Pakistan's desire to alter the status quo. Pakistan's military relationship with the United States in the Fifties was also directed to counter-balance India and erode its prominence in the region. This not only brought Cold War politics to the region, irretrievably puncturing the area of peace that Nehru had sought to build, but also considerably aggravated India's security concerns.

Pakistan's continued overtures to external powers, particularly the United States and China, for diplomatic backing and augmentation of defence capabilities remains directed towards eroding India's pre-eminence and power. It is not necessary here to go into the details of unresolved issues between India and Pakistan except to mention that Indo-Pak relations have remained lockjammed over a wide range of issues—Kashmir, Siachin, the Afghanistan crisis and the nuclear issue. For the past five decades, Kashmir has, however, remained the central and overriding concern for Pakistan.

Pakistan sees Kashmir as an unfinished agenda of partition which must be resolved on the basis of the UN Resolutions which have long been overtaken by the realities on the ground. India has made it clear that Kashmir is an integral part on which it can countenance no compromise. This is so not only for obvious strategic considerations but also because it would deal a blow to India's secular framework and open the floodgate to demands for separation. India, however, remains willing to discuss Kashmir and all other outstanding issues on the basis of the Simla Agreement which expressly enjoins bilateralism and non-recourse to force by both countries which is not what is on the Pakistani mind. Meanwhile, Pakistan's continued support—money, training and sophisticated weaponry—to secessionists in Kashmir makes for grave tensions for India.

This is not to underestimate the urgent need for India to take steps to put its own house in order but to point out that Pakistan's proxy war in Kashmir represents a direct and immediate threat to India's security. It is also important to bear in mind that Pakistan has never given up the option of going to war with India to get back Kashmir.

This has its own implications for India's security planning notwithstanding a growing recognition in both countries that the realities of a crumbling economy and sustained international pressure would militate against a full-fledged war. The world opinion has also decisively veered towards a peaceful solution of the Kashmir problem, with both the United States and China recognising the inevitability of a bilateral negotiated settlement. There is also a section of opinion which considers nuclear deterrence itself as a stabilising factor in Indo-Pak relations. Nevertheless, Pakistan's declared nuclear capability makes for India's heightened security concern, given Pakistan's less than peaceful intentions towards India. There is no gainsaying that India is faced with Pakistan's nuclear challenges at a time when the absence of a credible Russian nuclear guarantee in the post-Cold War world makes it more vulnerable than at any time before.

This also aggravates the existing pressures emanating from Chinese nuclear might and United States' insidious nuclear presence in the region. Although India has made it abundantly clear that it has the capability to respond effectively to any nuclear misadventure by Pakistan, India's security perspectives would have to reckon with a nuclearised subcontinent in all its future calculations. It also needs to be borne in mind that while the Indo-Pak Agreement on not attacking each other's nuclear facilities is a positive step foward in confidence-building, this or any other such confidence-building measure would remain essentially meaningless unless simultaneous exploration is made of the ways and means to resolve the underlying problems between India and Pakistan. It is thus that the recent resumption of Indo-Pak dialogue at the Foreign Secretary level, after a long period of tense silence, is a welcome development for the future of Indo-Pak relations. However, even as New Delhi's call for initiating a qualitatively new chapter of amity underlines its sincere desire for a more forward looking and constructive approach, Pakistan's usual style of blowing hot and cold and its recent efforts to militarily activate the ceasefire line do not at present give much cause for optimism for Pakistan's similar response. There is, however, no denying that it is in India's long-term interests to reduce hostility with its important South Asian neighbour. This would at the least call for proactive strategies to build greater trust and cooperation with Pakistan in a framework of mutual goodwill.

India's long-term security hinges perhaps in a larger measure on the future of Sino-Indian relations. It is, therefore, in India's abiding interest to work for peaceful and cooperative relations with its most powerful neighbour with whom it shares a long disputed border. A stalemate in Sino-Indian relations during the Sixties and Seventies only served to limit India's diplomatic manoeuvrability and potential role in the region.

Rajiv Gandhi's visit to China in 1988 marked a significant breakthrough in thawing the stalemate between the two countries. The agreement signed during the visit on maintaining peace and tranquillity on the Line of Actual Control (LAC), pending a final solution of the border dispute, was a momentous step forward in normalisation of ties between the two neighbours. Re-emphasis on Panchsheel and the decision to initiate confidence-building measures to reduce tensions on the borders underlined a new forward looking approach on the part of both countries. The formation of a joint Working Group at the level of Ministers to carry forward negotiations on the boundary question reflected the new political thrust at the highest level. The process of normalisation has been since carried foward by a number of steps. Agreements have been signed to re-establish the Consulate General in Shanghai and Bombay and to resume border trade across specified points along the Tibet border. A set of confidence-building measures have been set in motion: agreeing on joint verification of the LAC, meetings between the local commanders, mutually agreed pull-back of troops from forward areas and prevention of aerial violations. These measures have not only helped to effectively defuse tensions on the borders but have also considerably eased India's defence burdens. More important, for the first time since the Sixties, India does not have to reckon with the nightmarish prospects of a two-war front with China and Pakistan.

At the same time, India can ill afford to have a let up in its defence preparedness to meet the long-term Chinese challenge. Although China would be hard put to challenge India a la 1992 because of changed correlation of forces on the ground, there is no underestimating the challenge of China's emergence as a formidable power in conventional as well as nuclear capabilities which has resulted in a vast power gap between the two countries. China's defence modernisation is continuing to move apace. China also continues to be engaged in augmenting its nuclear arsenal as its launching of inter-continental ballistic missiles and underground nuclear tests amply underline. Notwithstanding China's foreswearing of "first use," India can hardly ignore the implications of a total nuclear asymmetry with China. China's major military build up in Tibet—reportedly deploying ballistic missiles of medium and intermediate range—makes for long-term strategic concerns for India's security.

It may be pertinent to note here that China's remarkably growing economy, which has received additional boost with the reversion of Hong Kong in July 1997 also gives it a definite leverage in international affairs as underlined by its manoeuvrability in its relations with the US. It has been in recent years showing greater willingness to assert its power in pursuance of its interests in the adjacent regions. China's flexing of muscles in the South China Sea and its increasing assertiveness vis-a-vis Taiwan illustrate this. Although at present China has great stakes in not upsetting its carefully structured political and economic equilibrium or aggravating tensions in its neighbourhood, given its growing economic and military power there would be continuing uncertainty regarding its future moves and projections. In recent years, more than posing a direct military threat, China continues to represent a challenge to India's role in South Asia.

China has, of course, visibly refrained from engaging in anti-Indian rhetoric in terms of its relations with its neighbours. It has also apparently softened its stand on Kashmir, urging Pakistan to virtually shelve the issue while working for improvement of relations with India in other areas. At the same time, it has remained committed to strengthening its political relations with all of India's neighbours. It continues to sell arms to Bangladesh, Pakistan, Sri Lanka and Burma which tends to hem India in a subtle way. In particular, its politico-strategic collaboration with Pakistan shows no appreciable change. China's help to Pakistan in developing its nuclear weapon capability is well-documented. Its recent supply of ring magnets and M-11 missiles has disturbing implications for India, seeking to threaten as it does the present balance of power in the region. China's supply of arms worth 1.6 billion dollars to Burma and its help in construction of naval and electronics facilities, and modernisation of its naval bases are also of concern to India in its strategic northeast and the adjacent seas.

China has, of course, come a long way since the Sixties in its national perspectives and world view, engaged as it is in consolidating its economic development, promoting regional peace and establishing a "just" new world order. This has led to a growing convergence of views with India which remains committed to world peace and a just and equitable world order. They have mutually shared perceptions on the need to preserve national territorial integrity and combatting challenges of fundamentalism, ethnic separatism and cross-border terrorism. There is also a broad understanding between the two countries on global trade issues and the pressures emanating from the industrialised world on human rights and good governance. All this augurs well for a more relaxed and cooperative relationship between India and China. It would, however, need to be clearly borne in mind for India's long-term projections that relations between the two Asian giants are bound to be marked by undercurrents of competition and contest, inherent in the logic of geo-political proximity and national rivalry. It also needs to be borne in mind that the border question has been shelved but not resolved. India has vital stakes in consolidating the process of normalisation with China but as long as the dynamics of military competition remains unchanged, a durable framework of Sino-Indian friendship would have to be underpinned by an overall balance of strength and a clear recognition of their mutual power status and stakes in the region.

It is clear from the foregoing that India has an abiding stake in peace and stability in its neighbourhood for its long-term security. India is going through a phase of rapid economic transformation and is poised to play a significant role in the global stage in the coming century. There is no gainsaying that India's projection on the world scene would depend in no small measure on its effective and constructive neighbourhood diplomacy. This would at the least call for evolving a framework of cooperative security in its neighbourhood. This would essentially mean striving to reduce tensions with China and Pakistan, its two powerful neighbours, without compromising on its core national strategic interests. This is so not only because they separately and together constitute a long-term threat to its security but also because stable peace in this region hinges on India's friendly ties with these two countries. India's recent agreement with China offers ground for finding a viable basis of confidence on which to build cooperative relationships. India's offer of several confidence-building measures to Pakistan is also a step in the same direction. These include the agreement on prohibition of nuclear attack on population centres and economic targets; the agreement on "no first use" of nuclear weapons; and upgrading of communication links between DGMO of both sides. In some ways, the Simla Agreement itself provides for an effective mechanism for confidence-building between the two nations to build durable peace in the subcontinent. Sustained efforts to initiate new confidence-building measures and strengthen the existing mechanisms would remain imperative for building a credible framework of cooperative security in the region.

India would also need to take a lead in setting the tone for a framework of relations with its smaller neighbours. New Delhi is today committed to evolve a fresh perspective on its relations with its neighbours in a framework of positive asymmetry. There is no doubt that in the short run, anti-Indian rhetoric would continue to be manipulated at will by these countries, depending on their domestic compulsions, but in the long run, deft handling of the neighbours with flexibility and sensitivity is bound to lead to a more relaxed political environment. This itself would lend a great credibility to India's role as a regional influential.

Peace and development in the region is in the long term a sine qua non for India's long-term security perspectives in South Asia which is facing staggering problems of poverty, illiteracy, malnutrition and under-development. The biggest challenge to regional peace and security emanates from its poverty and the under-utilisation of its vast resources to address the socio-economic needs of its teeming millions. Pressures of endemic poverty and population explosion are becoming critical in the region. South Asia has sunk to the bottom rung in terms of the number of its people living below the line of poverty. SAARC provides an effective regional institutional arrangement for South Asia to optimise its regional resources and capabilities to promote the welfare of its peoples and a cooperative framework for the socio-economic development of the entire region. India as the largest South Asian power has a special responsibility to give a visible push to SAARC and invest in policies which are informed by a larger and long-term vision of a cooperative and stable South Asia.

An important challenge to India's security lies in the unfolding security environment in its adjacent neighbourhood which has a vital bearing on its geo-political interests. The volatile situation in Afghanistan is of major concern to India. Afghanistan seems set to witness a fierce and long drawn struggle among the main contenders for power which, if unresolved, will lead to grave destabilisation in the trouble-torn country.

Although India does not share any borders with Afghanistan, it has fundamental geo-political stakes in the unfolding events there which can be detrimental to its own long-term security interests in the region. India, therefore, has a major stake in any outcome of the protracted Afghanistan crisis. India rightly views any fundamentalist regime in Afghanistan as an insidious threat to its own secularism as well as a potentially destabilising factor in the region. An important dimension of Indian policy is the inevitable antagonism of such a regime to India which has traditionally enjoyed close links with Afghanistan based on a shared perception of regional interests. The possible spillover of a Taliban style fundamentalist regime, in terms of impact of ideology, violence and narco-terrorism, into Kashmir makes for deep concern for India's internal security. India has, therefore, a stake in seeing the evolution of a broad based government in Afghanistan which takes care of the legitimate interests of all major groups to enable it to emerge as a stable and non- fundamentalist nation. It is in this context that India is keeping contacts with major groups within Afghanistan and supporting all broad regional initiatives from outside to solve the problem. A growing understanding with Iran and other likeminded countries is emerging as an important dimension of India's policy not only towards Afghanistan but also the politically sensitive Central Asia.

Of late, Central Asia has emerged as an area of major concern for India in view of India's long-term interest in this strategic area. This is because the situation in the region which continues to be fluid because of political instability and challenges of Islamic fundamentalism has wider implications for India's own vicinity. Central Asia has also emerged as a major strategic region in view of its vast untapped reserves of oil, natural gas and other precious resources. This has made the region a focus of sharp interest and struggle among most major powers, notably the United States, Russia, China, Iran and Turkey, who want to exploit the tremendous economic potential of the area. Although India can do little to influence the interplay of Great Power rivalry in the region, it has a stake in deepening and broadening its own interaction with the region. This would call for a more energised policy in building upon existing economic and cultural ties with the Central Asian countries making for its reinforced presence in this vital area. India is already engaged in an exercise of exploring the avenues for extending support in the field of infrastructure and technology. India has to continue to take into account in its larger security perspectives the region's great strategic, economic and political importance in terms of its energy reserves, strategic location and emerging political dynamics that are attracting wide attention and will have major implications for this whole region.

India also has vital interests in the emerging political and strategic dynamics in the Indian Ocean region. This is so because of its vital need for uninterrupted energy supplies and maritime trade through its strategic waterways. India is vitally interested in keeping the major sea lanes of communication in the Indian Ocean free for the movement of substantial portion of its trade, particularly in terms of access to vital oil supplies. Its objections to superpower presence in the Indian Ocean in the Cold War days was also a function of its concerns over escalation of tensions in its vital strategic vicinity. India's positive role in the newly formed Indian Ocean Rim Community also underlines its desire to evolve a cooperative framework of relations among the littoral countries of the Indian Ocean without undue interference of outside powers.

India's demand for oil supplies is slated to grow very steeply in the coming decades. Till such time that Central Asian vast reserves are fully exploited, the Persian Gulf which is currently accounting for 60 per cent of world's energy resources, would hold the key to global energy security. The potential of the South China Sea remains as yet largely untapped. West Asia and the Persian Gulf in particular would thus continue to remain a region of great strategic concern for all major powers, including some of the erstwhile self-sufficient countries like Russia, China and Indonesia whose reserves are getting fast depleted. Given India's strategic location to the area, India's has abiding interests in long-term stability and peace in the area because any potential destabilisation or conflict would lead to insecurity in India's strategic neighbourhood.

Given the external powers' continued quest for power and influence in the South Asian region, the need for diversification of strategic political options remains imperative for India as there is also evidence of new pressures in economic, security and nuclear fields. This calls for both restructuring the old ties and forging new relationships. India's policy towards the United States, Russia and China would have to be thus increasingly informed by the changing needs of national security and economic development as also the logic of its own role in the region. Strategic and geo-political considerations had been critical for Indo-Soviet ties in the Cold War period. But it was essentially the mutuality of interests that sustained those ties lending them a certain autonomous structure, irrespective of extraneous inputs. Mutual convergence between the two countries rested on the basic premise of Soviet endorsement of India's pre-eminence in the region.

The Soviet support was critical for India in coping with its problems with both Pakistan and China, singly and together. More important, it helped India to build a credible and self-sufficient defence structure at a time when there was visible reluctance from the West to do so. In the post-Cold War world, India and Russia have been able to credibly rework their relationship despite the initial hitches in the transitional phase in a qualitatively altered framework.

Although there has been some reduction in the volume of trade and economic interaction between the two countries, the question of repayment of loan and currency adjustment has been settled to mutual satisfaction. The new treaty of friendship and cooperation between the two countries is a reaffirmation of the abiding mutuality of the interests between them. India and Russia would continue to have a convergence of interests in the developments in their proximate regions—Afghanistan and Central Asia—where both have vital geo-political interests in promoting peace and stability.

There is also mutuality of interest on the need of averting internal destabilisation from ethnic conflict and trans-border terrorism in large multiplural societies. This has particular significance for India which faces a simmering problem in the sensitive state of Kashmir. India also has a continued stake in strengthened defence relations with Russia, given its large scale dependence for Russian modern military hardware—at reasonable prices—and advanced civilian technology in space and nuclear fields. India has been able to procure military equipment with provision for technology transfer, joint production and export to third countries. Recently, India and Russia have set up a joint working group to address the operative elements of a long-term military technological programme—the only such programme Russia has signed with any foreign country—which has been extended for another ten years beyond 2000. Russia has also offered to India the latest and advanced technology in all areas of the defence field.

At the same time, any talk of "strategic partnership" is still premature, given Russia's strategic alliance with China and its continued dependence on the West. There are also difficulties in the supply of sensitive technology—underlined by the problems in the cyrogenic deal and differences over nuclear disarmament, particularly after Russia's signing of the Comprehensive Test Ban Treaty (CTBT) and India's own position on it.

There is, of course, some satisfaction in India that Russia has now re-endorsed its stand on India's pre-eminence in South Asia and moved back from the projection of equidistance between India and Pakistan. Moscow has now reaffirmed its support for India's stand on Kashmir and its firm commitment not to supply arms to Pakistan. Indo-Russian relations, although qualitatively altered in the changed world context, would have continued relevance for India's long-term strategic perspectives. In the post-Cold War world, maintaining friendly and close relations with the United States, the only superpower today, which is capable of shaping the regional environment, would need to receive the highest priority in India's larger strategic calculations.

Indo-US relations have remained generally lukewarm over the years essentially for the United States' non-recognition of India as a power of consequence in the region. There has been no effort by the US to develop an autonomous approach to South Asia except in relationship to its broader global objectives. Shared democratic values have failed to provide a firm basis for understanding between the two countries whose divergent security interests lay at the root of the indifferent state of relations. This has remained so notwithstanding India's need and desire for improved relations with the United States, albeit on its own terms and from its own long-term security perspectives. The United States is seen in India as displaying singular insensitivity and disregard for India's vital security concerns in the region.

An important Indian objection to US policy in South Asia has been its commitment to the parity syndrome between India and Pakistan—including equating Indian and Pakistani nuclear policy—which India sees as not only immeasurably intensifying its security problems but also eroding India's pre-eminence in the natural balance of power in South Asia. Notwithstanding an improved phase of relationship in recent years, the United States' continued reluctance to deliver sensitive technology to India only serves to underline its disregard for India's sensitivities to the qualitative alteration of the military balance of the region over the years.

There are today greater opportunities for developing understanding between the two countries on promoting peace and stability in both South Asia as also the neighbouring strategic regions of the Persian Gulf and the Indian Ocean. Although differences persist over a range of issues—nuclear proliferation, Kashmir, trade related issues and restructuring of the Security Council—all of which have a vital bearing on India's larger security concerns there are some positive indications of Indo-US relations acquiring greater depth with evidence of more intense economic interaction and the evolution of a strategic dialogue between the two countries.

The United States which has emerged as India's single largest trading partner and investor, has an abiding interest in India's vast economy and burgeoning markets. India, of course, would need the US capital, technology and markets which remain crucial to India's future economic development. India has welcomed the recent US declaration—although belated—formally designating the Pakistan-sponsored organisation Harkat-ul-Ansar, operating in Kashmir, as a terrorist outfit. There is also some satisfaction with the US' full-hearted endorsement of the current Indo-Pak dialogue and its reaffirmation that it has no desire to intervene in Indo-Pak problems. All these would underline a growing US desire to build an independent relationship with India, notwithstanding Pakistan's continued relevance to its broader regional objectives. At the same time, a qualitative improvement in Indo-US relations would, in the long run, continue to remain contingent on the United States' recognition of India's regional pre-eminence in the building up of an independent policy towards India.

Given the inevitability of India's search for its own place in the global community, in view of its large size and power potential, and the growing complexity of its security challenges, India's nuclear policy would continue to have primacy in its national security agenda in the new world order. While nuclear disarmament must needs be India's long-term security goal, its nuclear policy has to take into account the given realities of the nuclear weapons having come to stay as an important bargaining leverage in international relations.

There is a growing recognition in India that given the current international realities and the situation of nuclear asymmetry in the region, mere retention of the nuclear option may not hold unconditionally in the altered scenario. India would have to give more sustained and serious thought to the timing of the exercise or non-exercise of its option in the days ahead. Developing a full-fledged nuclear weapon capability while continuing to press for total elimination of nuclear weapons will, of course, be the foremost challenge for India's future security perspectives.

Three or four factors deserve attention in this regard. First, time remains of the essence for India as domestic costs grow and international pressures mount on India to abandon its nuclear option and missile programme at a time when the nuclear powers are engaged in updating and refining their capabilities. Second, India has to reckon with the prospects of undeniable pressures from the US, China and Russia, should it operationalise its nuclear option. It may also find itself under increased Chinese nuclear threat in view of its unquestioned nuclear might today. Third, exercise of the nuclear option would bring to the fore the classic dilemma of development versus defence at a time when India's developmental goals require the greatest attention for sustaining its economic growth. Fourth, the goals of national security, short-term, as well as India's own aspirations, in the long-term, to play a global role of some significance, remain compelling for India's strategic perspectives. Last, can India afford to remain locked in continued confrontation with the nuclear powers—in the post-CTBT phase—and pay the inevitably high costs—economic, technological and political—without having actually exercised its nuclear option? It is clear that the whole range of possibilities—retaining the present ambiguity, opting for recessed nuclear deterrence and operationalising its nuclear option—would hold the centre-stage of the national security agenda demanding a well coordinated and well thought out nuclear strategy that would sustain India's long-term security projections. It is clear from the foregoing that India has to resolutely address itself to the emerging set of challenges and opportunities in the changed world order in a coordinated and comprehensive framework of paramount importance would be its ability to project its (long-term strategic perspectives and interests in responding to the interplay of domestic imperatives, regional balance of forces and global dynamics in the coming decades.

The overarching reality of India as a large independent nation which is destined to play an important role on the global stage would undoubtedly prevail over the present difficulties and obstacles. The need for India to come to grips with the complexities of the rapidly changing configuration of forces at the domestic, regional and global levels, however, remains self-evident. India's long-term strategic perspectives would have to show greater dynamism and flexibility in responding to the increasingly complex demands of national security, regional aspirations and global commitments. This would at the least call for clearly defining India's security interests and evolving a coherent and multi-layered framework of its security policy and perspectives. In the final analysis, India's own strengths and capabilities—political, economic and military—would alone add substance to India's future projections as a power of some consequence in the emerging global order.

INTELLIGENCE AND THE OPERATIONAL COUNTER-TERRORISM ROLE (RESPONSE)

To the extent that the MAC, the NIA, the IB and Union Government response agencies, such as the NSG, will presumably be housed within the NCTC, at least some of the connectivity concerns between intelligence and counter-terrorism operations will be met. However, the weakness in this area arises from the fact that the NSG (as a special weapons and tactics – SWAT – group) is only one small component of counterterrorism response.

The other components, such as state police first response, post-facto investigations, consequence management and deradicalisation programs for those arrested, rest predominantly within the state jurisdiction. Also the intelligence effort surrounding a terrorist event will still have all the problems of coordination and data matching mentioned above. This is the exact situation faced by Australia, which has derived a number of mechanisms to try to overcome the problem.

Other Missing Elements

The Indian reform process outlined above will go some way in providing a viable counter-terrorism and counter-insurgency base if fully and effectively implemented. It has several major deficiencies, however. Some of these, such as the need to concentrate on uplifting the South Asia region as a whole and on meeting the concerns of India's disaffected minorities, are beyond the scope of this chapter. But other important concerns about policing, governance and accountability need to be addressed. They particularly need to be addressed because – as argued above – the state and grassroots levels are key elements in counterterrorism and counter-insurgency.

The closely related factors of accountability and governance lie at the heart of the state and local-level security problems. Without accountability and good governance, governments will not be able to implement any programmes to alleviate the economic and political grievances of disaffected communities, such as the otherwise commendable NREGA. And the police, far from being able to act as the eyes and ears of the community, will actually be a part of the problem in that they will alienate those very communities.

INDIA'S NEED FOR DECLARATORY STRATEGIC DOCTRINES

India having formalised its "strategic vision" should then spell out in declaratory terms the strategic doctrines the country would follow henceforth. In the last 50 years, India has shied away from declaratory strategic doctrines. Declaratory strategic doctrines are necessary for the following reasons:

- India's strategic intentions are made clear in declaratory form. Ambiguity is the weapon of the weak and the passive. India should move away from ambiguous policies.
- Strategic doctrines should define in unambiguous terms the "red lines" whose crossing or attempts to breach by any country will not be tolerated. These "red lines"

should flow from the enunciation of India's national security interests. The use of force and swift retaliation should be declared in these strategic doctrines.

- Strategic doctrines so declared will leave no doubt to potential aggressors or those tempted to stir and generate internal security threats in India as to what India's responses would be.
- Declaratory strategic doctrines are especially necessary for combating terrorism, hijacking and other disruptive activities resorted to by adversaries. Doctrines should spell out that even the roots of terrorism and insurgency from across Indian borders will not be immune from India's retaliatory responses.
- On the practical plane, declaratory strategic doctrines would provide the template on which planning for India's national security apparatus and force-planning and force structures can be configured.
- Declaratory strategic doctrines should therefore essentially reflect India's will to use power both in terms of pre-emptive military operations and launching of offensive operations.

In the realms of Indian military strategy, the absence of declaratory strategic doctrines has been most keenly felt. India's military responses to both external and internal threats, so far, perforce, have been defensive and re-active in nature.

Our entire national ethos, political and military mind-sets and tactical thinking have been oriented in defensive terms

Such defensive and reactive policies have had a debilitating impact on India's military preparedness and also on India's intelligence machinery.

As soon as the crisis blows over, in the absence of strategic doctrines, combat equipment acquisitions and build-up of strategic needs is shelved. It has also led to neglect of our build-up of force-projection capabilities and the development of our offshore island territories into strong military bases for force projection capabilities.

India's Political Governance: The Need For a Qualitative Change

Good political governance is an imperative requirement of the power attributes of any nation aspiring to be a big power. Power status, decisive political leadership, strategic vision, military preparedness, economic advancement and national cohesion cannot be achieved without good political governance. The indicators of power potential which foreign countries look for pertaining to India all centre around and are focussed on political stability and good governance.

In India's march towards her future goals of being a major power, the weakest link in that achievement is India's political governance and the quality of her polity. This is not an individual opinion but the general opinion of one and all, namely, contempt for the politicians and their ethical standards.

Qualitative change in the polity and political governance of India can only be brought about by a conscious and deliberate effort by political leaders of major political parties. It is they who have to set irreproachable high standards personally and also ensure that party tickets are given to intelligent, mature and dedicated men and women of substance.

Leaders of major political parties need to discipline their unruly parliamentarians and legislators. India's polity should not take it for granted that they are not under scrutiny. Ironically this polity which claims to have a prerogative on national leadership stands paralysed qualitatively. This has a grave effect on India, strategically and militarily.

India's Strategic Culture: The Need for Re-Invention

India's geographical boundaries stood changed after 1947 and so also the nature and relief of terrain configurations on which present boundaries rest. Historically and culturally, India went through three widely separated stages–Hindu, Muslim and British, Each of these periods had a religious and cultural disconnect and therefore do not provide the consistency of the evolution of a strategic culture, like China for example. India today stands faced with the daunting task of re–inventing its strategic culture for two good reasons :

- India today faces strategic threats to its national security both external and internal, which are in marked variance to its earlier geographical, historical or cultural configurations.
- Secularism does not define or arise from any strategic culture. India's strategic culture needs to be reinvented by drawing on its most ancient and indigenous roots and blending it with India's contemporary strategic ambitions and the global strategic environment. It is India's political leadership and its elites who have failed to grasp this critical strategic requirement.

India's history of the last fifty years indicates that India was unable to re-invent a strategic culture, appropriate and commensurate enough to meet the threats to its security. India was passive, defensive, reactive and soft in her strategic cultures. India needs to re-invent its strategic culture in a more resurgent mode of proactive, directed and aggressive responses to threats to her national security.

National Security Issues Should Not be Politicised

India presents a regrettable phenomenon where political opposition parties, in the absence of any other political issue, tend to politicise national security issues. In this process and in their zeal to discomfit the ruling party at any cost, they fail to realise the impact it has on the Armed Forces of India – their morale, their will to fight and their entire confidence in the political structure of the Indian nation state is seriously jeopardised.

The most recent examples of this politicisation of India's national security issues pertain to the then opposition parties reaction to India's nuclear weaponisation in 1998, their ill-informed criticisms during the Pakistan aggression in Kargil in 1999 and thereafter and their attitudinal problems to the Indian Army operations against the Pakistan sponsored proxy war in Jammu and Kashmir State.

National security issues have hardly been discussed by political parties during Defence budget debates in Parliament. The parliamentary attendance then presents a sorry spectacle. Yet when grave national crises occur every second politician becomes a master strategist or tactician minus the grasp of the essentials of strategy and the intricacies of military operations and oblivious to the fact that the parliamentarians own strategic incompetence brought about the military aggression in the first place.

India's political leaders need to get together and work out conventions where during a crisis they can discuss the issues away from the glare of publicity and arrive at a consensus on how the Indian nation state has to meet the security challenges that arise.

National Security and Indian Media

The Indian media both print and electronic has developed imperialistic attitudes towards the coverage, analysis and projection of national security issues. Nothing exemplifies this more than the 'Tehelka Tapes' episode. In a bid to make money, national security interests were given a go by this portal. A noble mantle was sought to be worn by depicting it as a crusade against corruption. The media elite including notable editors-in-chief ganged up to support Tehelka not on the grounds of objectivity but for sheer defence of one of their flock. Some Indian journals, indulged in politicising the issues of military commanders performances on the basis of leaked classified documents. They did not even bother to think that such irresponsible journalism not only affects the national security of the country but also the morale of the Indian Armed Forces. It also affects the confidence of the uniformed personnel in the Indian media, who should really strive to be a pillar of the state rather than a money-spinning enterprise of some industrial house, depending on sensationalism for its wider circulation.

India as a nation state is still in the formative stages and many challenges both external and internal threaten its existence and integrity. The Indian media should refrain from applying western templates of journalism as neither the political & strategic context nor the national cohesion as existent in the West is presently obtainable in India.

POLICING AND GOVERNANCE IN INDIAN SECURITY

As with any large country, India's security mechanisms are required to meet multiple needs. They must defend the nation against attack by another country. They need to defend against terrorist attacks. They have to deal with insurgencies. They are supposed to investigate corruption and ensure the probity of government at all levels. A fundamental requirement is that they protect an individual from criminal attack. And they need to maintain order nationally and at the street level. In each one of these roles, and at each level of activity (national, state or local), security authorities and governance mechanisms can either be a part of the problem or the solution. Often, they act in different ways and are driven by different political imperatives at different levels.

Although security agencies have clear national goals, at the state and local levels, they can tend to become biased in favour of the government of the day through the political and economic nexus that develops between security authorities and politicians at the local level. There is nothing new about such bias. At the time of the assassination of Indira Gandhi in 1984, the Congress (I) authorities were accused of doing nothing to protect Sikhs in New Delhi from attack or in subsequently prosecuting alleged attackers. Similar allegations were levelled against the BJP government in Gujarat in relation to the anti-Muslim riots of 2002. The allegations against the Gujarat police and courts have several dimensions. One level of complaint does not involve government connivance as such, but rather the fact that the police simply reflected wider community anger over the killing of 58 Hindu activists at Godhra and therefore failed to control the anti-Muslim backlash that followed. This idea that the police can be 'biased' is reflected in The Sachar Committee Report (2006).

The committee found that in India as a whole, Muslims are under-represented in the police, constituting only 6-7 per cent of constables, whereas they constitute 13.4 per cent of the population. The situation is even worse for the Indian Police Service (IPS), where the committee reportedly found only 4 per cent Muslim officers. But arising from the Gujarat riots, there were also more troubling accusations of actual police connivance in supporting the riots at the behest of a biased political class. Although reports of police and political connivance are contested, the Special Investigations Team (SIT), established by the Supreme Court to inquire into the riots, has demanded the arrest of at least one senior policeman for complicity in the riots. And finally, there is the view that the Supreme Court of India was required to intercede in a justice system that was not affording justice to the victims at the level of the Gujarat High Court. In short, this case provides a ready example of the differing influences and perspectives at play in the different levels of India's justice system.

The justice system can be a part of the problem, but there are also many recent instances where strong, neutral political leadership has mitigated any supposed bias within the police. Although the Srikrishna Commission report implicated the government and police in the Mumbai riots of 1992-93, in recent years, strong action by the Government of Maharashtra has resulted in several potentially inflammable communal situations being contained. Despite two terrorist attacks on the communal 'tinderbox' of Malegoan, and despite the attacks of 26/11, careful handling by the Maharashtra government and the police managed to defeat the obvious purpose of such attacks – to trigger communal rioting and consequent polarisation of communities towards extremists. All too often, however, the reverse is the case: politicians have a leading role in manipulating the police for negative, rather than positive, purposes or at least they turn a 'blind eye' to police inactivity in the face of disorder.

Given the many different levels of performance of the Indian justice system, one of the challenges in a paper such as this is to obtain a reasonable measure of the state of internal security. The debate about internal security in India can be conducted in the 'glass half empty or half full' framework, depending on one's emphasis. In India, one can find the best and worst of policing at any one time. But the assessment of the extent of the reform process needed depends on the assessment of the degree of the problem involved, so an over-arching assessment is required.

The level of violence against individual citizens is one measure, even if a crude one, of the effectiveness of law enforcement and governance in India. On the one hand, those of us who follow security issues in India are assaulted on a daily basis by accounts of seemingly high levels of violence. On any given day, we can come across an account of a terrorist attack in a major Indian city in which dozens are killed and many more wounded and maimed; in which police fire on unruly mobs; in which Indian Maoists attack and kill whole contingents of police; in which women are set alight in so-called dowry deaths; or in which criminals or police are killed in major shoot-outs. Against this, those who travel through India are often struck by the way in which optimism and good prevail amidst extreme poverty and in which syncretic values persist and different religions and communities live in harmony and close proximity. Again, the booming economic data do not indicate that violence, dissonance and unrest in India are sufficient to dampen the economy in any significant way. But these are subjective views and the question still remains: how violent, corrupt and dysfunctional is India in comparative terms? This is a difficult issue. The data are hard to extract not only for India but also for other, possibly more violent, regions and sub-regions, such as Africa and parts of Central and South America.

In terms of violence, judged according to the statistics of violent deaths, India at first appears to be a dangerous place. Up to 2007, the US State Department continued to collect comparative data, but its findings are limited to the category 'terrorism'. Besides definitional problems with that term, in itself it does not cover the full spectrum of violence. Nevertheless, the 2007 report recorded 2,300 lives lost due to 'terrorism' in India (no comprehensive data were available in the 2008 report). According to data provided by the South Asia Terrorism Portal (SATP), India has lost 22,789 people to extremist violence between September 2001 and now. Even allowing for a flexible view of terrorism that includes all forms of extremist violence and taking account of India's population of 1.1 billion, this appears at first sight to be an alarming problem.

Measures such as the Global Peace Index are equally flawed as an absolute measure of violence. The index includes factors such as 'democracy' and excludes important areas such as 'domestic violence'. But nevertheless, the large South Asian countries rank relatively low (poorly) on the index (Pakistan 127; Sri Lanka 125; India 107; Bangladesh a surprisingly good 86).

Other data, however, paint a less alarming picture of the situation in India. The murder rate in India (which presumably also reflects deaths in terrorism and political violence) has somewhat fallen since Independence – from 3.7 per 100,000 in 1951 to 3.4 per 100,000 in 2007. Others put India's murder rate, at 3.8 per 100,000, still well below that of the US at 5.5 per 100,000, but well above many western European countries and the UK. China, perhaps a more valid comparison given its vast population, has a rate of 2.4 per 100,000. But China is a more homogeneous country and is more tightly controlled by its undemocratic political system. In terms of general crime rates, the officially recorded statistics are also reasonably positive. They report a declining rate for crimes under the Indian Penal Code (IPC – which fall towards the more serious end of the scale) in relation to population growth rate over the decade prior to 2007.

It would seem then that in per capita terms, India is not especially violent by world standards and is becoming less violent and crime-affected. While political violence, including terrorism, is concentrated in some cities and sub-regions, it does not, on the whole, stifle the daily lives and economic transactions of the majority of people.

Although India is in statistical terms not an especially violent place, there are nevertheless worrying signs that in some parts a destructive cycle of violence can intensify, possibly leading to a classic downward spiral of terrorism (or other forms of violence), excessive state response and further violence triggered by such response. Such was the pattern, indeed, that led to the inter-generational civil war in Sri Lanka. It would be particularly worrying if such trends were to emerge in key economic centres, such as Mumbai, Hyderabad and Bengaluru. As mentioned, another key area in terms of India's economic performance is the Maoist-affected regions. Violent separatism in Kashmir and India's North-East also has worrying strategic implications.

Moreover, crime statistics in India do not tell the whole story concerning governance, crime and violence. There is evidence that India's crime problem is seriously under-reported, and worse, that this under-reporting occurs in part due to a loss of faith in policing. It is impossible to know the extent of under-reporting of crime in any country, but there are ways we can explore the data to give an indication of the dimension of the problem. Crime victim surveys are a useful tool in this regard, but are not sufficiently developed in the Indian context to enable us to draw country-wide conclusions.

One survey of four major cities in Tamil Nadu (notably a state with more effective policing than many others) found that "many crimes occurring in India are not reported and that police (crime) figures are only the tip of the iceberg". A victimisation survey of Rajasthan conducted by Massachusetts Institute of Technology on behalf of the Rajasthan Police reportedly found that only 29 per cent of crimes were ever reported, and that of those that were, only 72 per cent received a First Information Report (FIR – the vehicle for setting the legal process in motion). Nevertheless, we need to note that the more serious the crime (such as murder), the more likely it is to be reported.

Serious under-reporting is also likely true of drugs crime. It is worth exploring this problem in a little detail, because serious drugs crime is usually associated with high levels of organised crime and corruption. Drugs crime and associated criminality, in turn, typically mount major, long-term challenges to legal structures, particularly when they become entangled with the so-called problem of 'narco-terrorism'. The Indian Narcotics Control Bureau (NCB) reports a virtually flat pattern of opiates seizures (at about one tonne of heroin annually and two tonnes of opium), suggesting India's trafficking in and use of this class of drugs is not rising markedly, or that interdiction has fallen markedly.

The United Nations Office of Drugs and Crime (UNODC), however, has another view. In a survey of India, the UNODC found that "in 2004, the number of chronic substance-dependent individuals were as follows: 10 million (alcohol), 2.3 million (cannabis) and 0.5 million (opiates)."

The report continued: "The survey not only points to the problem of India's population having twice the global (and Asian) average prevalence of illicit opiate consumption, but also shows that the treatment resources available are not commensurate with the burden of work (number of dependent drug users) requiring immediate treatment".

A national 'habit' of half a million chronic (highly addicted) users is indicative of consumption of massive quantities of illicit drugs, even allowing for the presumed lower levels of purity in India. This is, in turn, indicative of high levels of criminality.

The US State Department in its 2007 report also designated India as a major hub for illicit drugs. The State Department was concerned at the possibility of diversion of India's substantial licit opiate production and noted the sudden surge in discoveries in illicit growing in 2007.

The NCB notes: "It was decided to conduct an intensive survey of the probable areas (of cultivation) involving NCB, state authorities and other central authorities." Eight thousand hectares of illicit poppy were destroyed in that year compared with 218 hectares in 2006 and 623 hectares in 2008. Illicit harvesting of at least 8,000 hectares (the amount discovered and destroyed) suggests major criminal involvement in the purchase, consolidation and processing of the opium gum. For example, this area (which would be by no means the total area illicitly grown) constitutes nearly one-third of the estimated total illicit cultivation in Myanmar in the same year.

The concerns of the US State Department were reflected by findings of the Australian Crime Commission (ACC). Australia has reported an increasing quantity of South West Asian origin heroin (mainly from Afghanistan), with India supplying in the 2007-08 reporting year "the largest number of detections (as a global source of origin) over 500 grams."

This indicates that India is a major source of heroin transhipment from the Golden Crescent – reporting that is simply not consonant with the Indian Government's view of its illicit drug problem and the criminality involved with it. Just recently, a gang of Nigerians allegedly transhipping heroin from India to Australia was interdicted in Chennai.

US authorities also express grave concern about India's capacity to deal with money laundering. Although India passed legislation in 2009 that strengthens its anti-money laundering regime, the US Bureau of International Narcotics and Law Enforcement Affairs said in its 2009 report (issued annually through the State Department) that India was still falling well short of the Financial Action Task Force (FATF) recommendations.

The report noted that illicit hawala transfers for incoming remittances amounted to US$13-17 billion alone, leaving aside the fact that the majority of hawala dealings relate to criminality and tax evasion rather than remittances. The concern of this chapter is especially with India's counter-terrorism mechanisms; but we also assert that these in turn relate intimately to general issues of governance, corruption and policing. This relationship was recently defined on a practical level by the Minister of Home Affairs, P Chidambaram:

If intelligence-gathering is the corner stone of fighting insurgency or insurrection or terror, the foot soldier (police man or woman) cannot work in isolation. He must be enabled to gather intelligence from the people ... It is therefore important that State Governments adopt Community Policing.

In terms of developing a more sustainable approach to internal security (and consequently, the closely-related area of external security), the police and judiciary have crucial, even primary, roles to play. The police are the 'eyes and ears' of the system. They are a massive force that, if properly trained and networked, can observe intelligence at the grassroots and pass it upward to the strategic level. They are the ones in a position to pre-empt attack and provide a first response once it occurs. (We shall not quickly forget the images of police in Mumbai attempting to do battle with Kalashnikov-armed terrorists with World War II vintage Lee Enfield.303 rifles.)

A police service capable of providing these services should be more oriented to community policing than the paramilitary structure dictated by the 1861 Police Act. Under a community policing model, the constable is an independent, well-trained and educated operative, capable of making independent, street-level decisions on individual cases, which he or she encounters, rather than deferring to higher authority and acting purely according to direction.

This is the policing model conferred by the idea of the London 'bobby' patrolling the streets unarmed, as originating in the reforms of Sir Robert Peel in 1829. Under these reforms, the police were to be accountable, of un-impeachable integrity and to be at one with the public, who they were seen to serve.

Regrettably, the efforts to reform India's state police services, which still mostly operate according to acts very similar to the central government Act, which in turn dates back to the colonial legislation of 1861, have not significantly progressed. As expressed by Sanjay Patil in a recent report written under the auspices of the Commonwealth Human Rights Initiative,

When the British Empire first started wielding more control and influence on its colonies in South Asia, it modelled policing after the militaristic Irish Constabulary rather than the civilian London Metropolitan model. This was meant to subjugate very large and hostile indigenous populations with a relatively small force.

No lesser body than the Indian Planning Commission has pointed out that policing and legal structures in India are currently highly dysfunctional. Whereas the primary concern of the Commonwealth Human Rights Initiative is the rights of individuals, the Planning Commission is primarily concerned with India's economic and social performance as a nation. According to the Planning Commission, the poor performance of the legal sector is actually dragging India and its development down. In its words, "a more orderly society is the bedrock of planned development".

In 2006, the Indian Supreme Court also brought down seven requirements (six directed against the states and one against the Union) directed towards policing reform. These requirements, many of which reflected the recommendations of the Indian Police Commission, have never been implemented. The Police Commission had met eight times between 1988 and 1991. Its recommendations were wide ranging recommendations – from the establishment of proper, independent complaint mechanisms, to the replacement of the repressive and anachronistic 1861 Police Act, and to ensuring the independence of policing from the influence of the government executive.

One important factor apparently preventing reform is the nexus between the police and senior politicians in some states. Obviously, such states will be reluctant to introduce reforms attacking the cosy relationships that are of mutual benefit. So far, 11 of 26 states have implemented some kind of reforms, but often such reforms fall short of providing accountability and transparency.

Much of the above is common sense and covered elsewhere. What is sometimes overlooked, however, is that the ability to conduct successful investigations is a prime tool of counter-terrorism and that the police are the key investigators in counter-terrorism. Successful investigations can break up terrorist cells and organisations and provide far-reaching intelligence leads.

For example, B. Raman has pointed out that there have been no major attacks in India in the year since 26/11. In part, he attributes this to the successful investigation of the Indian Mujahideen series of attacks that took place on major Indian cities throughout 2008 and the consequent significant erosion of IM cells. The opening up of the investigations into the IM through an 'encounter' with three IM activists in New Delhi in September 2008 and the subsequent arrest of one has opened a whole chain of cases in India that had hitherto escaped detection.

But despite the successes against the IM, there is evidence that India's capacity to investigate terrorism and crime in general is still not always what it should be. Even crime scene management in important cities like Mumbai and New Delhi is often inadequate, as evidenced by the obvious and very poor crime scene control in Mumbai in the aftermath of 26/11. (Although it must also be said that crime scene management after any massive terrorist attack such as 26/11 is bound to be difficult).

In other instances, investigations have not always had early successes and have sometimes been characterised by poor practices and worse. For example, the investigations of the bombings in Hyderabad in 2007 resulted in a number of false arrests and accusations on use of torture by the police – accusations subsequently upheld in a report of the Andhra Pradesh Minorities Commission. The bombing of the Samjhauta Express train in 2006 has also not been resolved, despite a number of initial false arrests.

The attacks on the Mumbai rail system in July 2006 resulted in serious differences between agencies as to which terrorist group was responsible, with the Maharashtra Anti-Terrorism Squad (ATS) arresting Student's Islamic Movement of India (SIMI) members and the Crime Branch of the Mumbai Police arresting IM members.

Eventually, the Crime Branch was forced by the courts to release its arrestees. Following the blasts, about 300 Muslims were randomly 'rounded up' by the Mumbai police and held for questioning. Even the investigation of the 26/11 attacks was mired in controversy. And a suppressed, official report of the Maharashtra government reportedly points to poor policing practices in the response to the attacks.

All too often, Indian investigations seem to involve the arrest of a suspect on grounds of inadequate evidence and subsequent administration of the so-called 'truth drug' (Sodium Pentathal). Suspects are sometimes tortured in these encounters with the police, as occurred in the Andhra Pradesh case mentioned above.

These approaches seem to be based more on desperation resulting from political pressure to obtain a result rather than sound investigation practices. The otherwise cumbersome court system appears to bear out the view that the investigations process is generally poor in India.

The conviction rate for IPC (more serious) crimes in India in 2007 was 42.3 per cent. This compares with a conviction rate of 80.7 per cent in the UK. It is worth noting that conviction rates are a different data set than 'clear up' rates, which would be far lower than 42.3 per cent, given the fact that in 2007,14.5 million were awaiting trial on IPC crimes alone, suggesting that, on an annualised basis, the 'clear up' rates are extremely low.

On their part, senior police in India express considerable frustration with a legal system that can take years to bring cases to judgment and that is increasingly subject to the 'purchasing of justice' by the deployment of slick lawyers capable of finding loopholes in the system on technical grounds. In these circumstances, the police are increasingly taking matters into their own hands. In less serious cases, they are giving alleged criminals a thrashing and letting them go; in more serious cases, they are sometimes killing them in so-called 'encounters'.

In one of the most serious of these, three senior policemen have been arrested in Gujarat; but this is alleged to be only one of a number of such encounter cases in that state. Even a frustrated public is increasingly resorting to so-called 'lynch law'.

A video of a man in Bihar being beaten nearly to death by a mob shocked even the President, who remarked that something needed to be done to prevent ordinary citizens taking the law into their own hands, and also noted that "the realm of judicial administration is not without its own share of inadequacies and blemishes". While such methods might be seen to give temporary relief from criminality, they unfortunately also lead to grave injustices and further alienate disaffected minorities, who are often the targets of police bashings, torture and 'encounter' killings.

General crime and the police capacity to deal with it cannot be de-linked from counter-terrorism, especially in the South Asian context. In South Asia, there is a particularly close relationship between crime, corruption and terrorism. Criminal gangs like Dawood Ibrahim's 'D Company' have widespread networks for smuggling purposes, involving agents of corruption in the police and customs.

Court cases show that these were heavily utilised in the Mumbai bombings of 1993. Just recently, members of a criminal gang reportedly working on behalf of D Company were arrested for issuances of false passports. Given D Company's links with terrorists, the security implications of these activities are profound. According to the US Congress Research Service (CRS), Lending his (Ibrahim's) criminal expertise and networks to such terrorist groups, he is capable of smuggling terrorists across national borders, trafficking in weapons and drugs, controlling extortion and protection rackets, and laundering ill-gotten proceeds, including through the abuse of traditional value transfer methods, like hawala.

There is also a close nexus between firearms and explosives trafficking and terrorism and insurgency, between hawala and terrorism fund transfers, between the giant web of fraudulent under-invoicing and terrorism financing, and between all areas of criminality and the raising of funds to support terrorist and insurgent organisations.

Moreover, these problems are not specific to India, but are general throughout South Asia, which only goes to complicate India's situation. For example, India suffers from the fact that a major arms shipment route from South East to South Asia passes through the Bangladeshi ports of Cox's Bazaar and Chittagong.

The largest-ever such interdicted case involved a shipment of 10 truckloads of arms through Chittagong, allegedly destined for the United Liberation Front of Asom (ULFA) and allegedly involving corrupt senior Bangladeshi ministers and intelligence officers. India's porous border with Nepal also often features as a source of smuggled weapons and explosives, subsequently used in terrorist attacks and other crimes.

Given this close nexus between crime, corruption and terrorism in South Asia, it would be impossible to make India safe from terrorism and insurgency without also greatly improving the performance of the police and related agencies in investigating major crimes and corruption.

Policing, however, is predominantly a state government function and mainly still undertaken in India according to the authoritarian mould bequeathed by the perceived needs of the colonising power. Judging from the quotation of the Minister of Home Affairs, it is apparent that the Union government is well aware of the problems with policing in India and that the need to improve policing is integral to the counter-terrorism effort. Indeed, stimulated by the poor response evident to the attacks of 26/11, the government has commenced a major process of reform of India's counter-terrorism and security mechanisms. If implemented in full, these reforms will go a good way to meeting some of the major concerns about internal security in India. But as we shall see, they are still likely to have some serious limitations.

STRATEGIC CULTURE AND INDIAN NUCLEAR POLICY

Indian strategic culture – defined as a set pattern of thought and behaviour – with respect to nuclear weapons may be described as nuclear minimalism. Its chief characteristics are:

Low level of importance accorded to nuclear weapons. Nuclear weapons are viewed as dangerous and deeply problematic, and hence not central to the attainment of national security. Though potential nuclear threats have existed since China, soon after its war with India, became a nuclear power in 1964, there has never been a sense of urgency in India's nuclearization. The fact that India did not build an arsenal after the 1974 test and the absence of deployment after 1998 show that India remains a reluctant nuclearizer.

A political rather than a military approach to nuclear weapons. Such a view treats nuclear weapons as political instruments that are unusable for purposes other than deterrence, as opposed to an operational view, which would tend to regard them as extensions of conventional weapons. There is little interest in the concept of nuclear warfighting, even among military officers. Defence strategy as a whole, and nuclear strategy in particular, are completely civilian-dominated.

Emphasis on minimum deterrence. This involves the conviction that it does not take large numbers or a high degree of sophistication to deter an adversary. Immediately after the 1998 tests, the Indian government, backed by its nuclear scientists, announced that more tests were not needed. Moreover, from this standpoint, nuclear balances are of no consequence. Hence, India need not worry about China's far larger nuclear arsenal. This precludes arms racing, which is both costly and risky. It restrains unnecessary spending on a nuclear build-up and prevents the diversion of resources from the more pressing needs of economic development.

Strong commitment to arms control. This is a logical extension of the long-held apprehension that nuclear weapons are as much a source of insecurity as of security. India's preference is for comprehensive, non-discriminatory and multilateral disarmament, but the earlier unrealistic expectations of its feasibility have been toned down.

Today, bilateral as well as multilateral (non-discriminatory) arms control is considered acceptable. India has agreed on a number of pre-nuclear confidence building measures (CBMs) with China and Pakistan. In contrast with the United States and the Soviet Union, India and Pakistan agreed on a nuclear CBM even *before* they officially declared their nuclear weapons status when they signed in December 1988 an agreement not to attack each other's nuclear facilities. In the wake of the 1998 tests, the Lahore Memorandum of Understanding (February 1999) provided for mutual notification of impending missile tests. Currently, follow-up negotiations with Pakistan are being taken up.

However, there are some problems that appear to be inadequately resolved. Two significant ones – a failure to comprehend fully the relationship between different levels of conflict, and a lack of doctrinal clarity – are discussed below.

The Nuclear-Sub nuclear Linkage

A major problem with Indian thinking about nuclear weapons is its lack of clarity in relating the different levels of armed conflict, i.e., the relationships between subconventional, conventional and nuclear conflict. Initially, the advent of nuclear deterrence was regarded as having brought to an end *all* forms of physical conflict between India and its adversaries. Notably, it was expected by the leadership that Pakistan could no longer attempt to pursue its long-standing objective of obtaining full control over the disputed state of Jammu and Kashmir through military means.

Once India and Pakistan had established mutual deterrence, prudence would be the order of the day. Pakistan could no longer risk a conflict in Kashmir, the strategic status quo would be permanently frozen, and India would be able to deal with its Kashmir insurgency as an internal problem. This crucial error in Indian strategic thinking was exposed by the Kargil conflict of 1999. Accompanied by insurgents, Pakistani forces dressed in civilian garb occupied territory on the Indian side of the mutually agreed Line of Control (LoC) in Kashmir. The aim was to create a crisis without officially crossing the LoC, i.e., to obtain a military advantage while retaining official deniability. This would evoke a general fear of escalation from subconventional to conventional to nuclear conflict and thereby induce international intervention, compelling India to negotiate.

The attempt backfired for two reasons. First, India was able to use massive conventional firepower and throw out the occupying forces, whereas Pakistan could not overtly cross into Indian territory in response for fear of raising the conflict to a full-scale conventional war. Second, Pakistan's actions evoked a strongly critical international response, particularly from the United States, forcing it to announce a humiliating withdrawal of its campaign. However, the Kargil conflict did demonstrate to Indian leaders the problem of the "stability-instability paradox": that the standoff between nuclear rivals permits lowintensity or subconventional conflicts to occur between them. The working of the stability-instability paradox imposed on India a kind of strategic paralysis which Indian leaders found frustrating in the extreme. Though Kargil had failed, Pakistan was able to sustain its low-cost strategy of backing terrorist groups such as the Hizbul Mujahideen, the Lashkar-e-Taiba, and the Jaish-e-Muhammad in striking at will within India. Indian leaders struggled to devise a suitable response. The discourse among policy makers steadily shifted away from a search for political solutions to a quest for appropriate modes of force projection against Pakistan.

The options aired included hot pursuit of terrorists into Pakistani territory, limited strikes or special operations missions against terrorist camps in Pakistan, and a vague and undefined conception of "limited war." In January 2000, Defence Minister George Fernandes asserted that nuclear weapons "can deter only the use of nuclear weapons, but not all and any war," and that Kargil had demonstrated that Indian forces "can fight and win a limited war, at a time and place chosen by the aggressor." While admitting that under the nuclear shadow, there were "definite limitations if escalation across the nuclear threshold was to be avoided," Fernandes claimed that conventional war "has not been made obsolete by nuclear weapons." However, the likelihood that a resort to armed conflict might invite an adverse international response prevented action. The terrorist attacks of September 11, 2001 in the US altered the situation. The American intervention in Afghanistan created a favourable climate for a strong Indian response to Pakistan's support for cross-border terrorism. Furthermore, major terrorist attacks on the Jammu and Kashmir legislature in October, and on the Indian Parliament in December, sharply increased pressure on the Indian government to act. Indian leaders sought to break out of their straitjacket of inaction and turn the stability-instability paradox against Pakistan through the exercise of coercive diplomacy.

They initiated a massive conventional build-up along the Pakistan border and threatened to launch an unspecified form of limited war unless Pakistan stopped abetting terrorism in India. Though nuclear weapons did not enter the picture directly (there is no evidence so far of nuclear weapons being readied by either side), the mobilization did have a strong nuclear-strategic component. India's strategy was a two-pronged one. It attempted *direct compellence* in pressurizing Pakistan to back off in the face of a looming full-scale conventional and possibly nuclear conflict. It simultaneously attempted *indirect compellence* by causing the United States, fearful of a regional holocaust, to pressurize Pakistan to reverse its strategy of supporting cross-border terrorism.

Thus, a linkage was established between subconventional and nuclear conflict through conventional mobilization. India warned that if Pakistan chose to bring nuclear weapons into the fray, it (Pakistan) would suffer far more than India. On December 29, 2001, Fernandes warned:

Pakistan can't think of using nuclear weapons despite the fact that they are not committed to the doctrine of no first use like we are. We could take a strike, survive, and then hit back. Pakistan would be finished. I do not really fear that the nuclear issue would figure in a conflict.

In effect, what the Minister was saying was that nuclear balances do matter. This was in direct contravention of his government's doctrine of minimum deterrence, which rests on the belief that they do not. Besides, the idea that India could tolerate some damage from nuclear weapons seriously undercut its deterrence philosophy.

In the end, the whole exercise was fruitless. Despite considerable US pressure, Pakistan's promises to end support for terrorists operating in Kashmir were tactical and temporary, and, in the face of Pakistani counter-mobilization, India had to withdraw its forces in October 2002 after a ten-month-long deployment. It could not take the risk of treating a smaller quantum of nuclear damage as acceptable in practice, as opposed to its rhetorical argument. Deterrence overrode compellence. While the Indian government has not abandoned the possibility of other forms of limited conventional action, it is evident that the experience has taught a lesson. The episode revealed the difficulty involved in attempting to create strategic space for limited armed conflict in a nuclear environment. This explains the BJP-led government's October 2003 decision to resume negotiations with Pakistan.

Lack of Clarity on Minimum Deterrence

Where does India stand today? The picture is not yet clear. Its doctrine of "credible minimum deterrence" has yet to be articulated fully, and has undergone significant changes between 1999 and 2003. After the 1998 tests, Prime Minister Vajpayee made a brief announcement in Parliament on the elements of his government's nuclear doctrine. He stated that further testing was not necessary for credibility, affirmed India's commitment to the principle of no first use (NFU), and declared that arms control and disarmament remained central to the national agenda. But he said nothing about the sources of threat, the nature of deployment, the types and number of weapons desired, targeting, and other details which are normally considered the primary components of a deterrence strategy. Much of the public understanding of India's minimum deterrence doctrine till recently was based on the Draft Nuclear Doctrine (DND) released by the National Security Advisory Board (NSAB) in August 1999. The DND envisages "credible minimum deterrence" based on a capacity for "punitive retaliation with nuclear weapons to inflict damage unacceptable to the [nuclear] aggressor." For this, the requirements are "sufficient, survivable and operationally prepared nuclear forces" and the organization and will to employ nuclear weapons in the event deterrence fails. It proclaims NFU as well as non-use against countries which are not nuclear and are not allied with nuclear powers. It also calls for robust conventional forces in order to raise the nuclear threshold.

The DND supports a triad of air, land and sea-based delivery systems whose "survivability will be enhanced by a combination of multiple redundant systems, mobility, dispersion and deception." It distinguishes between an unspecified mode of "peacetime deployment" and a shift to "fully employable forces" in the event of a conflict arising. There is an emphasis on credibility – "any adversary must know that India can and will retaliate" – and on effectiveness based on "reliability, timeliness, accuracy and weight of attack." The document goes on to outline the requirements for command and control, security and safety, and research and development, and concludes by focusing on disarmament and arms control. The DND has been criticized for its lack of clarity and its open-endedness. Its call for a triad of delivery systems, and its emphasis on effectiveness and survivability go against the grain of a minimum deterrence posture since they reflect the typical Cold War approach used by the United States and the Soviet Union, both of which built needlessly large forces on the basis of such arguments. In short, the DND reveals a distinct preference for the operational rather than the political aspect of deterrence.

However, as Minister of External Affairs Jaswant Singh told an interviewer subsequently, the report was released in order to generate a national debate and was "not a policy document of the Government of India." Singh's interview provides a much more political exposition of Indian nuclear thinking. There are, certainly, a number of common elements in the DND and the interview. Both declare that India will not be the first to use nuclear weapons; that its retaliation-only posture will be based on the mobility and dispersal of assets as well as on an unspecified level of redundancy; that a distinction has to be made between peacetime and active deployment, implying the possibility of a normally de-mated disposition of warheads and launch vehicles; and that ultimate authority over the arsenal must be civilian.

But Singh's enunciation of nuclear doctrine differs from the DND in important respects. While noting that nuclear assets must be survivable, he does not endorse the DND's stress on India's need for "multiple redundant systems" as necessary for survivability.

The latter implies a discomfort with imbalance and a penchant for arms racing because its points of reference are the operational characteristics of an adversary's inventory. Singh explicitly states that "parity is not essential for deterrence," that India will not engage in arms racing, and that minimum deterrence is only a question of "adequacy," not specific numbers – a point not made clear in the DND.

Singh also makes the crucial point that retaliation need not be instantaneous. The implication for stability is clear: there is no need for Indian nuclear forces to be on high alert status, ready for instant retaliation. This facilitates a relatively stable nuclear posture.

This is a question that is not addressed in the DND. Further, whereas the DND does not focus on the question of targeting, Singh observes that "we have discarded the Cold War reference frame of nuclear war fighting," and that "we do not see nuclear weapons as weapons of war fighting," which is an unambiguous rejection of counterforce doctrine.

Another difference is with regard to the development of a nuclear triad. While the DND calls for a triad, Singh's position is that though development of diverse capabilities will go on, it is "premature" to talk of a triad and, more important, that a triad is not a "pre-requisite for credibility." The overall effect of the interview is to convey a relatively strong sense of commitment to nuclear minimalism based on a restrained posture with few weapons.

In this respect, Singh is more reassuring than the DND. His delineation of nuclear doctrine is in keeping with a pattern of strategic preferences that treats nuclear weapons with circumspection. This helps explain the early initiative taken by Prime Minister Vajpayee in February 1999 (less than a year after the nuclear tests of 1998) to travel to Lahore in an attempt to establish regional strategic stability.

The brief announcement on nuclear doctrine and on the establishment of a National Command Authority (NCA) in January 2003 added something to our understanding of official Indian thinking. Its main points on doctrine were:

1. Reaffirmation of "credible" minimum deterrence;
2. Reiteration of NFU;
3. The threat of "massive" retaliation in response to a first strike against Indian forces anywhere;
4. Non-use of nuclear weapons against non-nuclear weapon states;
5. The option to retaliate with nuclear weapons against a chemical or biological attack;
6. Adherence to strict export controls; and
7. Renewed commitment to arms control through participation in the Fissile Material Cutoff Treaty (FMCT) negotiations, continued observance of the national moratorium on testing, and sustained commitment to universal disarmament.

Though these commitments do tell us something about India's deterrence posture, none of them has a direct bearing on the central character of *minimum* deterrence. NFU is a promise rather than a guarantee, and adversaries are unlikely to take it seriously in their calculations of risk. Besides, in comparison with earlier statements, it is diluted by the exceptions made with regard to chemical and biological weapons.

Massive retaliation is a threat that will in any case be expected by an adversary, for nuclear weapons, inevitably, are conducive to worst-case assumptions. Perhaps the pronouncement nearest to conveying a commitment to minimum deterrence is the pledge not to test, since a sophisticated arsenal of diverse and "reliable" weapons would require testing.

The critical aspects of minimum deterrence are *not* mentioned in the announcement: the perception that deterrence can be achieved with a small number of weapons, with weapons of relatively little variety and sophistication, and with weapons that are not deployed or even assembled.

If these aspects of minimum deterrence were to be spelt out, then a truly minimalist doctrine would have been articulated. That they have not been officially declared does not mean that a minimum deterrence doctrine does not exist. Quite clearly, it does. That is evident in its practice. However, the continuing search for diverse capabilities – land, air and sea-based – shows that the concept of minimum deterrence is not consistent. The only argument in favour of a triad is that it will reduce vulnerability, which is a standard Cold War argument. Sufficiency has to be defined in terms of the risk of retaliation faced by the adversary in contemplating the use of nuclear weapons, not one's own risk in being devastated by a first strike.

This brief review shows the lack of clarity and consistency in India's understanding of minimum deterrence. If ambivalence is allowed to persist, the possibility of nuclear thinking and practice drifting toward an open-ended operational conception of deterrence will increase. As India's nuclear infrastructure grows and takes shape, operational pressures led by military personnel, whose job, after all, is to treat nuclear weapons as usable weapons, will also grow.

Questions about vulnerability and reliability – and above all "credibility" – will be raised in the quest for more and "better" weapons. Unless minimum deterrence is clearly and thoroughly understood, there is always the possibility that some combination of intellectual drift, organizational pressures, and sustained threats will push doctrine toward open-ended expansion.

7

India's Military Policy Challenges in the 21st Century

The first macro problem that must be resolved, if India is to rise as a great power, is achieving higher rates of economic growth. The reason for that is simple. A competent military costs money and modern defense capabilities, which are sophisticated and effective, are priced in numbers that boggle the imagination. For a country like India, which has to deal not simply with questions of defense but also questions of development simultaneously, high economic growth becomes the only solution especially in those situations when India cannot choose between the objectives of defense and development. When one begins to think of the revolution in military affairs — the kind of capabilities today that characterize the military forces of the great powers — it is simply impossible for India to acquire such capabilities without sustaining economic growth of at least 7 to 9 per cent per annum consistently.

China is a good example. A country that has experienced close to double-digit growth for more than twenty years since 1978, still finds it hard to develop the kinds of sophisticated military capabilities it seeks to acquire across the board.

Therefore, one must be prepared for the fact that even if the Indian economy were to grow between 7 and 9 per cent consistently for the next twenty years, the best India would be able to do in the area of cutting edge defense technology is to acquire niche capabilities. But those niche capabilities may be enough for the specific strategic circumstances that it faces. The second macro problem that India needs to engage and satisfy is the development of an appropriate national vision and appropriate institutions designed to manage the acquisition of great power capabilities.

What substantive goals, defined in terms of national interest, does India really seek to service? The answer to this question cannot be defined in terms of platitudes like a "just world order." That is a useful phrase for a political campaign. It is a terrible criterion for defense planning and force structuring. The other aspect of this question of defining India's goals and creating the appropriate institutions pertains to the issue of whether India will be able to achieve the right balance between state control and societal autonomy. It is very important to realize that successful states in the modern era have been those that have maintained this balance in the most creative way possible.

The third macro challenge that I would highlight for your consideration is whether India is capable of exploiting the existing structure of the international system to its advantage. In this context, I think India should get rid of the notion of a multipolar world order as a practical outcome in the relevant future. Pursuing chimerical goals like multipolarity does not make for good policy. The international system, for all practical purposes, is going to remain a unipolar system for at least the next half century. By all indicators, if you define power in terms of comprehensive national strength, it is unlikely that the United States will face serious peer competitors for at least another fifty years.

Consequently, the challenge for India becomes, can it develop a viable strategic partnership with the United States that serves both mutual interests and India's own unilateral interests? Can India develop a relationship with the United States that helps it enhance and magnify its own power?

This is not to suggest that the United States is the only power in the international system. Clearly not — there are many others. This is also not to suggest that India's goals ought to consist solely of developing a relationship with the United States, or that India somehow is constrained solely to develop a relationship with the United States and no other. Not true. India has the flexibility to maneuver within the interstices of the international system. But at the end of the day, there is one eight hundred pound gorilla that has to be engaged. And that is the United States. That gorilla is not going to go away. That gorilla has already put its nose for the first time in modern history, into the physical environment of the subcontinent. And it is in India's national interest, and important for its capacity to generate and magnify its power, to develop a productive and a collaborative relationship with the United States that enhances the interests of the two countries.

First, India has to deal with the challenge of neutering internal security threats without undermining its capacity for effective external defense. This is harder to do than is sometimes imagined. It is unfortunate that the principal security threat that India is going to have to deal with on a day-to-day basis is the threat to internal security. There is no running away from this problem. Historically, India dealt with this challenge by essentially throwing manpower at the threat instead of technology. And the reason it did this was simply because it enjoyed a surfeit of manpower and a deficit of technology.

There were two consequences to this strategy. One was that its approach to preserving internal defense was probably not as effective as it could be, because technology could provide that valuable supplement which was not available to India. The second consequence was that preserving internal security became extremely expensive and has now come at the cost of being able to acquire the new technologies required to raise a modern military force. It is a myth that India's manpower is cheap. Maintaining the size and kind of forces that India does, if maintained over the secular period, will undercut its ability to acquire the kind of RMA capabilities that wins modern wars. And this is going to require India to make very painful choices — painful choices about reducing its manpower strength and changing the inter-service budgetary balances, choices that it cannot make today because of the gravity, importance, and burdens of its internal security commitments.

The next micro issue is the need to preserve effective external defense, now in a nuclear shadowed environment. This brings us face to face with the vexed question of whether India has the capacity to successfully prosecute a limited war. Most commentary so far has focused on the issue of limited war as an example of Indian recklessness. People have chastised the Defense Minister, Mr. George Fernandes, for arguing that limited war in fact represents a solution to India's external security problems. My take on the issue is somewhat different. I believe that limited war should be viewed not as a product of the proclivities of the state, but rather as a predicament resulting from a specific set of structural circumstances.

The transparent presence of nuclear weapons in the subcontinent for the first time makes unlimited wars untenable as a matter of state policy.

This is not simply India's choice — it actually represents a dilemma of the nuclear age. And it is a challenge that faces India both with respect to Pakistan and with respect to China. In both cases, unlimited war is not feasible. There is also no guarantee that war is obsolete. And therefore the challenge of limited war confronts India squarely, both with respect to its northern and its western borders.

What does limited war mean for Indian defense policy? It means that India is now confronted with the task of being required to hit hard and effectively enough to punish an adversary, but not hit so hard or so effectively as to cause inadvertent escalation. This in turn leads to questions like "how do you avoid escalation?" Most commentaries have focused on this aspect of the problem. But there is another aspect to the problem, which has largely escaped attention. Because it is going to demand of India a new style of war fighting that New Delhi traditionally has been uncomfortable with and which historically it has been relatively incapable of. It is a style of war fighting that puts a premium on achieving very speedy decision on the battlefield and then terminating offensive action either before the international community intervenes or before the conflict degenerates into unavoidable attrition. Getting the Indian military to successfully prosecute a fast paced war that generates quick decisions is something that we have not seen in fifty years of India's independence. It is also the kind of war that traditionally the United States was not very good at. We preferred wars that allowed us plenty of time to mobilize, plenty of time to deploy, and then plenty of time to be able to grind down the adversary at our convenience. If India is to be able to prosecute the opposite kind of war, as the United States is now proficient at — fast, decisive, and yet limited — it is going to require an investment in new technologies and new operating skills apart from new doctrines and new concepts of operation.

Third, if India is to become a great power of the sort that it seeks to become, it also has to become a net provider of regional security, both in the sub-continental and in the extra sub-continental arenas. This is easier said than done; yet at one level it is the quintessential part of the definition of a great power. After all, what is the meaning of having great power capabilities if at the end of the day you cannot extend net security to others? And yet any Indian attempt to provide the kind of regional security that I am talking of, even in the sub-continental arena, is fraught with hazards because it risks deepening intra-regional rivalries and it risks deepening the suspicions India's weaker neighbours have of its capabilities and its intentions. Finally, will India develop the organizational structures that are required to maintain and operate these capabilities if it seeks to provide the kind of regional security that is to be expected of a great power?

The fourth micro problem pertains to whether India can acquire an effective nuclear deterrent without breaking the bank. My view is that nuclear weapons are important for India's security in some limited sense, but it is also essential to remember that they are actually relatively obsolescent technologies. Nuclear weapons are now over fifty years old and they are generally unusable as instruments of international politics.

SITUATION IN INDIA

Effecting major organisational changes in the management of the armed forces has to be politically driven from a full understanding of the issues involved, the benefits to be derived, the efficiencies and savings to be achieved, without undermining operational effectiveness. A pre-condition has to be that the highest political executive be convinced of the necessity for change, has a hands-on familiarity with the management of defence issues in broad terms, and has the will, time, and organisational, legislative and people skills to see the changes through. Such conditions existed in varying degrees in the USA, UK and most European countries during and after the major wars, and urgency was provided by the people's instinct for survival in the face of possible nuclear holocaust. In India, the necessary conditions for driving change are largely absent, despite the dysfunctional nature of the organisation for defence planning and endemic delays, cost overruns and failure to meet specifications.

Planning for defence is an extremely complex matter abounding in uncertainties. Since the state is dealing with future requirements, the success of research or design effort, availability of material resources or skilled personnel, capability of the builder, manufacturer or supplier, or even assurance of funding and stability of policy cannot be taken for granted. This is further complicated if foreign governments or manufacturers are involved, introducing uncertainties of licensing, sanctions, denial regimes, end-user issues and even unrelated matters such as diplomatic pressure. There are also the complications of offsets, sweeteners, kickbacks and disinformation/misinformation by competitors and interested parties.

Integrated Defence Planning

Whatever the complications, it would seem self-evident that comprehensive integrated planning for the defence of India would reduce duplication and waste, better utilise technical and manpower resources, make for more efficient and cost-effective procurement for the armed forces, and simplify their logistics management. This is of course easier said than done. The first difficulty is the vastly disproportionate size of the Indian army compared to the Navy and the Air Force, the nature of its operational role and its special equipment requirements, very little of which is common to the other two services. Until more common platforms such as the Advanced Light Helicopter (ALH) and the Light Combat Aircraft (LCA) enter service, shared logistics will remain restricted to basic items such as ammunition, transport vehicles, rations, medical supplies and the like. Some commonality also exists in indigenously developed missiles, UAVs, radars, communications equipment etc, but the list could be expanded.

Nevertheless, there is a modest degree of integration in the Indian armed forces, starting with the common training of officer cadets at the National Defence Academy which began in January 1949 long before the concept gained favour with leading military powers. The Indian armed forces have been moving towards integration at the higher levels of the defence organisation too with deliberation, within the limitations of the security environment, the infirmities of the political system, the shortcomings of bureaucracy and the doubts within the military establishment itself.

The Service Headquarters are now styled as the Integrated Headquarters, Ministry of Defence (Army/Navy/Air Force) as the case may be, and there is limited integration of civil and military staffs on a functional basis. There is also more devolution of financial powers, the positive effect of which is discernible even at the unit level. However, despite strenuous efforts and comprehensive recommendations by a "Group of Ministers", the nettle that is yet to be grasped is that of the Higher Defence Organisation at the level of the Defence Minister, the Chief of Defence Staff (CDS) and his charter and responsibilities, and the reorganisation of the Departments of Defence, Defence Production and Research and Development.

No integrated staff can function effectively unless there is a common professional superior, and none exists. All joint planning and proposals routed through the Chiefs of Staff Committee (COSC), are agreed to (or shelved) on the basis of consensus and promulgated under the authority of the rotational Chairman, COSC. Consensus is not a bad thing; it causes less frictions and has a greater chance of succeeding. But it is critically dependent on the cooperative relationship between the services, mutual accommodation, goodwill, personalities of the three Chiefs, their interpretations of parochial service interests and willingness to moderate them for common objectives. Instances are known of a single service secretively processing cases that have implications for the other two, in cooperation with some civil servants for their own ends, and together, misleading the minister. Naturally, trust is the biggest casualty, with not only administrative but operational implications.

Since budgets are always tight, no consensus is possible on the equipment plans of the three services if it entails sacrificing a major service project. Budgetary proposals are, therefore, merely aggregations of each service requirements, and no matter how justified, result only in separate rough and ready budgetary provision for the Army, Navy and the Air force in the national budget.

This by no means implies authority to spend the amounts on the proposals submitted, which have to be again justified individually up the tortuous chain for approval by the "competent authority", whosoever that might be in a given case. Delays and shortfalls are in-built into the system and seem to worry only the military that has to live with the consequences in terms of diminished operational capability or personnel hardship and morale. Another major deficiency is that the Department of Defence under the Defence Secretary, who is the *de-facto* Chief Staff Officer to the Defence Minister, does not participate in any meaningful way in formulating and developing the proposals received from the armed forces before they are moved for financial and executive approval, preferring instead to "examine" them for ministerial endorsement, often without being technically or professionally equipped to do so.

Because of the staffing pattern, its competence lies in procedural matters, but as "examiner", it feels obliged to raise numerous, supposedly searching queries that are often based on superficial information.

INDIA'S MILITARY AND DEFENCE POLICY

India inherited some defence industries from Great Britain. They included Hindustan Aeronautics Limited (HAL), which is today India's largest defence public sector undertaking (DPSU), Mazagon Docks Limited (MDL), the largest shipyard in the nation, and more than half a dozen ordnance factories. The growth of the domestic defence industry has, however, been sporadic since Independence. It did not follow any definite plan though emphasis was placed on enhancing indigenous defence production capability.

Some analysts have also traced certain vigorousness in the Indian effort at developing an indigenous defence capability to the early 1960s spawned by the 1962 India-China war. The war is seen as having underscored the urgency of building a domestic defence industry through foreign assistance. It was also in consonance with Nehru's policy of building a strong industrial base patterned on the Soviet model. But while the war with China has been identified as the catalyst in the effort at developing a domestic defence base, there was no concerted, systematic and well-orchestrated effort towards the achievement of this goal.

There were many factors that stood in the way of India building a strong military-industrial base. India's comparatively easy access to various types of defence equipment from the former Soviet Union (FSU) and their purchase against deferred rupee payments and on "friendship" price were some of them. Sophisticated defence equipment was transferred to India under the favourable rupee-rouble arrangements from FSU. Some license production facilities were also established in India, for instance for the Mig-21 aircraft. The Cold War also ensured that India continued to have a favourable and preferred source of defence systems and equipment from FSU. It did not find the superpower wanting in any critical manner in fulfilling India's defence requirements. However, this had the unintended consequences of dampening any sense of urgency in India to develop an indigenous defence industry. Coupled with this was the reluctance of the US to help in India's effort to develop a domestic defence production base. Nevertheless, trudging along, India was able to develop the largest defence industry among developing nations.

However, with the collapse of the FSU, India lost easy access to sophisticated defence equipment at cheap prices. The problem was compounded by the absence of an alternate source of modern defence equipment. The situation became worse with the almost complete disruption in the supply of services and spare parts necessary to maintain the predominantly Soviet-equipped Indian armed forces. The navy was particularly affected, as it was dependent on Soviet designs and equipment for some of the ships that were under construction in India. This led to huge cost and time overruns in the indigenous construction programme of naval vessels.

Ironically, the need to service and maintain various kinds of equipment imported from FSU compelled India to seek ways and means to develop some level of indigenous capability. Towards this goal, certain technologies and know-how were obtained, both for the repairs and for the local production of some critical spare parts. These efforts were, however, largely case-specific and were not components of any systematic strategy for the comprehensive development of an indigenous defence industry. They were also service-driven in the absence of any coherent strategy to achieve self-reliance. However, the liberalisation of the Indian economy that almost coincided with the collapse of FSU and promised to unlock India's productive capabilities gave impetus to the goal of developing a domestic military-industrial complex.

It was, however, not until 2005 that India formulated a defence offset policy to contribute to the nation's goal of developing its domestic defence industry. This policy was incorporated in the Defence Procurement Procedure (DPP) 2005. The policy introduced a 30 per cent offset in contracts valued above Rs 3 billion under "buy" and 'buy and make" categories.

Under the policy, foreign vendors had the liberty to discharge their obligations either through the execution of defence exports of Indian items and services or through investments in India's defence infrastructure. They also had the option of selecting Indian firms in consultation with an industry associate of their choice to implement their offset obligations. The hallmark of this policy was its non-obligatory nature, or in other words, these offsets were non-mandatory. It was left to the Services Capital Acquisition Plan Categorisation Committee (SCAPCC) to recommend the incorporation of offset obligation in acquisition proposals. The offset policy was, however, in the nascent stage and it lacked clarity in many areas. It also suffered from the absence of any designated agency in the Ministry of Defence (MoD) for guiding, overseeing, executing and monitoring the implementation of the policy. In reality, confusion reigned in equal measure in the corridors of South Block as in the minds of the vendors on how to implement the offset obligations. Consequently, the offset policy did not yield any dividend.

The absence of any offset benefit to the Indian defence industry led the Government of India (GoI) to make significant changes in DPP 2006 and they included the following:

- offset was made mandatory in defence contracts of the size and nature as prescribed in the 2005 policy;
- foreign firms were allowed the flexibility of forming joint ventures (JVs) with Indian firms, and;
- a new organisation called the Defence Offset Facilitation Agency (DOFA) was established comprising of representatives of all stakeholders; the Services, DPSUs, Defence and Research Organisation (DRDO), etc.

Defence Offsets

Offsets have been variously defined. In essence, offsets in defence, as in civil trade, are compensations that a buyer seeks from the seller for the purchase of goods and/or services. The demand for offsets in defence has exhibited an upward trajectory since the 1950s. It gained further momentum in the 1980s and has been growing ever since. From around 20 nations about two decades ago, this practice has now been now adopted by more than 130 nations. European nations have been able to generate more offsets than others. During the period 1993-2004, European countries were able to obtain offsets valued at 99.1 per cent of their defence imports while non-European countries achieved 46.6 per cent of their imports. Significantly, 72.9 per cent of the offsets obtained by European nations were 100 per cent or more of the value of the weapon systems imported by them. The data on arms sales and offsets show that demands for offsets "are increasing over time in all regions."

India was, however, late in adopting an official offset policy though it had obtained some compensatory benefits since Independence through a series of bilateral arrangements. It was only in 2005 that the nation, through its Defence Procurement Procedure (DPP), announced an official policy to secure offsets for its defence imports. The policy was amended to give it greater clarity and direction in 2006 and again in 2008. Consequently, as a late entrant in the field, India's polices are yet to be fully tested against the complex process of managing offsets and it is yet to traverse the path of achieving its declared objective of creating a vibrant military-industrial base.

Objective of Paper

This paper seeks to critically examine the salient features of India's offset policy and answer the following questions.

- Will the policy outlined in DPP 2008 contribute substantially to the development of a military-industrial base in India?
- What are the shortcomings of the policy?
- What modifications are required in the offset policy and connected government procedures to maximise the benefits that can accrue to the nation from capital acquisition of defence equipment?

In order to understand the basic arguments contained in this paper, a few concepts relating to offsets in general and in defence trade in particular are explained.

Offsets Explained

Offset, as the term implies, is an element that counterbalances or compensates an act. It is a set-off from a development, in this case, military acquisition. However defined, the term offset primarily signifies an element of 'compensation' as the predominant import of the term. It occurs "when a supplier places work to an agreed value with firms in the buying country, over and above what it would have brought in the absence of the offset."

As is commonly understood, in trade, offsets have been classified as direct or indirect offsets. Direct offsets are those that are directly connected with the item being sold by the seller and can take the form of co-production, component production, licensed production, etc. Indirect offsets are those not directly related to the product being imported and here compensations can be secured in any other area with the aim of obtaining for the economy what would otherwise have not been available to the buyer but for the purchase.

Though the above two forms characterise the two widely-accepted compensatory strategies, it is necessary to add a new terminology to describe a hybrid form of offsets that is between the direct and indirect offsets that India is seeking to obtain. This may be termed as quasi-direct offsets. It can be defined as compensation given in the sector under which the purchase falls, but is not directly connected with the product that is being imported. For instance, when tanks are imported, and the offset is obtained in the form of assistance for the co-production of a warship, then it will fall within this definition (quasi-direct) as it enhances the defence capability of the importing nation, though the compensatory arrangement is not directly connected with the item being imported. Therefore, though analysts have largely described India's policy as seeking direct offsets, it would be more accurate to describe it as quasi-direct offsets.

MAJOR TRANSITION IN INDIAN MILITARY POLICY

Recently the US journal Defence News reported that the Indian government is working on a program whereby Israel would replace Russia as India's largest supplier of weapons and defence equipment by 2008. Since Russia now supplies some 70 percent of India's weapons imports, this report, if true, would mark a major transformation in Indian defence policy. Under the terms of the program, India would identify the products it wants and ask the Israeli government to negotiate with domestic firms on its behalf as Jerusalem does with regard to its own weapons.

Israel is already the second-largest supplier of military systems to India, so this program could affect a major transformation in India's security relationships. The potential repercussions of this project, which would clearly show a serious break with Moscow's arms salesmen, are immense. Given the deep ties between the US and Israeli defence industries, if this program does materialize it will also probably enhance the United States' competitive position in the Indian defence market and result in further substantial increases in the already rising amount of US arms sales and security cooperation with India. Those sales could either be bilateral or brokered through Israel, such as weapons made jointly by Israel and the United States, including missile defence systems that India reportedly is interested in acquiring.

This program would then also strengthen the developing tripartite relationship among Israel, India, and the US in regard to defence sales. We can see this already occurring, because the United States has brushed aside Pakistan's objections to India's receiving the Israeli Phalcon radar, made with US technology and thus subject to US veto on its transfer to a third party.

Realization of the projected Indo-Israeli project would also simultaneously symbolize and express India's rising continental Asian status as a great power with interests and capabilities across the continent, allowing it to break free of its confining chains as merely a major South Asian power if not the regional leader, something that both Indian and foreign observers have labeled as a prerequisite for a full partnership with the United States. Not only would those trends strengthen Indo-Israeli ties, they would provide fuel to the oft-reported desire on the part of at least some US elites to create a tripartite alliance with India and Israel against terrorism (if not for other, broader objectives that would emerge later). Joint Indo-Israeli defence collaboration on a scale envisaged above would also, or so these advocates hope, tie into the US alliance and Israeli partnership with Turkey, creating a kind of pan-Asian bloc. The new program grows out of India's difficulty in negotiating a US$10 billion multi-year defence acquisition program with Russia. Three areas in particular seem to have caused some anxiety in New Delhi.

In March 2002, The Times of India reported that the Parliamentary Standing Committee had urged the government to avoid overdependence on Russia for armaments and spare parts. The committee reportedly acknowledged Russia's previous contributions and reliability as a provider of defence equipment to India but cautioned that the current dependence on Moscow for almost 80 percent of its arms imports is unhealthy. It also observed that Russia was not providing military hardware on the same beneficial financial terms that it had during the Soviet era. Therefore the committee also urged the Indian government to cease making advance payments for weapons acquisitions from Russia, and that in the future it seek to put more defence contracts up for competitive tender. Russia also has come under criticism because of India's difficulty in obtaining and negotiating speedy delivery of spare parts for these weapons systems. At the same time it became clear that given its worsening relations with Pakistan, India is seeking to diversify its foreign purchases and use foreign partners to develop its own defence industrial capability, eg by conditioning purchases on obtaining offsets from the sellers to develop its own indigenous capability. The alliance, if it were to materialize, would build on the already greatly improved Indo-Israeli relationship that has led to large-scale military sales from Israel and to India's rapprochement with the United States as well. As the Phalcon deal suggests, it could become possible to envisage tripartite collaboration among these states on missile defence, especially if India's great goal of securing the end to all US sanctions on the transfer of both civil and military technology is realized.

Moreover, the broadening of India's ties and reach in political-military terms through the acquisition of top-quality defence systems would enable it to play the kind of role that analysts in both India and the US postulate as being essential to any serious strategic partnership with the United States. And that role also accords very much with some of the deepest aspirations of India's foreign and defence policy elites, thus highlighting a congruence of visions concerning India's future international position. In effect India's aspiration to play a major role "from Socotra to Sumatra" would have been both realized and blessed by the United States, as Secretary of State Colin Powell implicitly suggested in 2001. India would then become not just a South or even Central Asian power but a major player in the Persian Gulf, the Middle East, and Southeast Asia.

At the same time, India's search for new vistas in defence acquisition and production relates very much to its rising economic, technological, and military-industrial capabilities as well as to its desire to strengthen existing long-standing partnerships, eg with Russia. For example, beyond the existing $10 billion weapons sales from Russia to India, India is collaborating with Russia on joint production of a fifth-generation fighter that Russia feels vital to its military future. Both are also collaborating on research that is probably tied to missile defence and nuclear systems as well. More broadly, India is the only country with whom Russia is collaborating on joint production of sophisticated and futuristic weapons systems. Likewise India, not China, gets the best weapons currently being produced in Russia, systems that not even Russia's armed forces can obtain. Moscow offers offsets in the form of technology transfer of production skills and know-how to India, one of its largest customers. Although India obviously seeks to diversify its sources of foreign procurement, Russian producers have until now been confident of their ability to obtain the bulk of Indian defence contracts. Whether or not this confidence is misplaced, time will tell, but diversification and strengthening of India's own capabilities surely would increase India's scientific-technological and manufacturing capabilities for weapons production. This objective also appears to be a major goal of the deals now being made with Russia, Israel, and presumably the United States. We see similar deals with Italian and French firms for joint manufacture of weapons systems.

India's leading defence firm, Hindustan Aeronautics Ltd (HAL), is also pressing an outsourcing program whereby it would help private Indian companies find and choose foreign partners to undertake such high-tech projects as avionics integration, weapons-system integration, and other related efforts to "lay the foundation for a credible domestic aerospace industry base that could meet the majority of India's military aerospace requirements in the next 10 years".

And it is no less logical to assume that India would be thrilled to duplicate this particular kind of relationship with Washington, especially as India already has a large space program with military applications and very much wants US conventional-weapons systems and technology transfer.

Indeed, a Pentagon-commissioned study of Indo-American perceptions reported that on the basis of many interviews, a uniform conclusion was reached that "for Indians, technology transfer from the United States is military cooperation's touchstone". Other Indian assessments confirm the great importance that India attaches to transfer of both civil and defence technology as a critical and essential element in any partnership with the US. While India's aspirations in the defence industry are common to other countries that seek the capability for indigenous production of most, if not all of their weapons, it is nevertheless clear that this deal, if it materializes, would utterly transform defence relationships among major players in the defence business: India, the US, Israel, and Russia. The major transformations in Asian security that accelerated after September 11, 2001, have clearly not yet run their course. Nor is it clear when the overall Asian situation will stabilize or when also the rising tide of weapons sales will abate.

THREAT SCENARIOS

Indian force levels must be adequate to meet the following contingencies.

- Full-scale war with Pakistan. This combined with a holding action against the Chinese in Tibet and containment of insurgencies;
- Full-scale invasion by China with a holding action against Pakistan and containment of insurgencies;
- Low-intensity operations against large-scale infiltration in Kashmir;
- Naval operations in the Indian Ocean, Bay of Bengal and Arabian Sea.
- Policing of adjacent areas on request, e.g., Sri Lanka, Maidives, etc.

The Indian strategy should aim at force levels to counter these threats. The most likely threat scenario in the short term can be stated thus: Pakistan with subsidiary threat from China. In the long term the main threat is from China.

The major combat components of the armed forces of India and Pakistan are given in Table 1. In the case of China, Chinese capabilities of waging an offensive from the Tibetan plateau are relevant.

Though Chinese armed forces total more than 3 million China's capability to deploy troops on the' Tibetan Plateau is restricted by terrain infrastructural problems and logistics. An assessment of capabilities is as follows:

Ladakh	1 army plus 3-4 divisions
Sikkim	1 army plus 3-4 divisions
Arunachal Pradesh	3 armies 9 divisions

(A Chinese Army consists of a basic 3 divisions)

The total assessed capability is that of 17 Infantry Divisions. China's Navy has a blue-water capability. Presently her ability of operating in the Indian Ocean and Bay of Bengal is restricted to her submarine arm which has more than 100 submarines, a proportion of them having nuclear propulsion. She has got Burma to agree to a railway connection to an Indian Ocean base for the Chinese Navy. Such a base will have a decided effect on the potential naval threat in the Bay of Bengal.

Table 1

	India	**Pakistan**
Army		
Armoury divisions	3	2
Infantry divisions	22	19
Independent armoured brigades	5	9
Corps independent artillery brigades	3	9
Mountain divisions	10	-
Independent infantry brigades	7	9
Army aviation squadrons	14	15
Air defence brigades/groups	6	8
Para brigades	1	-
Navy		
Principle surface combat vessels (including 2 Indian Aircraft Carriers)	24	14
Submarines	15	6
Patrol and coastal	40	18
Inshore/Offshore	21	7
Air Force		
Combat aircraft *conisisting of :*	707	393
Fighter ground attack squadrons	23	7
Fighter air defence	17	9
Recconenance squadrons	1	2
Naval air combat aircraft	64	4
Helicopter (armed)	75	10

Defence Expenditure

India's defence expenditure has been sinking in real terms. Inflation, currently around 11 per cent, is expected to rise. India's defence expenditure as a proportion of GDP declined from 4.04 per cent in 1986-87 to 2.53 per cent as against Pakistan's 6.88 per cent and China's official figure of 6 per cent (actual reported to be significantly higher).

As a proportion of total government expenditure, Pakistan spends 26.52 per cent, China 23.8 percent and India14.94 percent. India's defence expenditure share of governmental expenditure has come down from 17.27 per cent in 1987-88 to 14.94 per cent in 1993-94 and 13 per cent in 1994-95.

Defence allocations in 1994-95 were Rs 230 billion. This has been increased to Rs 250 billion in 1995-96.

The breakdown percentage in 1995-96 was : Army 53.96%, Navy 13.29%, Air Force 25.69%, Defence production 1.76%, R&D 5.28%

Lack of funds has resulted in mothballing tanks, ships and aircraft. This reduces immediate combat readiness. Pensions for defence personnel have been taken out of the defence budget and are met, from the consolidated fund of India.

Defence Production

There are 39 ordnance factories. These meet the armed forces' requirements and to some extent the paramilitary forces'. The production by the eight public sector undertakings particularly Bharat Earth Movers and Bharat Electronics has gone up.

Indian ordnance factories are producing a vast range of products, battletanks, infantry combat vehicles, self-propelled guns, field guns, anti-aircraft guns, mortars, small arms and ammunition, rockets and projectiles, bombs, grenades, mines, depth charges and other items. They also supply the railways, coal industry, paramilitary and police. Production of the 5.56 rifle has begun. India also exports various defence items.

In 1987, procurements from ordnance factories wore shifted from the defence production head to defence allocation. This has had the impact of reducing the Army's allocations correspondingly.

Though R&D funding registered a growth in the last ten years from 2.05 per cent to 4.39 per cent in the last budget, the money allotted is inadequate. In 1987, the transferring of R&D to defence as a consequence had an effect on the total defence allocations. Funding for R&D despite the increase of 105.13 crore in 1995-96 is far less than what is required. Since R&D for defence also has a bearing on other allied research agencies it would be preferable that R&D is funded under a separate head and its funding suitably enhanced to meet defence research needs. The priorities are for the :

AIR FORCE-LCA, helicopter (ALH) and Agni

ARMY-main battle tank, missiles, radar and artillery

NAVY-weapons systems, missiles and sonar equipment

Not only has Pakistan's defence expenditure increased significantly, the Pakistani Military Capital Stocks have also increased, both qualitatively and quantitatively. During the last few years Pakistan has fabricated nuclear warheads (estimated at 15), and built up fissile stocks to fabricate a similar number. Pakistan has added to her arsenal during the last five years 600 main battle tanks, 775 armoured personnel carriers (M-113-A2), 185 combat aircraft/ Mirage and the Chinese F-7P). The navy bought 3 frigates from the UK. 3 modern submarines at US $600 million are on order from France. 18 missiles HATF 1/11 have already been deployed. An unspecified numberofChineseM-11 missiles have been inducted. Those have a capability of carrying nuclear warheads. Pakistan's defence budget for 1994 accounted for 34.53 of government expenditure at a total of Rs 237,795.2 billion.

Pakistan has received loans from Saudi Arabia and US for arms acquisition. Pakistan is reported to have siphoned off some 60 per cent of the weapons and equipment intended for the Afghan Mujahideen for equipping terrorists operating in

Jammu and Kashmir. Accurate figures for China's defence expenditure are difficult to assess. Estimates place it at US $31.18 billion. The Chinese armed forces are being modernized and more professional forces are being created in place of the cumbersome structure obtaining. China has developed a blue-water navy and is actively spreading its influence in Burma with a view to obtaining naval and air facilities in the Bay of Bengal.

In our case with an inflation rate currently around 11 per cent and soaring international prices for military hardware there are insufficient funds available for modernization. Approximately 60 per cent of the budgetary allocations are appropriated for the revenue account, pay and allowances, etc. The proportion available for the capital expenditure for combat and combat related stores including fuel and oil is hardly sufficient to maintain existing force levels. No major weapon system has been inducted since the Bofors deal.

The defence budget has increased by some 10 per cent. With inflation now at 11 per cent this would mean in real terms a decrease in defence allocations. It will be insufficient to maintain the status quo particularly as the proportion allotted to the revenue account will increase as a result of the upcoming recommendations of the pay commission.

The armed forces' expenditure in aid of civil power is increasing due to insurgency conditions in Jammu and Kashmir and the North-East. So far these costs have not been recovered from the Home Ministry allocations. Recovery of these dues will increase availability of funds for the armed forces.

The raising of the Rashtriya Rifles has not come up to the initial expectations. It was intended that these 36 battalions (enough infantry for 4 divisions) to be increased to 40 battalions would be financed by the Home Ministry. This has not been the case and the financing has to be borne out of the Army allocations. In the circumstances the Army could have raised regular infantry battalions which would have given the flexibility of using them both for counter-insurgency and if so required for induction into regular divisions or brigades.

For the record this was the system earlier where regular infantry battalions were raised on a reduced counter-insurgency establishment. These modified infantry battalions wore used in the 1971 war with minimal reorganization. This system had the advantage of using the existing regimental layout and avoids the hybrid composition of the RR with all its attendant problems of milking regular units, postings, promotions and morale. It has aggravated the shortage of officers which is now in the region of 12,500. This is seriously affecting the operational efficiency of the Army.

The Army is manpower-intensive. The Army's ability to generate firepower and mobility are not commensurate with its manpower structure. Manpower has to be trimmed and firepower increased. The armed forces require new weapon systems and force multipliers. Obsolescent equipment requires upgradation.

Provisioning of maintenance spares and ammunition, petrol and oil are essential. Planning presently is for a short war. A future conflict is likely to be protracted. Due to the vulnerability of our sealanes it is essential that stocks and reserves should be held for a conflict of longer duration than those of 1965 and 1971.

The armed forces for their part should pay more attention to interior economy. Savings can be effected in manpower and consumption of petrol and oil. Establishments should be reviewed to cut out nonessentials. It will be noticed that the Pakistan Army has comparatively much fewer headquarters. A number of headquarters can be eliminated. The staff at Army Headquarters and lower state formations can be reduced. The present ratio of teeth to tail is too low. The establishment of units should be reviewed in this light. The armed forces must work out priorities of 'musts', 'shoulds' and 'coulds' as there will never be sufficient funds to meet all projections.

CHANGES OF MAJOR POLICY IN DEFENCE INDUSTRY

It is almost seven years since the first set of major policy changes were promulgated by the Government to give a fillip to our stagnating and moribund defence industry. The fundamental underpinnings to the policy changes were two: firstly, bring in the private sector; and secondly, opening the door for foreign companies by permitting up to 26 percent investment, so that technology inflows are facilitated. It was perhaps rightly believed that these were the two principle measures that were required to catalyse our ailing military industrial capabilities.

While most observers welcomed the policy announcements, there was considerable scepticism over the Governments' resolve to implement them. Could a system that was wedded to the philosophy of state led industrialisation for almost fifty years, change course that easily? Unlikely! Then there was the problem of our establishments' recognised and reputed talent for conceptualising great ideas, but seldom demonstrating the capacity to execute them. However, after having out-of-habit taken recourse to castigating the Government, it would be prudent to also try and understand its compulsions and concerns. The first is that given the nature of the UPA Government, no reforms can be implemented without the Left's concurrence.

The Left's dogma is to stonewall any measure that appears to threaten the interests of the PSUs and the Ordnance Factory Board (OFB). Thus the Left would not be inclined to acquiesce to proposals that contemplate the relaxation of state control over most core industrial sectors. Similarly, the defence PSUs and the OFB, would also not be willing to dilute their monopoly of their defence market.

Then there is the problem of the huge investments and the capacities created in all our Government owned defence industrial under-takings. Logically, it cannot be any one's case, that these assets are permitted to decay instead of putting them to optimal use. With the private sectors' case for a level playing field, the fear that over time, the Government owned defence industrial establishments would be progressively edged out of business, is genuine.

The third concern, and not easy to counter, pertains to the argument of national security. Since the private sector is not under Government control, in times of a crisis it may not respond to national requirements in the same manner that a Government owned unit would do. It is a combination of the preceding concerns that explain the Government's hesitation in letting go the control that we have witnessed since the policy changes were promulgated in May 2001.

Having acknowledged the issues, it must be conceded that these are not new or unique to us. All nations have had to grapple with the same set of dilemmas, and since we are in the catch-up game, our problems ought to be easier to solve, for we have the experience of other countries to learn and benefit from.

So, while the Government at one level remained wedded to the policy of reforms, in its implementation, it dragged its feet. Consequently, the practice of doing business only with the Government owned industries did continue unchanged for three to four years, much to the frustration of the private sector. This ambivalence of the Government impacted negatively on the private sectors' attempts at collaboration with foreign companies. It should therefore be accepted that foreign partnership was, and is, vital for our industry to take off. Indigenously we do not have the technology, nor the know-how, for state-of-the-art systems that the defence services aspire for. Since foreign defence companies were unclear of the Governments' intent, they were not prepared to enter into collaborative arrangements with the private sector. For quite a while they remained cautious, indulged in fence sitting-hedging their bets.

The air was finally cleared with the Government's announcement of the Defence Procurement Policy of 2006. The most significant features of this policy were its 'offset clauses' and the concept of RURs (Raksha Utpadan Ratnas). Of the two, it is the offset policy that has the potential to yield spectacular results in energising our defence industry.

The billions of dollars of business that this policy will bring to the Indian industry has generated unprecedented excitement among our domestic players. In excitement lies the challenge. They will have to be prepared to absorb complex technologies and engineering skills, and then manufacture components, assemble sub-systems, and systems, at a cost that is competitive and sufficiently profitable.

Ever since the idea of the offset policy was mooted, all foreign multi-nationals have been lobbying intensely to sabotage it. Arguments-that the policy would push up prices, that the Indian industry is incapable of absorbing high technology 'direct offsets', that monitoring mechanisms cannot be effective etc-have been in the air for a while.

A few days back, it was reported, that the Government is considering some relaxation in the policy. The areas mentioned were the adjustment of the cost of technology transfer against offsets, banking of offsets and the acceptance of indirect offsets. Though these issues may merit consideration, it would be somewhat premature to accept policy changes even before we have begun. The pressure on foreign vendors to fulfil their offset obligations must remain undiluted. Concurrently, we must concentrate on finding satisfactory solutions to the issues being raised. Having dwelt somewhat cursorily on policy issues, an objective assessment of our present industrial capability and its growth potential would now be in order. The Defence industry cannot be viewed in isolation. It has to be a manifestation of the nation's overall industrial and technological capabilities. Often we tend to ignore this fundamental.

The first place to begin this survey would be to look at the captains of our industry. There is a growing realisation that they have arrived. Globally, they are winning admiration and recognition. In the early nineties, when the first steps of liberalisation were initiated, they nurtured apprehensions about their survival.

Having successfully negotiated that phase of transition in our economy, they have at the beginning of the twenty first century emerged with renewed strategic sense that has a global sweep. Witness the takeovers and the expansion plans of quite a few of our companies. Just a decade ago, who could have imagined, that the Jaguar brand car would be owned by an Indian Company? They have in the recent past displayed vision, and matched that vision with the capacity to implement. The next requirement is of the work force. It is abundantly available in all categories; managerial, technical and in terms of working hands-our biggest asset being the young age profile of our people. Some intervention can be expected from the government in its labour policies. But being a politically sensitive issue, the Industry will have to live with this problem, till a change becomes environmentally possible.

In terms of spheres in which we have advanced to global standards our range has remained somewhat limited to the automobile sector, pharmaceuticals and a few other disciplines. We have hardly any capabilities in electronics, communications, optics and in the field of aviation. Our industrial policies should focus on these voids. To become a meaningful player in the defence sector, these technologies are vital.

Our biggest strength is software services. Infosys, Wipro and TCS are globally among the best. In addition, there are a host of second tier companies, clocking rapid growth, while doing both domestic and international business. Unfortunately, this strength has not been effectively harnessed to give the requisite impetus to our defence industry. Particularly, because the new generation of weapon systems and related support systems, are all heavily dependent on extremely sophisticated software, the cost of which may be as high as 30-40 percent of the total value of the platform. Electronics we know takes up another 30-40 percent.

The Left and a few other groups have consistently opposed the opening up of the defence industry to the private sector. They have repeatedly been claiming that the public sector units can produce all that our armed forces need. A brief look at their track record will establish that such confidence in the state owned establishments is quite misplaced.

We have 39 Ordnance Factories, 8 Defence PSUs and 50 Defence Research Laboratories, ie. close to 100 establishments, all well equipped, extravagantly staffed, with some excellent scientists and managers, and yet no creditworthy achievements to show. And what equipment do they produce which is to the satisfaction of our Armed Forces? It would be difficult to list any, other than the ALH from HAL, which has the potential to be a good product. The DRDO might want to take credit for the Agni (1 and 2) and the Prithvi. These are good systems but lose a fair amount of their sheen since they come twenty to thirty years after similar systems were inducted in China.

Our process of reforms in the management of the Government controlled defence research and production establishments, have regrettably floundered. Many studies have been done, yet-to all intent and purposes-the drift continues. Over the last three to four years the Government has been pushing for public private partnership. The idea being that such association would bring about the desired efficiencies in the public sector. But the problem is that such forced marriages do not really work. Driven by expediency, some private companies, may consider coming to an under-standing with PSUs for the short term, but such arrangements are not likely to be conducive to the real growth of the defence industry.

The policy of opening up of the defence industry to the private sector was successful in attracting quite a few industrial houses-large, medium and small, to enter the fray. Even prior to the formal opening of the defence sector, some had indirectly been in the business by manufacturing components, sub-systems and systems-for integration by the defence PSUs.

Besides, our nuclear and space programmes had involved the private industry. Such companies have executed sophisticated design and engineering jobs that include special metals and alloys, and therefore have acquired the confidence to take on the development and manufacture of defence systems.

L&T, Tatas, Mahindras, Godrej Boyce, Bharat Forge and more recently Punj Lloyd, are some of the major industrial houses that have staked their claim for defence contracts. Following them, are a large number of second and third tier companies covering a wide range of technologies.

The basic handicap of all these companies at the time the policy change was announced in 2001 was their lack of domain knowledge. They did not know weapon systems, or what force multipliers were, or how the procurement procedures worked. They also did not know how the global arms market operated. They were equally unaware of the equipment profile of our armed forces and their future requirement.

Even though these companies inducted service officers whose advice was available, lack of personal knowledge of the business inhibited executives from pursuing projects that entailed taking investment decisions. Increased involvement in the defence sector; and interaction with the defence services, the procurement arm of the Ministry of Defence, and the big multi-national defence companies, over the last five to six years; has impacted positively on the confidence levels of company executives.

The role of defence service officers in galvanising the industry merits special attention. Other than these officers, not many in India, have any idea of modern warfare, military organisations, weapon systems, munitions and the support systems. Such domain knowledge within the industry is imperative. All over the world companies engaged in the business of military hardware extensively employ service officers to develop products and promote business. Not only this, even governments in order to support domestic industries, lend serving officers and men to participate in trials or make presentations. We may recall some of the service-industry seminars held in Delhi in the recent past which had serving officers endorsing products.

Unfortunately, the environment that we have nurtured in India discourages our retired/retiring officers from being employed. If employed they cannot be optimally used because of the establishments' attitude towards them. Who benefits? Only the foreign companies and maybe our adversaries!

This must change. By encouraging the absorption of service officers by the defence industry, the nation will reap multiple benefits. Firstly, the users would have access to informed inputs on developments, which would contribute to better decisions on choice of systems and the formulation of specifications. Rather the industry would gain from the expertise of these officers in an area which they have much to learn about. Secondly, to some extent, the problem of rehabilitation of officers who retire at relatively younger ages would get addressed. It is important that the Government revisits this issue.

The central issue facing the defence industry is access to contemporary technology, its absorption and assimilation, and then the use of domestic research and development to graduate to next generation systems. South Africa, Israel, China, South Korea, Brazil, and even Singapore, have learnt to successfully navigate this cycle.

There is no reason why we cannot emulate their example. In our case, so far, technology transfers have taken place only to the OFB and the defence PSUs. Their experience should not become the only basis for drawing conclusions on this subject. The appetite for growth of the private sector, and its new found confidence, would undoubtedly yield different results.

A survey of the global defence market will reveal that we are currently the biggest importers of defence systems. The US and China do spend more but they mostly buy domestic. The figures of our projected purchases are being regularly quoted in thousands of crores.

They do give us sufficient strength to extract terms that could be used to considerable advantage. Look at the pending procurements: some 200 helicopters, 126 advanced fighters, approximately 800-1000 artillery guns, and half a dozen submarines. Each of these would run into billions of dollars. The conclusion is obvious-buy sensibly.

With these purchases in the pipeline, if we did not get all the technologies we need, we will have only ourselves to blame. Procurement terms must state our purchase imperatives unambiguously. As a matter of fact we could consider modifying our procedures when acquiring big ticket items.

Take the case of advanced fighters. All contenders have proven comparable systems. The differences essentially stem from design philosophies and the source of sub-systems and systems that have been selected for integration.

The gaps in features are so narrow that quite often the choice can be a matter of individual predilection. The same arguments can be applied to the helicopters we want or the submarines. Selection could therefore be based on the totality of the package a vendor offers and not just the L-1 criteria after qualifying. To what extent and in what manner is technology being offered? What are the long term buy back agreements?

What kind of investments is the vendor making in India? For such high value transactions we must extract much more than what we have done hither to. We need to therefore delve deeper into the manner in which we pursue major acquisitions. There could also be a case for some coordination with say the Civil Aviation Ministry taking into account the carriers that Air India would be planning to induct. An important caveat at this point would be in order: under no circumstances should the views of the concerned service headquarter not be the ultimate deciding factor.

While charting the strategy for the development of our domestic defence industry we must identify technologies that require special attention; technologies where our capabilities merit quantum upgradation. It can be assumed that the DRDO, the services headquarters, and also the CII, would have undertaken studies on this subject. Our acquisition plans must look at integrating the road map that we should have drawn for technology inflows and digestion. Electronics, optics, communications and avionics, are generally the areas that we should be focussing on. We have for a few decades depended exclusively on Bharat Electronics for all our communication requirements as also all our electro-optical products.

Today Bharat Electronics may be a profit making company but has little to offer in terms of future technologies or next generation products. The same story applies to HAL, notwithstanding the successful development of the ALH, which should have been offered at least ten years earlier.

There is therefore a strong case to encourage private sector companies to enter these fields. The logic that since the Government has made investments in creating capabilities, all orders must be confined to these companies has proven over time to be counterproductive. A change in approach is long overdue. India urgently needs an HAL/BE in the private sector. The Government must encourage and support their emergence.

The subject of exports has also been grossly neglected. There may be a Joint Secretary in the Department of Defence Production responsible for promoting exports, but he can do little under the present dispensation. Pakistan's Ordnance Factories have consistently exported more than us. No defence industry can expect to sustain itself purely on the basis of sales in the domestic market.

Our private sector, unlike our Government owned establishments, have understood this. But they need much more support. The Government and the industry have to work together in a closely coordinated manner. Witness the way in which over the past few months the Heads of Governments of Germany, UK and France have brought with them the captains of their defence industries to India. The agenda requires no amplification. Here again we must push to get our act together

If India's defence industry is today on the threshold of transformation, considerable credit must be given to the role played by the CII. FICCI has also contributed, but only marginally. We may recall the first Army-Industry Partnership Seminar conducted in the mid nineties under the aegis of the CII. Many of us sceptics murmured-'what's the point?' But CII persevered. It continued with its efforts to nudge the industry and simultaneously influence our policy makers. It has also been actively persuading the big global players to look at teaming with the Indian industry. The results though slow, in the coming times would soon be there for us to witness. Having reached thus far, the CII must not take its foot off the pedal. Much more still needs to be done.

Before concluding, some of the suggestions made are listed below:

- Protection to the PSUs and the OFB from domestic players must be progressively withdrawn.

- A major overhaul of the functioning control, organisation and functioning of the OFB and the defence PSUs has been long overdue. Can we not figure out a way to move forward on this issue?
- Pressures to dilute the 'offset clause' of the DPP must be resisted. What we should be focussing on is the mechanisms for monitoring post contract implementation.
- Encourage the absorption of service officers in the defence industry. The rules of interaction with industry representatives must change. The MOD and the services headquarters should be more accessible to domestic industry. Currently doors for foreigners open up much more easily.
- Put in special efforts to promote and assist the growth of the private sector in the areas of aviation, communications, electronics and sensors (optics). There should be a comprehensive action plan for the acquisition of key technologies. The Government and the industry should work in concert on this issue.
- Re-examine our procurement policies and strategies for major purchases. Given the nature of the global market we can perhaps extract much more from our big deals.
- The growth of our defence industry can only be sustained if its business model takes into account the imperative of exports for sustenance.
- The laudable role played by the CII merits recognition. Both the Government and the industry should continue to encourage the CII to step up its activities to accelerate reforms and change.

Our vision for India in the next two decades would be flawed if it did not envisage a sizeable, vibrant and sophisticated defence industry for us that is globally competitive and has the capacity to research and develop new state of the art cutting edge technologies. Our industry has acquired a new found confidence. All it needs is direction and support form the Government. The launch of the Nano within four years of it being conceived has been inspiring. We hope the global awe it has attracted is repeated time and again. We want Nano clones now coming out of India's defence industry stable

With increasing outsourcing opportunities, the Indian aerospace and defence industry is emerging as a key participant in the Asia Pacific aerospace and defence market. Apart from India's perceived viability as an outsourcing hub for aerospace and defence products, the overwhelming involvement of the Government in areas of supply and demand cements its advantage in the industry.

The Government's pro-active soliciting of international cooperation has seen production moving to India, generating more opportunities for the country. Export competitiveness has been given priority, hence, there has been an increased thrust towards reduced import dependency.

The Indian economy is one the fastest growing in the world, reflecting the successful reform process initiated in 1991.

The Indian Government has gradually opened its key sectors to foreign participation and foreign investment in the Indian aerospace and defence industry which currently has a 26 percent cap. Meanwhile, since two-thirds of the Indian population depends on agricultural income, reforms in this area are widely considered necessary to aid economic growth.

Development of the agriculture sector, trade, as well as capital liberalisation, and improvement in investments, are some vital areas being focused upon by the current Government. The *Frost & Sullivan* Country Industry Forecast service for the Indian aerospace and defence industry uses a macroeconomic perspective to provide a focused analysis of the industry.

This service covers an array of issues pertaining to the industry including political stances, trade policies, industry regulations, as well as their overall impact. Besides enabling decision makers to assess the impact of non-market forces, this analysis also helps in identifying new opportunities in the industry. In addition, it provides a strong base for preparing business contingency plans.

ASSESSMENT OF MOVES TOWARDS PRIVATISATION

As a result of the above, increase private sector participation in defence production is increasingly being pursued: according to the latest reports more than 300 companies have already registered their interest in participating in the defence sector. Thus far, the following areas appear to have borne the greatest fruit.

IT and Communications. According to the MTCL India's capabilities in areas such as super-computing and software development are very strong indeed. With this in mind, it is understandable that a number of senior military figures have recently made clear their desire to upgrade the Armed Force's communication and IT capabilities through private sector involvement. Speaking during an August 2000 CII seminar, for instance, General V.P Malik observed that: "the private sector, which had not previously participated in defence production, had expanded in size and reach and now has the capability to produce non-lethal items such as communications and IT related' products He also stated that: 'the army would be requiring radios of all types, ATM switches, optical fibre cable, satellite systems, power sources of all types and micro and macro cellular systems' and that the Army was looking at buying these technologies off the shelf from private companies.

Service Contracts and Outsourcing: There is a growing interest in outsourcing to the private sector within the military The IAF, for example, is exploring the possibility of privatising its base-repair depots, accounts, and areas of administrative work. According to the Chief of the Air Staff, Air Chief Marshall A.Y. Tipinis, there is also scope to involve the private sector in the maintenance and operation of fighter aircraft, air-launched guided missiles and ground to air missiles as well as support equipment such as radars, communications networks, and specialist vehicles. Outsourcing is also an option for the PSUs; indeed they are increasingly shedding the production of low technology items to the private sector. For example, both

Bharat Electronics and Garden Reach Shipbuilders have developed a network of small-scale industries and ancillary units around them. Likewise, the ordnance factories have been sourcing various raw materials and small parts from a range of indigenous industries. Some effort has also been made to involve the private sector in the production of middle level technologies: for example, at one stage Kirloskars was involved in the development of an indigenous engine for the Arjun tank.

Foreign Participation. There is mounting evidence to suggest that the country's eight PSU's will be allowed to enter into 'strategic alliances' and partnerships with foreign defence manufacturers. On 12 October, for example, George Fernandes, stated that 'India provides an excellent opportunity for the developed and developing world to source cost-effective goods and services from our defence production industry' He also talked of the 'opportunities that India offers for joint-ventures, technology transfers, and co-production facilities for export to other markets'. Currently the amount of foreign investment in the Indian defence sector is small. But a number of foreign manufacturers have already taken him up on the offer. During the visit of the Russian President Vladimir Putin to India this October, for example, the two sides signed a new military and technical co-operation agreement to establish joint ventures for the production of a variety of armaments and military hardware and establishing joint sales and marketing structures for the products. The Russian government is also thought to be considering investing a share of proceeds of its recent sales to India for creating after-care and upgrading facilities in the country. Looking to the future it is possible that Russian companies will invite their Indian (and Chinese) counterparts to participate in the development of next generation weapons systems. Russia is not the only country assessing this option. Somewhere in the region of 20 partnership agreements covering a range of cooperative arrangements, including co-production of aircraft equipment, joint development of communications equipment, and co-operation in software and electronic design, are believed to have been signed between British companies and the eight PSUs. Similar discussion have also been held with France, Poland and others. Every effort is also being made to ensure that these partnerships are not limited to the public sector.

Research and Development: There is some reason to believe that private companies will be encouraged to participate in defence R&D. Participation in this area received a significant boost following the May 1998 nuclear tests, when the imposition of sanctions on India prompted the Defence Research and Development Agency (DRDO) to open up eight labs in non-strategic areas to private participation. In addition to this, the DRDO now claims to have 'various levels of partnership' with 250 industries.

Defence Exports: In a related development, the government is now actively assessing the possibility of increasing exports of defence related equipment. Traditionally, modern India has eschewed the option of selling arms abroad, and relatively speaking its defence exports are minimal, although a defence exports cell was established in 1973. In recent years, however, the country has held a number of defence export shows in co-operation with the CII, while Indian PSUs have participated in defence shows abroad. Currently, the main products exported are from the country's ordnance factories and include small arms ammunition, explosives, rockets, spares for rifles and guns, clothing items, parachutes, aeronautical stores, communications equipment, and components and sub-systems. India's main export markets are Asia and Africa although some equipment has gone to Europe. Old export markets are also being expanded and new ones being sought out: following a visit to Vietnam in March 2000 by George Fernandes, for example, both countries, who signed a Protocol on Defence Co-operation in 1994, initialled a new agreement to enhance defence cooperation in areas of training. Algeria is also considering buying defence equipment from India, including spares for its MiG combat aircraft, and helicopters, vehicles, night vision devices and communications equipment. India's hope is probably that it will be able to use the revenue from sales to reduce its own unit purchase costs as well as provide an extra flow of money into defence R&D.

Future Prospects

Despite these positive signs, at this stage there are still a number of factors inhibiting increased private sector (and possibly even foreign) involvement in defence production.

The main stumbling block is that in order to increase private sector involvement the Indian government would have to scrap the 1948 and 1956 Industrial Policy Resolutions. This is unlikely at this stage because many of the country's bureaucrats and politicians fear that such a decision will lead to mass lay-offs and possibly social turbulence. (Incidentally, these same individuals are also against the privatisation of India's other PSUs). As is traditionally the case, pressure against change is also likely to come from both the management and the workforce from within the sector. In short, the momentum and support for the economic reform programme in India has yet to gather the momentum necessary to allow fully fledged private participation and competition in defence production. Private participation in the sensitive areas of defence R&D is likely to be limited due to concerns about security. Substantial foreign participation in the form of joint ventures particularly with Western companies, meanwhile, is likely to be limited by concerns about security and the reliability of Western suppliers in meeting their obligations. (By way of an example, the fact that a number of Indian Navy SeaKing helicopters have been stranded in Britain because they contain American parts, which the country is restricted from selling to India as part of the sanctions imposed following the May 1998 nuclear tests, is believed to one of the reasons why the deal to sell the BAE SYSTEMS Hawk has been further delayed) Organisational problems within the MOD are also likely to hinder any advantages to be gained by through the greater involvement of the private sector. The isolation of defence production from defence R&D, for example, is seen by many in India as inhibiting sensible planning and management of India's defence programmes.

Despite all the problems and challenges of the past decade India is unlikely to abandon the dream of establishing its own defence industry. Paradoxically, however, it is becoming increasingly apparent to all concerned that the only way that the country will be able to fulfil (even partly) its ambition of designing and manufacturing its own top-end defence equipment will be to dismantle the system of public ownership on which it is based. As the process of globalisation and consolidation in the defence industry continues to gather pace and the price of designing, developing and producing modern defence equipment increases rapidly, India's aspirations would also be greatly helped if it could rapidly involve foreign companies in the process of defence production.

Five to Ten Year Forecast

In the near term (5-10 years) the evidence collected in the paper suggests that this is unlikely to happen. Rather, the development of a hybrid model in which the core of PSUs and the DRDO will be maintained, while private sector participation will be sought in non-sensitive/peripheral areas such as IT and communications will probably dominate. This process will be complemented by an increased effort both to seek partnerships with largely Russian put possibly some European defence companies. However, if past efforts to establish joint ventures with Indian companies in both the civil and defence sector are anything to go by the scope of these will be limited. India's attempts to increase its defence exports profile partly as a way to fund its indigenous R&D programme will also be limited to the sale of low and middle level technologies to cash-strapped and politically isolated regimes, such as Algeria and Vietnam.

The perceived need to modernise its armed forces quickly, which has taken root in the wake of the Kargil crisis and the impending obsolescence of many of its existing platform, however, means that India will continue to look abroad to full-fill the majority of its top-end defence needs. This will be reflected in the division of resources within the defence budget, which is also likely to continue to grow over this period.

Ten to Twenty Year Forecast

Potentially, India's long term prospects (10-20) years are better. There is a good chance, for example, that by 2010 the Indian government will have made real advances down the path of economic reform and that the climate for private sector participation and perhaps even the privatisation of the PSUs will be more favourable. Crucial to India's success, however, will be its ability to bring together its civil and military R&D capabilities, not only in non-military/dual use areas, but across a broad spectrum.

India could also use its strength in IT to strengthen its partnerships with foreign defence manufacturers and secure maintenance, upgrading and possibly production facilities in return. Parallel to this, and bearing in mind the fact that future defence platforms, such as the JSF, are unlikely to be single country ventures, there are also added advantages to be gained from India linking itself into those foreign companies associated closely with this process; indeed it may even be able to contribute in certain key areas. If this happens, although it is unlikely that India will be able to produce 70 per cent of its requirements domestically, it will certainly be able to source more from domestic producers, and more crucially will benefit from its access to technology, and participation in R&D programmes. (It is possible that India will be able to reduce its total reliance on imports to 50 per cent, although it is still unlikely to be able to produce whole systems indigenously).

Final Assessment

Naturally, this rather rosy outlook depends on India's willingness to accept not only the advantages of privatisation, but more importantly the direction in which defence industries today are going.

Arguably, the room for companies focused solely on their home markets and expecting to provide their militaries with state of the art defence equipment, not only in the developed world but also in the West, is shrinking rapidly, due to the rising cost and sophistication of the systems involved.

Put another way, participation in regional or global defence programmes will become the norm. India, with its growing strength in the new economy, has the chance this time not to miss the boat, although there is always a danger that misplaced nationalism and an unclear understanding of developments will prevent it from making the most of the opportunity.

INDIA'S DEFENCE INDUSTRY IN THE 21ST CENTURY

Major Policy Initiatives

India's defence industry entered a new phase of self-reliance on the eve of the 21st century. Since the mid-1990s, several initiatives have been undertaken by the government to effect changes in the defence industry. Soon after the liberalisation of the economy was announced in 1990/91, the defence industry started realising the importance of civil-military interaction in the industrial sector. The private industries in India, which were thus far debarred from entering into defence production and whose role in the defence sector was limited to supplying spare parts and other minor contributions, started demanding a share in defence production.

In 1994, the then Defence Minister founded six Task Forces on major areas of defence modernisation, of which reforms in defence industry was an important part. This was carried out by the government in consultation with institutions like the Confederation of Indian Industries (CII). The CII, on its part was instrumental in bringing out a series of proposals in the broad field of private participation in the defence sector and armed forces–industry cooperation. Soon after this, the government initiated a programme called 'Army-Industry Partnership', under the auspices of CII which highlighted the importance of cooperative arrangements between the armed forces, defence industry and the government. After India's nuclear tests, various sanctions were imposed on India, of which sanctions related to the import of military and dual-use goods and technologies were considered the most important.

Sanctions were imposed on more than 150 items, which affected the progress of many defence products. However, the impact of sanctions on military technology was taken up as a another phase of challenge for the defence scientists as they had faced similar sanctions after the test in 1974. At that time they had faced more difficulties as the defence industry was not in a position to withstand such severe cuts which had resulted in delays in many major programmes. This time around, the defence industry had made significant progress to be able to withstand sanctions. After the Kargil conflict in mid-1999, the government started looking into security gaps and founded a committee under Mr K. Subrahmanyam. He brought out a major report on this conflict, which is known as the 'Kargil Committee Report'. This report, among other recommendations, highlighted the importance of reforms in higher defence management and reforms in institutional processes in the security sector.

The Government also founded a Group of Ministers' committee to look into major aspects of the overall security management of the country. The committee submitted its report to the government, which is known as GoM Report on 'Reforming the National Security System. This report highlighted the importance of self-reliance in India's defence industry and recommended several steps to introduce institutional changes into the system. Coupled with changes at institutional and organisational levels, India's defence industry entered an entirely new era after the Government announced a major change in policy by outlining codes of conduct for and inviting private participation in the defence industry. This is seen as by far the most important policy shift in the defence-industrial sector in the last fifty years. By doing so, the Government, through an official notification No. 5(37)/2001-FCI, allowed private sector participation up to 100 percent and permitted foreign direct investment (FDI) up to 26 percent. This decision has been hailed by both the private industry and the government-owned defence industry. Institutions like CII and FICCI, which represent interests and views of the private sector, have been instrumental in influencing such a marked change in policies. According to Mr Sushanto Sen, the Director General of CII, such a policy change is certainly going to benefit both the defence industry and the private sector.

In tune with the stated objectives of India's defence industry to achieve a higher degree of self-reliance and a desire to make its flagship units globally competitive, thus entering into competitive defence markets, the Government has also introduced some institutional changes that are expected to smoothen operations both at structural and organisational levels. Earlier, procurement procedures were considered cumbersome, and there were overlaps in organisational responsibilities of respective organs responsible for procurement.

Under the new system, the Services Headquarters were integrated into the Ministry of Defence to provide closer interaction. The procurement structure is now a three-tier structure with the recent establishment of the Defence Acquisition Council (DAC) at the apex.

Its primary role will be to accord in-principle-approval of long-term perspective plans (15-20 years), acceptance of necessity for the capital acquisition plan (5 years), identify 'Make', 'Buy' and 'Make and Buy' projects and monitor progress of the three Boards under it – the Defence Procurement Board, Defence Production Board and the Defence R&D Board.

The Defence Procurement Board under the Defence Secretary will have the primary role of capital procurements and coordination. The Defence Production Board will be headed by the Secretary Defence Production and Supplies and will oversee all activities related to indigenous manufacture, progress in 'make' projects and will provide support to DAC.

The Defence R&D Board will be headed by the Secretary Defence R&D and will oversee progress, monitor and report on all R&D proposals in consultation with the user service and production board. Other measures at institutional level include direct linkages between the armed forces and the Ministry of Defence through integrated headquarters, which include respective perspective planning branches. In sum, organisational and institutional changes brought about recently seem to complement policy changes.

Problems and Prospects: An Assessment

India's quest for self-reliance has produced mixed results. Some of the lessons that India has learnt in the past fifty years are worth noting here.

First, a combination of factors have led to the indigenous design and development component of self-reliance slowing down to almost zero for over a quarter of a century after 1962. This has led not only to a huge technology gap but also contributed to severe difficulties in technology assimilation in the industrial sector.

However, since the mid-1980s, activities toward achieving a greater degree of self-reliance have taken up momentum. The technology gap also widened the scope for acquisition of production technology rather than design technology from foreign sources.

This in turn has created a license production regime at the cost of indigenous production. During the 1990s, the activities to encourage joint ventures and co-production in the defence-industrial sector is largely seen as a step to reduce license regime and boost indigenous industrial capabilities. How far this will achieve desired results are yet to be seen as such activities are only of recent origin and they need lead time to prove themselves.

For example, the market for Brahmos missiles is estimated to be large, but it depends on how much is it likely to penetrate the cruise missile market at a global level. Success of this kind will not only validate India's defence-industrial capabilities to meet domestic demands but also increase its confidence in many ways.

Second, private participation in the defence-industrial sector has started after a long delay. This is attributable to several factors, ranging from the socialist and protective nature of the defence sector to fears of what is called 'security diffusion'.

The latter especially relates to a fear of below-expectation performance by the private sector as it is hardly specialised to meet strict high military standards, hence compromising security standards. This kind of fear has been criticised by many who argue that private participation is essential in the defence sector which is primarily technology driven and capital intensive.

The recent opening up of the defence sector for private participation has generated a lot of interest in the country. Institutions like CII caution that while such initiatives are always welcome, the government should come out with a clear 'road-map' for the private sector participants in defence so as to enable them to prepare themselves for the new reality.

Fears regarding the ability of the private sector to match expectations of the country in the highly demanding and technology-dominated industrial sector are countered by industrialists like Atul Kirloskar (Chairman of Committee on National Defence, CII), who claim to have absolute faith in their abilities.

Many also claim that given a chance, the secondary role of the private sector can be turned into a primary one in a short period of time. Some of the leading industrialists even claim that they have or intend to possess capabilities to produce complete weapons systems.

Several companies like Mahindras and Mahindras (M&M), the Tata Group, Kirloskar Brothers, Larsen and Toubro (L&T), and many others have already jumped into the fray to obtain orders from the defence industry. Since 2002, the Government has received more than ten applications from the private sector to manufacture weapons systems. It has recently awarded five licenses to L&T and M&M to produce military vehicles and some weapons systems.

Third, the government has emphasised measures to enhance the defence industry to cope with future challenges. Such measures are carried out by both OFs and DPSUs, apart from respective branches of the Government and the armed forces. Digitalisation, strict quality control, performance-related benefits, professional management systems, allowing the private sector to carry out R&D activities in the government-owned laboratories, are some of the measures which have come up in recent years and are likely to impinge the defence-industrial landscape.

A simplification of production and procurement rules promise better buyer-seller relations. There were some protests coming from employees' unions of OFs and DPSUs against privatisation. The Government has assured these unions that employees' interests will be borne in mind but that it will give priority to performance.

In one instance, the Defence Minister is reported to have appealed to the workers in one DPSU to not to worry about possible relocations due to privatisation and assured them to take effective steps to safeguard their interests. It seems that rationalisation of the defence industry is on the cards which might bring some unrest in the form of reduction of employment in the defence-industrial sector.

There are even rumours that some of the units, especially from the ordnance sector might be closed down. The private sector participants are, however, optimistic.

They argue that their factories can effectively be converted into profit making civilian units. In several rounds of interviews with senior officers and industry analysts by the author, it seems that some of the industrial units may come under close scrutiny. Conversion to civilian production in their cases is not ruled out. In brief, significant rationalisation, diversification and closer private participation are coming and are likely to influence India's defence industry in many ways.

INDIA PROJECT MILITARY POWER IN THE FUTURE

There is good reason to believe that India will have at least as great a need for military power projection in the future as it has in the past. New Delhi's primary strategic priority over the next decade—deepening internal consolidation— requires sustained economic development and enhanced internal security.

This, in turn, is at least partially dependent on developments in the country's immediate neighborhood. As current National Security Advisor Shivshankar Menon has argued, "[U]nless we have a peaceful and prosperous periphery, we will not be able to focus on our primary tasks of socioeconomic development." Furthermore, the achievement of regional peace and stability in South Asia will be a necessary precondition for India to claim great-power status.

Unfortunately, many of the countries on India's periphery are weak or fragile states. For example, *Foreign Policy* magazine's 2010 index of failed states included five of India's neighbours (Afghanistan, Pakistan, Bangladesh, Burma, and Sri Lanka) in the top 25. Although many of the challenges plaguing India's immediate neighborhood are political and economic in nature, and therefore not necessarily directly amenable to solutions based on the application of conventional military power, New Delhi may periodically require the ability to shape events in these countries that military power projection provides.

Further afield, successive political leaders in India have identified the arc from the Persian Gulf to the Straits of Malacca as "a legitimate area of interest . . . for the first quarter of the 21st century."

As a result, the Indian Navy's maritime strategy states that "whatever happens in the [Indian Ocean littoral region] can affect our national security and is of interest to us." India's interests in this region are largely economic in nature, with energy access and growing regional economic engagement meshing with concerns about the safety of ships transiting the entire Indian Ocean littoral.

In recent years, official statements have been increasingly blunt about the importance India attaches to energy security, which is deemed "vital for an assured high rate of [economic] growth." At present India imports over half of its natural gas and 70% of its oil, the vast majority of which comes from the Persian Gulf. Over the next 20 years, India's oil consumption is expected to grow at an annual rate of 5% to 7%—more than three times the global average rate of increase—which will more than double present day consumption by 2025. To sustain its high rates of economic growth, India must secure access to new sources of hydrocarbon energy.

The ability to influence events in this broader region may take on increasing importance as India's comprehensive national power grows. Scholars of international relations argue that as a state's wealth and material power increase, it "will select a larger bundle of security and welfare goals than a less wealthy and less powerful state."

In terms of foreign policy preferences, scholars also argue that rising powers have generally sought to expand their spheres of influence— as state power increases, so do political interests abroad. This expanded material capacity and broadening of political interests are expected to translate into an increased interest in favourably shaping the state's strategic environment. Therefore, it is reasonable to assume that India will have at least the same level of need for power projection missions going forward as it has in the past. It will, in fact, most likely make increased use of such tools in the future.

The New Delhi has already employed its power projection assets to provide regional public goods (e.g., humanitarian relief, non-combatant evacuation operations, and securing sea lanes of communication) in parts of the Indian Ocean littoral in a manner befitting a regional hegemon.

One key difference between great powers and other states is that great powers create external security for their region beyond merely protecting their own borders. Any country can have regional interests, but great powers also have regional responsibilities.

As the dominant regional power in South Asia and an aspirant to a seat on the U.N. Security Council, India is likely to be called on in the future to take an increased role in ensuring international peace and security, either under U.N. auspices or as a part of various multilateral coalitions. While some in New Delhi may hope India can free-ride to great-power status, including ducking hard decisions and avoiding shouldering a burden, this status is unlikely to be achieved without bearing more responsibility.

It is not possible to precisely identify in advance the specific contingencies that could compel India to project hard military power abroad, but, beyond the historical instances already noted, India may find several additional reasons to send its armed forces beyond its borders.

Examining Military Power Projection

To some, the phrase "power projection" suggests imposing regime change on a state far away from home for strategic gain. In this view, a prototypical example might be Operation Iraqi Freedom, the 2003 U.S.-led invasion of Iraq. While such a conceptualization captures some key elements of power projection, it is far too narrow.

The U.S. Department of Defense (DoD) defines power projection much more broadly as being "[t]he ability of a nation to apply all or some of its elements of national power—political, economic, informational, or military—to rapidly and effectively deploy and sustain forces in and from multiple dispersed locations to respond to crises, to contribute to deterrence, and to enhance regional stability."

Focusing specifically on the final element of national power in the DoD's definition—the use of military tools—it is possible to disaggregate military power projection into nine different aspects based on the political goals being sought and the level of force employed.

Four of these relate to the employment of "soft" military power (securing sea lanes of communication, non-combatant evacuation operations, humanitarian relief, and peacekeeping), and five are primarily concerned with "hard" military power (showing the flag, compellence/deterrence, punishment, armed intervention, and conquest).

Soft Military Power Projection

Securing Sea Lanes of Communication. The protection of shipping lanes from attack by hostile states or irregular threats. As the Indian Navy's maritime doctrine notes, trade is increasingly critical to the Indian economy, which makes the protection of the sea lanes transiting the Indian Ocean a significant priority.

Following the attacks of September 11, 2001, the Indian Navy played a high-profile role in escorting U.S. shipping through the Straits of Malacca.

More recently, Indian naval vessels have been deployed to the Gulf of Aden, where they have thwarted several attempted hijackings by pirates.

Non-combatant Evacuation Operations. The evacuation of Indian or friendly third country civilians from a foreign country when they are endangered by war or civil unrest. For example, during Operation Sukoon (Urdu: Relief) the navy evacuated 2,280 Indian, Sri Lankan, and Nepalese civilians from Lebanon ahead of the 2006 Israeli-Hizbollah War. Several orders of magnitude larger was the airlift of over 100,000 Indians from Iraq and Kuwait ahead of the 1991 Gulf War.

Humanitarian Relief. The use of military forces abroad to assist in the aftermath of a natural disaster.

Following the 2004 Asian tsunami, the Indian Navy mobilized 32 ships and over 20,000 naval personnel to evacuate casualties, as well as provide emergency sources of power and water to the peoples of Sri Lanka, the Maldives, Indonesia, Thailand, and Malaysia.

Peacekeeping. Military operations designed to support diplomatic efforts to reach a long-term political settlement to an ongoing dispute. India has been one of the most significant contributors to U.N. peacekeeping missions. As of 2009, the Indian Army had roughly 8,000 personnel deployed in the Democratic Republic of Congo, Lebanon, East Timor, the Ivory Coast, and the Golan Heights.

Hard Military Power Projection

Showing the Flag. The symbolic deployment of military forces to a region to demonstrate political interest, resolve, or willingness to take more forceful military action. For example, in June 1987 the Indian Air Force violated Sri Lankan airspace when it undertook Operation Poomalai (Tamil: Garland), the forced airdrop of relief supplies to ethnic Tamils during the siege of Jaffna. This action sent a clear message to the government in Colombo about New Delhi's desire to see a negotiated end to the conflict and helped lead to the signing of the Indo-Sri Lankan accord. More recently, the Indian Navy has undertaken several high-profile deployments to the South China Sea and the Persian Gulf, which have been interpreted as important signals of Indian interest in these regions.

Compellence and Deterrence. The use or the threat of military force against another state to induce it into or dissuade it from pursuing a given policy. In this form, power projection acts as a diplomatic tool, attempting to influence the decision-making process and calculus of foreign actors.

For example, the governor of East Pakistan's decision to surrender to India in 1971 has been attributed to the compellence effect of well-timed air strikes on his residence in Dhaka at the very moment he was conducting a crisis response meeting. In the same conflict, the destruction of East Pakistani airfields after the air force in the territory had been attritted was an exercise in deterrence by denial that sought to preclude intervention by an outside power.

Punishment. The punitive use of force against another state in response to its pursuit of a given policy. Aside from limited punitive strikes on Pakistani posts across the Line of Control in Kashmir in response to militant activity (not an expeditionary use of force), punishment has not been widely employed by the Indian military.

Armed Intervention. The forcible movement of military units into another nation's territory to influence the internal affairs of the target country, short of outright conquest.

Historical examples in India's immediate neighborhood range in size from the 1988 deployment of a parachute battalion to the Maldives (Operation Cactus) to put down a coup to the 1971 intervention in East Pakistan by three corps of the Indian Army to assist guerillas fighting for independence.

Conquest. The offensive use of military assets to forcibly occupy non-contiguous territory controlled or claimed by another state.

This has not been an aspect of power projection pursued by independent India, although at the time some observers believed that the use of military forces in Hyderabad (Operation Polo), Goa (Operation Vijay), and elsewhere as part of the post-Independence consolidation of the Indian Union was "an act of military aggression and conquest."

Given this disaggregation, it is clear that power projection is a much broader concept than mere invasion seeking regime change. Military assets, depending on how they are employed, can advance a state's foreign policy goals by facilitating the projection of either hard or soft forms of military power. Moreover, since Independence, India has employed at least seven, and perhaps eight, of the nine aspects of military power projection.

India's Conventional Military and Power Projection

The three varieties of conventional military power—sea power, air power, and land power—all contribute to power projection in different ways.

Sea power has a high degree of fungibility across various power projection missions and will likely form the foundation of India's global reach in coming years. This is particularly true in India's "extended neighborhood," since the region stretching "across [Asia's] sub-regions—be it East Asia, West Asia, Central Asia, South Asia or Southeast Asia" is largely a maritime domain. In contrast, air and land power play more limited, but nonetheless important, roles in India's power projection capabilities.

Sea Power

In light of the fact that roughly 90% of India's external trade by volume and 77% by value is seaborne, Indian maritime power has a role to play in sustaining domestic economic development.

Indeed, a host of observers dating back to the pre-Independence period has argued that India's economy is "at the mercy of the power which controls the sea." In the northern Indian Ocean, securing sea lanes of communication will be facilitated by the Indian Navy's ability to exercise "sea denial" (negating an enemy's ability to use the sea but at the same time making no attempt to control the sea itself) in a region stretching from the Arabian Sea in the west to the Straits of Malacca in the east.

Moreover, as India looks farther away for energy resources, its political and military leaders are explicitly linking this effort with the need for the Indian military, particularly the navy, to be able to "protect the country's economic and energy interests" in key parts of the Indian Ocean.

Aircraft carriers, surface ships and submarines equipped with land-attack cruise missiles, and amphibious landing ships—the latter of which are discussed with land power below—are the key maritime power projection platforms that can influence events on land from the sea.

While submarines can rely on stealth to approach an enemy coastline, task forces of cruisemissile-armed surface platforms, amphibious assault ships, and aircraft carriers require the assistance of attack submarines, maritime patrol aircraft, and modern destroyers to protect them from hostile submarines, aircraft, and anti-ship cruise missiles.

Tankers and supply ships sustain maritime forces with food, fuel, and ammunition when operating a significant distance from friendly ports.

In 2008, then-Chief of Naval Staff Admiral Sureesh Mehta foresaw that the navy of 2020 would be "capable of influencing the outcome of land battles and performing a constabulary role in the Indian Ocean region." Achieving this will require a significant upgrade in capabilities. Naval planners envision a three-carrier fleet as the cornerstone of India's future blue-water navy: the 44,500-ton, Russian-built INS *Vikramaditya* (Sanskrit: Brave as the Sun) which is expected to join the fleet after 2012, and two domestically built aircraft carriers of the Vikrant class weighing in at 40,000 tons (INS *Vikrant*) (Sanskrit: Powerful) and 64,000 tons (INS *Vishal*) (Sanskrit: Great), scheduled to enter service in 2015 and 2018, respectively. At the same time, the introduction of the fourth-generation supersonic MiG-29K Fulcrum provides India with the most powerful naval strike aircraft in the region and increases its force projection capacity by an order of magnitude.

However, these optimistic projections mask a dark reality: at present India's existing 28,000-ton aircraft carrier, launched in 1953, is on its last legs. Should the induction of the *Vikramaditya* or the *Vikrant* be delayed beyond the middle of the decade, as some informed observers speculate, the navy could find itself without a carrier for several years. At the same time, only 11 of the 30 Mk. 51 Sea Harrier fighters that were in service in the 1980s remain, and at the time of this writing, there is yet to be a test flight of the naval version of Hindustan Aeronautics Limited's domestically designed Tejas lightweight fighter, which is supposed to replace the Harriers in providing air defense to the carriers.

Furthermore, the *Vikramaditya* and the *Vikrant* will carry only 16 fighters each. Assuming that the bigger *Vishal* will accommodate a larger complement of aircraft (50–60), analysts say it would have to operate in tandem with one of the 40,000-ton carriers to produce "as much striking power as a single U.S. Nimitz-class carrier.

Even armed with precision-guided munitions, a contingent of this size could sustain only a modest land bombardment, and only for a modest time." Moreover, a three-carrier fleet will only ensure that the navy has at least one carrier at sea at all times, given the repair, training, and deployment cycles for modern naval vessels.

To be able to implement Admiral Mehta's constabulary role in the Indian Ocean, the navy would need to have the ability to maintain two carriers at sea at all times, which would suggest a need for twice as many flattops. With an estimated unit cost of $1.5 billion, against an annual naval procurement budget of $2.3 billion, building each additional carrier over six or seven years could easily tie up 9% to 11% of the acquisition budget per platform, making a rapid expansion of the fleet unlikely.

The Indian Navy's surface-strike capability centers on the 290-kilometerrange supersonic BraMos cruise missile. A joint venture between Russia and India, the BraMos can achieve Mach 2.5 speed, which is three times faster than the U.S. Tomahawk cruise missile. While highly effective in an anti-shipping role, the BraMos is less useful as a land-attack weapon because it possesses only one-tenth the range of the U.S. Tomahawk. This latter characteristic is also true of the land-attack variants of the Russian-designed 3M-54 Klub cruise missile (275 kilometer range) also in service with the Indian Navy.

The relatively short range of these missiles would render surface-launched cruise missile strikes against a state with even modest anti-access capability (attack submarines, anti-ship missiles, or supporting surveillance systems) a risky proposition.

According to published reports, the Defence Research and Development Organization is currently developing a subsonic cruise missile with a reported range of 1,000 kilometres. Code named *Nirbhay* (Sanskrit: Fearless), it could fill an important gap in the navy's land-attack capability. However, test flights of the missile have been repeatedly delayed.

Finally, the Indian Navy's ability to project maritime power in the Indian Ocean and beyond is constrained by the fact that it is currently decommissioning surface ships faster than it is adding them.

At present, large portions of India's fleet of 57 surface combatants, including five of its eight destroyers and seven of its 11 frigates, are approaching the end of their service life. The navy requires these types of platforms, equipped with advanced anti-aircraft and anti-submarine systems, to operate in hostile littorals. Moreover, to achieve a real power projection capability, the navy will require several additional fleet replenishment tankers and modern replacements for its cadre of Soviet-era minesweepers.

Air Power

Air power projection comes mainly in two forms: strikes against ground-based targets and the transport of ground troops. Since the latter role is primarily a supporting one, it is taken up in the discussion of land power below. As a tool for power projection, the use or threat of air power is primarily used for compellence/deterrence or to punish another state, should the initial efforts fail to bring about a desired policy change. Affecting targets at a range beyond a few hundred miles requires advanced strike aircraft (typically operating in conjunction with refueling tanker aircraft) capable of penetrating enemy air defenses, longer-range cruise missiles, or ballistic missiles.

The chief of the Air Staff, Air Chief Marshal F. H. Major, has argued that Indian air power needs "a strategic reach to safeguard our national interests," which requires a "long-range presence, persistence and 'forward-basing arrangements'."

In this vein, the IAF's revised war doctrine is reportedly structured around "both pre-emptive action and swift retaliation" across a region stretching from the Persian Gulf to the Straits of Malacca. However, the air force has long suffered from the piecemeal acquisition of aircraft, and much of its fleet is facing obsolescence—raising questions about future combat power.

Nonetheless, the IAF has pushed for an independent strategic role in future conflict, arguing that air power can influence the battle space through deep-strike missions. The air force "aims to achieve this objective by operating advanced, long-range platforms with air-to-air refueling capability" and "must be equipped for long-reach, persistence, all-weather, precision, air dominance, networked, and space-enabled force capabilities."

Future Military Roles

Support Forces Deployed on Peacekeeping Missions. It is hardly inconceivable that Indian peacekeepers (or those of friendly nations) could be targeted by belligerent parties during the course of their duties, thus potentially requiring a forcible extraction or rescue operations along the lines of Operation Khukri in Sierra Leone, where Indian forces rescued 230 U.N. peacekeepers who had been held hostage for over 75 days by the rebels of the Revolutionary United Front. Because India's local U.N. partners in the region were too weak to respond effectively, the success of this operation depended in large part on the rapid introduction of a battalion of Indian grenadiers and para-commandos airlifted directly from the Kashmir Valley, as well as a flight of Indian Air Force (IAF) attack helicopters.

Protecting Indians Abroad. Several recent events highlight the increasing salience of this issue. Following the 2000 coup in Fiji that ousted Prime Minister Mahendra Chaudhry, an ethnic Indian, there was significant pressure on the Indian government to take steps to protect Fiji's large Indian community. However, the lack of naval capacity rendered such an operation impossible. Of even more concern are the five million Indians employed in the Persian Gulf. A contingency in this region is hardly unthinkable, given the 1991 and 2006 emergencies that required major evacuations of Indian nationals from conflict zones.

Bibliography

Ajey Lele: *Strategic Technologies for the Military : Breaking New Frontiers*, Sage, Delhi, 2009.

Alperovitz, Gar. *The Decision to Use the Atomic Bomb*. New York: Vintage Books, 1996.

Anil, K.C.: *Military and Democracy in India: Challenges, Politics and Power*, Sumit Enterprises, Delhi, 2009.

Banerjee, Sumanta: *In the Wake of Naxalbari: A History of the Naxalite Movement in India,* Calcutta: Subarnarekha, 1980.

Bellamy, C.: *Knights in White Armour: The New Art of War and Peace*, London, Random House, 1997.

Benjamin, Joseph : *China-Pak Relations : Prospect and Retrospect*, Reference Press, Delhi, 2004.

Bhat, T.P. : *India and China : Trade Complementarities and Competitiveness*, Bookwell, Delhi, 2008.

Budge I: *The New Challenge of Direct Democracy*, Oxford, Polity Press, 1996.

Chitkara, M.G. : *Indo-Pak Relations Challenges Before New Millennium*, APH, Delhi, 2001.

Clinton, William J. *A National Security Strategy for a New Century*. Washington, DC: Government Printing Office, 1998.

Damrosch, L.F.: *Law and Force in the New International Order*, Boulder, Westview Press, 1991.

Dasgupta, B.: *The Naxalite Movement*, Bombay: Allied Publishers, 1974.

Dixit, Prabla: *Defence Economics: A Struggle for Power*, New Delhi, Orient Longman, 1981.

Fletcher, Arnold: *Afghanistan, Highway of Conquest*, Ithaca, New York, Cornell University, 1965.

Friedman, G.: *The Future of War of Cyber Crimes*, N.Y., Random House, 1996.

Gaur, Mahendra : *Indian Policy of Neighbour*, Delhi, Kalpaz Pub., 2006.

Ghosh, Ajoy : *China-Pak Conflict : Threat to South Asian Security*, Reference Press, Delhi, 2003.

Hays, Peter L. and others: *Countering the Proliferation and Use of Weapons of Mass Destruction,* New York, NY: McGraw-Hill, 1998.

Huntington, P. : *The Soldier and the State : The Theory and Politics of Civil-Military Relations*, Natraj Pub, Delhi, 2005.

Huntington, S.P.: *The China Modernisation Military and the State*, N.Y., Vintage Books, 1964.

John M. Seidl: *Politics American Style: Race, Environment and Central Cities*, New York, Prentice-Hall, 1972.

Juvale, R.P. : *Military Strategy and Diplomacy*, Cyber Tech Publications, Delhi, 2010.

Kumar, Raj : *Weapons and Military Technology*, Sumit Enterprises, Delhi, 2009.

Martin H. Greenberg: *Studies in Nuclear Terrorism*, Boston: G.K. Hall & Co., 1979.

Mary, W.: *Asian Power and Politics: the Cultural Dimensions of Authority*, Cambridge, Belknap Press, 1985.

Peter G. Tsouras: *Dictionary of Military Quotations*, Manas, Delhi, 2006.

Posen, B.R.: *The Sources of Indian Military Doctrine*, Ithaca, 1984, Cornell Univ. Press.

Radhakrishna: *Handbook of Military and Defence Services*, Sumit Enterprises, Delhi, 2009.

Rosen, P.: *Societies and Military Power: India and its Armies*, Ithaca, Cornell University Press, 1996.

Rudolph, Heimanson: *Dictionary of Military*, N.Y.: Oceana Publications, 1967.

Singhal, D. P.: *India and Afghanistan: 1876-1907. A Study in Diplomatic Relations*, St. Lucia, University of Queensland, 1963.

Strange, Susan: *The Retreat of the State: The Diffusion of Power in the World Economy*, Cambridge: Cambridge University, 1996.

Sutton, J., *Technology and Defence Market Structure*, MIT Press, Delhi, 1998.

Index

M

N

O

P

S

T

❑❑❑